F

Will Randall was born in 1966 and educated in London.
He taught languages in   years
before going to live in   ook,
Solomon Time, was the s   and
since then he has lived ir   *lian*
Summer, 2004), Africa (B   ...... numerous
parts of France (*Another Long Day on the Piste*, 2006). He
continues to travel, teach and write.

Visit the author's website at: www.willrandall.co.uk

Praise for Will Randall

For *Botswana Time*
'This is a good-humoured book, written by a man who went
to Botswana with an open heart. The result is a wonderful,
amusing and affirmative book about that remarkable
country, filled with laughter, colour, and simple decency.
Bravo, Mr Randall. Bravo'

Alexander McCall Smith, author of
The No.1 Ladies' Detective Agency

For *Indian Summer*
'Many great writers have written about their time in the
East; Somerset Maugham, E. M. Forster and Rudyard
Kipling among them. Even if he never writes about India
again, Will Randall should be added to this illustrious list'
Daily Express

'Randall kaleidoscopically evokes his changing perceptions
of the country's extraordinary diversity in a travelogue full
of sensuous detail, humour and poignancy'   *Observer*

LIMEY
GUMSHOE

THE HAPLESS ADVENTURES OF
A HIGH-VISIBILITY UNDERCOVER DETECTIVE

WILL RANDALL

ABACUS

First published in Great Britain in 2008 by Abacus

A CIP catalogue record for this book
is available from the British Library.

ISBN 978-0-349-12039-3

Typeset in Palatino by Palimpsest Book Production Limited,
Grangemouth, Stirlingshire
Printed and bound in Great Britain by
Clays Ltd, St Ives plc

Abacus
An imprint of
Little, Brown Book Group
100 Victoria Embankment
London EC4Y 0DY

An Hachette Livre UK Company

www.littlebrown.co.uk

*This is a book for anyone who likes to know that the
truth has finally been brought out into the light.*

Author's Note

Although the main cases dealt with in this book are true and I hope that *Limey Gumshoe* realistically demonstrates the working methods of a modern private investigator, some names and places have been changed to protect the innocent – and me.

Acknowledgments

Much to my delight, I was welcomed with open arms into the world of US licensed private investigators and it was with great pleasure that I learned from the anecdotes, methods and experience of the men and women whose job it is to seek out the Truth. Naturally, there were a number of individuals who featured large on my American horizon. Mike Friedman was the inspiration for this book and proved a bottomless source of kindly advice and information. His roving spirit makes him a man after my own heart. Brandon Perron is a true professional and an inspiring teacher as well as a generous host. His book *Uncovering Reasonable Doubt: The Component Method* is required reading for any would-be PI. I am exceedingly grateful to him and all his team – good friends. Thomas P. Shamshak was a genial guide to Boston, a born instructor and great company as were Drs Jeff and Beth Davies. Thanks for the hospitality.

Nearer home, all at Abacus have been immensely supportive of my various projects and Richard Beswick has a keen eye for an interesting idea. Kirsteen Astor annually undertakes the Herculean task of keeping me on track with an impressive assurance born of (bitter) experience. Kate Hordern, as always, keeps my affairs, at home and abroad, very much in order and is a source of inspiring new projects. Angie Sen managed all things secretarial with an awe-inspiring swiftness and precision. Tanya Demidova's illustrations add another dimension to my tales and are much complimented.

Family and friends offer me much encouragement and an endless source of welcome when I pass by. I am appreciative of them all.

Lastly, of course, I am thankful to Raymond Chandler, creator of my alter ego Philip Marlowe. He, too, is always out there looking for the 'truth that warms the heart'.

WR

The Loire Valley, France
January 2008

Contents

Prologue

Peeing into a bottle is never easy.

Naturally the task is made that much harder when the receptacle in question is an empty magnum of admittedly very good Washington State Pinot Noir 2005 and you are driving, as I was, at nearing the speed limit, on the Massachusetts Turnpike. If I had only had the presence of mind when I had lurched out of bed in the city-lit dawn, I would have chosen a container a little more suited to the job. Buck Burnett, my erstwhile surveillance partner, swore by orange juice cartons, customised for the task. Practical and easily disposable apparently.

Of course, I would not even have had to touch upon this less than attractive aspect of the professional life of a private detective had the subject in the car that I was following not had a bladder capable of resisting the same pressures as a bathyscaphe. Sadly, ever since we had left downtown Boston, hours earlier, he had not once indicated or manoeuvred in the direction of one of the brightly decorated gas stations that lined the highway and which now looked surprisingly less gaudy in the morning sun than they had in the neon night.

Really, of course, it was Buck's fault, I mused. If he had not crashed his vehicle into another in a parking lot in Brookline and then got involved in an impressive contretemps with its owner, now he and I would still be engaged in a common or garden two-car moving surveillance. Swapping our positions but remaining in the box formation, Buck slowing down to pull back behind the target, whilst I zoomed in front, would have meant that I could have sped ahead, careered into one of the lay-bys, made use of one of the roadside loos and been back on the road within minutes – all the while remaining within walkie-talkie contact with Buck.

To take my mind off pressing matters I shifted my seat belt a little bit, and had another go at understanding the cruise control buttons on the steering wheel. Once I had given that up, I checked again hurriedly, with a knot of anxiety suddenly tied tightly in the pit of my stomach, that I still had visual on the subject's vehicle – the private eye jargon meaning that I could still see it. This, thankfully, I did as he was now toodling along in the outside lane, an arm out of the driver's window, no doubt humming bluegrass tunes, whatever they sounded like.

To keep my mind closely focused on the job, and off anything else, I consulted the Surveillance Manual that lay open on the passenger's seat of the Dodge Stingray. It had been given to me the day before by Nelson Mason, the proprietor of Chestnut Investigations Inc. and my new boss. The pages fanned and flopped randomly, which was as confusing as it was irritating, so I pinned them open with the magnum and between snatched glances at the road, read the next section:

THE SURVEILLANCE OPERATOR

1) Surveillance operators do not conform to any specific type in regard to physical characteristics such as gender, race, or size.
2) Surveillance operators should use timely reason and logic in reacting to a given set of circumstances.
3) Surveillance operators should have a keen sense of perception.
4) Surveillance operators must thrive from the thrill of the chase.

Well, this particular surveillance operator would have been more than happy to fulfil all the above criteria had he not thought he was going to explode as we crossed over the state border into New Hampshire that sunny early afternoon.

In quiet desperation I stared out of the driver's window. Although the scenery did not change in a hurry, I sensed a wildness about this state that was greatly different from the genteel atmosphere of Massachusetts. The inscription on the bottom of the state licence plates here seemed to underline this:

Live Free or Die

There was nothing complicated about following the subject now as the road was wide and there was just a convenient amount of traffic behind which to hide. What was not so convenient was the recognition, once more, that at some stage – the Pinot Noir bottle option having been discarded – I was definitely going to have to visit a 'restroom' – Must Pee or Die, in fact. I tried to take my mind off the problem again, this time by whistling along with the radio, but soon discovered that tapping my foot along to the beat was in-advisable in my present condition. Switching it off, I contented myself instead with trying to build up a comprehensive list of American euphemisms for the lavatory.

As the sun began to tip over the horizon and I had just remembered 'comfort station', which was definitely in the top five along with 'the john' and 'the little boy's room', the subject suddenly started to indicate.

1

Russia Revisited

Gazing over the emerald algae that lapped against the shores of the Charles River out to the elegant skyline of Boston, I had felt tired and confused by the choice available at the 'Formal but Bohemian Eatery' in which I sat. Take, for example, the sandwiches, the thousands of fillings and the myriad different breads: *pain ordinaire* or pumpernickel or rye, Italian rye, American rye, Marble rye, New York rye, light rye. Then, rather disappointingly, there was wheat bread or, indeed, rather bizarrely, flour-free bread – surely the black hole of baking. And the coffee: latte, mocha, cappuccino, espresso, machiatto, Romano, granita, ristretto or a long, skinny, semi-something, the list was endless.

Eventually, I gave up and spent a happy ten minutes attempting to fold up the origami-style menu whilst I waited for my lunch guest to arrive. Watching a light aircraft, its advertising tail fluttering gaily like a movie star's scarf, gently putter over the cranes and building sites of the latest phase of the Big Dig – the monstrous reengineering of the city's transport routes – I wondered how I was to fill my afternoon. Tackle another chapter perhaps? This was after all why I had decided to accept a request to house-sit for some English friends who were researching medical matters at Harvard University. They had headed back home for a stint of maternity leave, delighted by a new baby girl, and I was happy to have the house, in the 'South End' area of the city, to myself in which to attempt to finish off my latest book – an account of a recent sojourn in the French Alps. Boston's attractions were unfortunately many and made it all the more difficult to get back to the task that needed to be completed by a rapidly approaching date. Going out for lunch was, I knew, just another excuse although I was much looking forward to seeing Makepeace after all this time. Perhaps later, for digestive purposes, I would just take a stroll down Newbury Street to admire the spectacular boutiques and their equally spectacular customers before dragging myself back to my desk.

Some minutes later I was considering my longer-term future – a regular and unnerving pastime – when I was distracted by a rich baritone voice behind me.

'Hey, Will, long time no see!'

'Well, Jack, this is great!' I responded happily, rising to my feet and turning. 'It must be fifteen years at least, I should think.'

Fifteen years it might have been but I recognised him immediately. Although he had swapped the quasi-military buzz cut – sported when I had first met him in St Petersburg, Russia – for a regulation city slicker hairstyle with side parting, it was his face that remained immediately recognisable. His cheek bones were movie-star high, and his features were gaunt, slightly lined, the attractive result of too much laughing. Two of the bluest eyes were twinkling with amusement as he came up to the table and flung a photographer's padded holdall onto the floor and pulled open the pop buttons of his army surplus jacket. Dropping it over the back of his chair he punched me cheerfully and not too painfully on the upper arm and sat down.

'So, what's new, buddy? You gotta tell me everything you've been up to.'

'And so have you!'

Carefully, I gave Jack a rundown of my movements over the last ten years and he the same. It is not easy. People get bored very easily, although the only reason that Jack's nicotine-stained fingers fidgeted together as we spoke was the non-smoking atmosphere of the café. Within the first minute or so of meeting him again I was reminded that he is almost more talkative than I am.

Philippines, Saudi, Afghanistan – he gave me his impressions and we swapped judiciously chosen anecdotes.

'I suppose pretty much everybody that I knew out there in St Petersburg has moved on by now,' I said and Jack nodded.

'Yeah pretty much all gone – even the Russians!' He laughed his choky, smoky laugh and we pondered awhile on the speed at which people change location, and even career, in the modern world. Heaven knew I'd held down a few different jobs in the last few years. The small band of European friends that I had made when I lived in the Solomon Islands a few years earlier now lived in France, Vietnam, Australia, Vanuatu, New Zealand and South Africa respectively. Interestingly, not one of us, for reasons that ranged from the political to the personal, had returned to their country of origin.

In the early nineties, after the Wall came tumbling down, Eastern Europe, pretty much unseen by Western eyes for a generation, became a magnet for any young or not so young would-be adventurers. It was virgin territory. Almost a clean sheet for the jaded Lonely Planet generation. For them it seemed almost as exciting as it had been discovering Africa in the nineteenth century. My younger brother, possessed of a rather more rugged approach to life than me and a good degree in Russian, decided to up sticks, at about the same time as I was settling into a rather cosy teaching job in the West Country, and chance his luck in the then limited world of 'free' journalism in the former USSR. Replying to an advertisement in a magazine he gained employment as the news editor of an English-language daily in St Petersburg and quickly found himself accommodation in the shape of a small apartment just off Nevsky Prospect not far from the Fontanka Canal. Naturally, as soon as the first school holidays came around, I had flown out to investigate his strange new world.

By coincidence, my birthday fell some time during the course of my stay and he offered to organise a party for me. I accepted, of course, but wary of my brother's culinary skills, I offered to buy and cook the food for the evening celebration.

'OK, you do the food then and I'll get the drink. Who do you want to invite?'

As I had met no one apart from a couple of barmen in the few days since I had been in the 'Venice of the North' I suggested that he invite anybody he chose, making this a slightly surreal surprise party. I did know that the bash was to take place, I just would not know anybody coming to it.

The following day I visited the covered market some streets away from my brother's apartment with his girlfriend, soon to become my sister-in-law. We shopped for meat and vegetables, all of which were plentiful, and then she led me by the elbow to what she considered the most important corner of the food hall, the gherkin counter. Five or six trestle tables had been placed end to end along one wall. Laid out on them were bowl after bowl of gherkins pickled to a greater or less degree. As she expertly ordered I could not help noticing that the gherkins were being scooped from recycled bed pans and popped into clear plastic bags, the diagrams on which made clear that they had originally been designed as blood transfusion bags. As we packed them into the wicker shopping basket I trusted that they too had not been recycled.

Some hours later I was making the most of my brother's single frying pan in the kitchen-cum-bathroom of his apartment, and was listening to the plastic People's Radio when a clinking in the stairwell announced his return from work.

'Here we go, then,' he announced as he negotiated the front door and deposited two plastic bags onto the table in the sitting-cum-dining-cum-bedroom. 'This should cover it.'

Poking cautiously at the bags I peered in to see what he had bought.

'Here you are. Some wine.' He pulled out two bottles of red wine and held them out by their necks for me to inspect. The labels were written entirely in Cyrillic and on each was pictured the rear view of a peasant woman bent over what might possibly, observed with an open mind, have been grapevines.

'Bulgarian, all the rage right at the moment, doncha know?' he joked. At that time in Russia no other wine existed except something from Georgia that would have permanently stained your insides.

'Looks fine,' I said doubtfully. Back then my oenological knowledge was minimal. Today, after a very great deal of practice, it is much improved but even in those days I imagined that the words on the label were probably some kind of a health warning.

My brother emptied the rest of the plastic bags, despatching them to the floor, to reveal their contents. On the table stood an army of bottles of vodka all from Finland – surprisingly the best to be had in Russia.

'Blimey, how many have you got here? One, two, three,

four, five . . . ten! That's ten litres of vodka. How many
people have you invited for goodness sake?' I looked around
the comfortable but distinctly limited flat.

'Oh, twelve, I think, at last count,' my brother said airily,
lining the bottles up like soldiers in a war game. 'Why?
Don't you think it will be enough?'

The evening turned out to be a pretty international affair.
Shortly past eight o'clock through the door trooped two
Germans, two, possibly three, Finns, some English, some
Americans and Canadians, a number of Russians, the
inevitable Irishman and a New Zealander who got very
grumpy when someone suggested he might be an Australian.
Now that I do the maths perhaps we were more than twelve
but despite the cultural and linguistic mish-mash of the
evening everyone seemed to get on very well. Appreciative
remarks about the food were made and, initially anyway,
the Bulgarian red wine was sipped delicately from an eclectic
variety of glasses. After the warming but rather heavy
Russian bread-and-no-butter pudding, brought by one of the
guests, a young man called Sergey at the far end of the table
stood up quite unexpectedly and raised his glass announcing
something in Russian most gravely as he did so.

'Oh, God, yes, I nearly forgot.'

My brother looked unexpectedly flustered. Leaping from
his seat he dived into the bottom of the sideboard. He re-
emerged clutching two bottles of Finlandia and these were
quickly passed around the table so that glasses might be
filled. Finally some order was restored and Sergey gestured
that one and all should stand, but as I struggled to my feet
I found myself pushed down again by well-meaning hands.

'So a toast! A toast to our most illustrious visitor who
celebrates his birthday today,' the young Russian roared and
my brother simultaneously translated with similar gusto.

Of course, I was delighted and lifted my glass as everyone

raised theirs to me. I had certainly never been called illus-trious before. Now he mentioned it, though, I wasn't sure that it didn't suit me rather well.

In those days I had perhaps a slightly less practised eye for working out the way that things are done in different cultures and countries. Here, now, I realised immediately that the Russian approach to vodka toasts did not involve anything as effete as sipping. A dozen heads snapped back as glasses were drained in a single fiery shot. Half a second elapsed and then twenty-four eyeballs simultaneously bulged as two dozen buttocks hit their seats again. Of course, the initiated amongst us managed to hold back the desire to cough, splutter, clutch their throats and make any number of unseemly noises. Nonetheless, after another seven or eight toasts that included ones to absent friends, the government (anybody's), the weather, the food, the apartment, and the cat (which as far as I knew my brother did not possess), everybody seemed to have developed a certain expertise in the consumption of vodka shots.

It was well past midnight before my brother began to check through the bottles to see if there was enough for one last round. Just as he was beginning to think we might have to draw a veil over the proceedings, which would have been no bad thing, there was first a ring at the door and then a loud thumping. Someone went to release the latch and after quite a lot of crashing and bashing a figure appeared in the doorway of the room where we sat by the light of two slightly noxious oil lamps. Wielding two bottles of vodka in one hand above his head and in the other some Russian champagne was the man who was now sitting opposite me in this genteel coffee house in Boston. (By way of public information I think it worth suggesting that this latter beverage is best avoided. It tastes exactly like washing-up water with bubbles.)

'*Do Svidania,*' he roared and in a single breath expended my entire knowledge of the Russian language before addressing himself to my brother with no excess of formality. 'Hey, you goddamn Limey, I told ya I'd make it. Not gonna miss a party like this!'

He peered curiously about the room through the thick cigarette smoke before his bright blue eyes lighted on me and he rasped a laugh.

'So this must be the birthday boy! Recognise the Randall features anywhere!' He waved over at me and I greeted him with a smile that had come automatically, gleefully to my lips as my brother introduced the newcomer.

'Ladies and Gentlemen. Mr Jack Makepeace!'

Lurching across the room, Makepeace, as I discovered he was universally known, slung an arm around my neck and gestured to the guests to replenish their glasses with the vodka he had brought. Its garish label announced it to be a brand known as Okhta. At the time it cost fifty pence a litre and, as a sign of quite how bad it is, has now officially been banned for human consumption by the Russian government. The several hundred thousand litres of unconsumed Okhta are regularly used to clean office floors. But all this did not stop us that night. When my brother and I found ourselves at the top of a tower overlooking the Neva River dressed in fur hats and old Soviet military greatcoats, each gripping an unsteady Makepeace by a shoulder, life was for living and the talk was for talking. That was until daylight broke in the east and we extinguished the cardboard butts of our last cigarettes in the greying slush. Slowly, at the first hiss of the grand underground trains, we crept off to bed to wake a dozen hours later as fresh as if we had just come round from a general anaesthetic.

Makepeace, the son of some farmers from Connecticut, had spent some time in the military before chucking it in to learn the guitar and travel the planet. He had decided to take American entrepreneurship around the world with him and was the first to have brought it to the USSR. This at least was his claim. By the way things were working out for him, it must have been something of a new concept for the local population. He was importing radios and hoping to sell them to the masses who after umpteen years should, by all reason, have grown tired of Soviet marching tunes. Regrettably, the radios were not flying off the shelf. Someone had pointed out to Jack that this might well have been because there were as yet no commercial stations broadcasting.

'But they'll come,' Jack had announced confidently. 'They *will* come.'

And indeed they had, any number of them. By this stage, sadly, Jack had gone bust and had finally, after a stint as a freelance photographer – a sure sign of a dip in fortunes – been reduced to returning to America, where he had been employed making public information movies. Of an adult nature, my brother had maintained, perhaps jokingly, on one of the occasions that we had reminisced about my first meeting with Makepeace. Despite the fact that over the fifteen or more years since that memorable evening in Russia we had often thought about him, we had only communicated sporadically with Makepeace. Time zones and distance made it more difficult for us all, more than most, to keep in touch but the fondness that we had for him remained undiminished.

So it was that when my brother heard that I was proposing to house-sit in Boston he had reminded me that our man was a New Englander and had suggested, no, *demanded*, that I look him up as soon as I arrived.

'So yeah, doing some writing and that? That's what your bro told me, isn't it?' Makepeace asked as we applied

ourselves again to the lunch menus having enjoyed a traveller's digression about meetings, coincidences and other
serendipitous experiences.

'Yes, that's what has kept body and soul together for the
last few years,' I replied enthusiastically and then was very
nearly swept from my chair by a tidal wave of guilt about
the unfinished manuscript that lay on the desk in the flat
back in the South End.

'That's just great!'

'Yes, yes, it has been. But, uh, anyway what about you?
The last my brother told me you were out in Manila selling
armoured SUVs to the Philippine government. What
happened there?'

Makepeace looked crestfallen and I was immediately
sorry I had asked. Happily his good cheer returned almost
immediately.

'Oh, that was pretty good. You know it was like . . . a
good experience. I loved that shit. Of course you've always
got a problem when the Mob get involved so I pulled out.'

'Oh yes, of course you would have. Absolutely. If that
sort of, uh, thing, uh, went down,' I concurred with some
degree of enthusiasm.

'Yeah, I had some trouble with them. Bad times, you
know. Had to get out pretty quick. Decided I'd spend a
little bit of time at home. Hasn't been so bad so far. Bit of
R'n'R. You know what I mean?'

'Oh yes. What? Oh, Rock 'n' Roll. Jolly good idea . . .
Er . . . Too right.'

I stopped talking. Not for the first time it seemed like a
good idea.

'Hey,' Makepeace said, quickly changing the conversation for no better reason than he seemed to be boring
himself. 'So, do you like baseball?'

'Oh, well . . .' I replied vaguely. Then, suddenly seized

with curiosity again, I pushed Jack Makepeace a little harder. 'So what are you doing now that you're back?'

'Oh, this and that,' he replied evasively.

'Well, looks like you're busy,' I said nodding to the padded bag that he had brought in and which now lay on the floor. 'Looks like you're into photography or film or something?' The moment I said this I regretted it as I remembered my brother's suspicions about the nature of Jack's filming activity.

'Oh, well, being as observant as that maybe you should be in my new line of business too!' Jack laughed. 'Yeah, well, now that you ask. I have had a bit of a change of direction. I've been working pretty much full time as a private investigator.'

'Ha, ha, a private eye! What, a private detective? Ha, ha!'

I was still laughing as the pneumatic waitress came over to take our order.

2

Sherlock Holmes and the Ponster

'Oh yes, I suppose you do find it all rather bizarre. Sorry about that,' Makepeace replied not very apologetically. After our mountains of food had finally appeared and we had done our best to wade our way through them, I had eventually controlled myself and asked him to be serious.

'A private detective! Don't be ridiculous.'

'Here you go, this should prove it for you,' he said as he reached deep into the pocket of the jacket that hung on the back of his chair. After a moment or two of digging around he pulled out a card and spun it by one of its sharp edges across the table to me. It landed face down and I slowly picked it up like a nervous tarot card reader. I really did not know what to expect.

It was white and plain. At the top was a fanciful crest featuring an eagle and some doubtful Latin. Below was written:

Jack J. Makepeace
PRIVATE INVESTIGATOR
CHESTNUT INVESTIGATIONS INC.

At the bottom were some telephone numbers and an email contact but no postal address.

It was just a business card but I looked up at Makepeace astonished. Smiling, he explained.

'When I got back from Manila I was kinda all washed up, you know. No money, not really got anything lined up that was kinda interesting. Way back I did some film classes, you know, just video and that, so I answered a small ad in the back of the *Globe*, you know. Just asking for a cameraman to make short movies.'

He grinned at me and I looked back quite innocently.

'I know what you're thinking, aren't you . . . ?'

'Thinking? No, not thinking anything, no . . .'

'You're thinking the adult industry, right? Bit of triple X action, right?'

'What? Oh, no! Adult films? Oh, do you mean . . . Oh no, oh no . . .'

My face blazed.

'Well,' he chuckled. 'That was exactly what I was thinking. But no, it weren't nothing like that. Maybe wish it had of been. No, just kidding.'

'Oh.'

'So yeah. Just turned out to be a small outfit. Got themselves recruited by the City of Boston to make public information clips for local TV.'

'Oh, public information, really?' It was difficult to get the correct measure of seriousness into my voice.

'Yeah, kids crossing the road, what to do with your trash . . . You know the kind of thing. Kinda boring but OK, I guess.'

'Well, yes certainly not as interest— But OK, yes . . .'

'Stuck it for about six months then one day this guy who does the sound, he tells me he was working part-time for a PI firm. Sounded kind of interesting. Started to do some work for them. Now I'm pretty much on the payroll.'

Makepeace picked up the bill that had arrived via the shiny, happy waitress, who wished us a good day and teetered off. Waving me away and pulling his wallet from his hip pocket he counted out some notes; I thanked him and we stood to go.

'Are you all set?' he asked as he scooped up his bag and swung it over his shoulder.

'Sure am!' I replied. So intrigued was I by what he was telling me that I did not bother to think about where I was off to next.

'Yeah,' he continued. 'So, it's been pretty good. Gotta pack it in pretty soon though. Had a bit of an accident in Petersburg. Involved an elevator shaft and a bottle of vodka but unfortunately no elevator. Long story. So, yeah, well anyway one of my knees went south. Got it patched up but it's gone to hell just recently. Got an operation booked for next week and then rehab. Waiting to see the specialist now. Takes one heck of a long time with the physio and that.' He shrugged and grinned. Only then, as we headed for the moving staircase that took us down into the heaving hell that was the shopping mall, did I notice his pronounced limp.

'Well, that's very bad luck. Sorry to hear that,' I said quite genuinely, and then rushed on perhaps a little too quickly. 'So, what kinds of things do you ... er ... investigate?' I looked over my shoulder then turned back to him and ducked my head as I whispered, 'I mean, what sort of "cases" do you cover?' I felt rather thrilled.

'Oh, this one I been working this morning, it's pretty much bread and butter for us guys. Just a covert surveillance.' He slapped his bag. 'What we call a cheatin' spouse case. Husband thinks his wife's running around town with another guy. Client just wants to know where she goes, where all his dough gets spent. I follow her around, take a few snaps, write down her movements, write up a report. That's the dull bit, of course. Find out what the old man wants to know, if there's a guy, who the guy is. Maybe see if maybe she's got a drug problem or something.'

Stepping out into the street I skipped along, trying to keep up with Jack, who, despite his knee problem, was zooming over the pavement occasionally flipping his watch down his wrist and glancing at it.

'Wow!' I let slip before adopting an entirely more thoughtful demeanour. 'Really. I see. Very interesting. Yes, so do you think that she is, you know well, er . . . "running around" then?'

'Hell, no. Not this one. You can see she's not cheating for a start and she doesn't have any real problem – apart from a little too much shopping and a lot too much food. But she ain't out on her own there. Just bored, I guess. Guy's a jerk.'

'I see. So what other stuff do you do? Must be plenty,' I added, hoping to tease some more exciting stories from him.

'Look, sorry, Will, actually I got to head for the office right now. Gotta do an undercover for a big fraud case we're on. Kinda tricky one but we're getting there.' We had stopped on the kerb and Makepeace was looking back down the traffic searching out a cab.

'Undercover? Really? Fraud, is it? I see . . .'

Makepeace smiled at me, his face cracked with lines, as he crushed out the second Marlboro he had smoked since we had arrived in the open air.

'Find it kinda intriguing, don't ya, buddy? I guess it is.' He thought for a moment and checked his watch again. 'How 'bout you come on over to the office with me? I gotta drop this shit off and get some other gear. If you like I'll introduce you to the other guys. They're always good for a talk and a coffee. That is unless you gotta get back to your book?'

'Book? Oh, no. There's absolutely no rush about that.'

This was, in fact, quite untrue but this was too interesting a lead to pass up. No one would mind. I was just going for a chat.

'OK, OK,' laughed Makepeace as a taxi screeched up and we climbed in. He gave some instructions to the driver, who nodded from his plastic, bullet-proof-screened position behind the wheel but did not stop for a breath talking what, I think, was probably Haitian Creole into his mobile phone. We sat back on the hard wipeable seats as he took us down along the Charles River and back over the bridge at Fenway Park, home to the Boston Red Sox. Before long we found ourselves driving past Boston University and on into the old quarter of the town. Swinging back and around onto Charles Street, we pulled in left and up one of the steep, narrow streets of red-brick town houses and low apartment blocks with their black, zig-zagging fire escapes that made up 'historic' Beacon Hill. The taxi driver pulled over after a tap on the plastic from Makepeace who struggled his way along the back seat and popped out of the door.

'Right here,' he said pointing up. Looking up through the leaves of the plane trees that lined the road I could see a window behind which was drawn a Venetian blind and onto which was stuck a large, silvered transparency. As I peered more closely I suddenly realised that it was the outline of a piercing human eye.

An all-seeing eye.

A private eye!

By the time that I had made my way up three narrow

sets of stairs I was quite puffed. Makepeace and I stumbled into a crowded suite of rooms and through the glass panel door of an office. As we did so I saw a huge man sitting on a groaning swivel chair behind an overloaded desk.

His hair like an ill-tended horse's mane sat over his enormous crown completely covering his ears on either side and hanging over his shoulders in thick tresses. Its whiteness reminded me of the snowcapped summit of some enormous mountain whose sides ran down over great jowls and dewlaps of cheeks onto wide, enormous, sloping shoulders and down over the foothills of a colossal stomach. His collapsed features and his heavy breathing gave a sense that he was not in the first flush of health. Nevertheless, as I caught his gaze, within the first few seconds of meeting this man I thought I detected a certain integrity, a genuine humanity that hangs over some people like an ineffable scent.

Before Makepeace could introduce us the great man spoke.

'Hey,' he said, sticking out an oversized Punch and Judy hand, on the little finger of which he wore a heavy rhinestone ring. 'The name's Mason, Nelson Mason.'

Amused by the 007 form of introduction, I smiled at him.

'The name's Randall, William Rand—' I replied, but before I could finish he interrupted me with a wheezy cough and a laugh.

'Good to meet you, Randy, good to meet you.'

'No! No, no, no, my name is not—'

Over the last few years I have become increasingly exasperated with people's inability to get my name right. How difficult is it?

'So I guess you're a Limey, is that right, Randy?' Mason continued and I was so amused by the Limey bit that I quite forgot my irritation.

'Yes, well I'm English, that's right, but my name is not—'

Before I could get any further, rather as Vesuvius might erupt, Mason slowly and shudderingly stood to his feet.

'Goddamn bladder. Goddamn bladder like a goddamn peanut. Gotta go to the bathroom. Goddamn . . .'

With that he lumbered for the door. Makepeace smiled at me and I grinned back in bewilderment.

Finally, Nelson Mason made his shambling return, pulling closed what must have been a good two foot of trouser zip. Sitting down again, heavily, he winked at me and asked me if everything was OK.

'A friend from England,' Makepeace introduced me rather belatedly and peremptorily, made his muttered excuses and left the room.

'Hey, isn't that just crazy? I just love you Limey guys.' Nelson Mason clearly did not find the circumstances of our meeting nearly as odd as I did. 'Here let me give you a gift. Hold on. Yeah. OK. Now you know who is the greatest of all you guys?'

'Er, no, no I'm not sure I do,' I replied politely surprised.

'Yeah, the greatest Englishman who ever lived – it's that Sherlock Holmes.'

I didn't see the purpose of pointing out the illogical nature of this statement and anyway there was no room for interruption.

'Yeah, the greatest is that Sherlock Holmes guy, he's the best.'

'Yes, that's true, er . . . I guess. The best . . .'

'Yeah, we only got Elmore Leonard, Mickey Spillane, Columbo, Perry Mason, even Magnum, jeez – but you guys, you got your Hercule Poirot, well, OK, he's like a European, and that English Lord, Sir Peter Wimsey and Miss Jane Marple, she's a cutie, isn't she? She just kills me. Yeah, hell, there's a whole load of great ones. Even so, they don't mean shit next door to Sherlock. I mean Sherlock, he's seriously the best.'

Nelson Mason clearly felt this sentiment peculiarly strongly because now he slapped down one hand like a huge ham on the table top.

'Hey, Nelson,' called a woman's voice from a reception area. 'Hey Nelson, aren't you gonna ring that Susie back this afternoon? Says her husband's setting off next Tuesday and she needs to meet with you to set up a surveillance, give you the background.'

'OK, OK, Rita,' Nelson replied to the unseen Rita. 'Give me a break, why don't you? Jeez!'

Then he gasped and coughed and spluttered horribly. Finally he appeared to be on the way to recovery, although he still did not look very well.

'Oh, hey, Rita, this here is a new buddy of mine from England. I want you to meet him – Randy, Randy Williams. Why don't you give him a coffee or a soda or something? What'll you have, Randy?' Without waiting for my answer, he carried on talking to the unseen Rita, all the while rummaging in one of the drawers of his desk. 'While I'm thinking about it, get me a glass of water will you please? Thank you, Rita, thank you.'

He then collapsed into another frightening bout of expectoration. I half stood, put out my arm, retrieved it and sat down. Any comfort or assistance I could bring him was beyond my capabilities.

Concerns that I might have had that Nelson was on the point of expiring were put to the back of my mind as around the corner and through the door came an angular, spiky figure. A woman in a smart business suit, who could not have been any greater contrast to the seething mass that was Nelson, introduced herself.

'Hey, Randy, good to meet you.'

Meekly, I shook her hand. Resistance was useless. Randy, it appeared I was to remain.

'How you doing?' said the woman. 'I'm Rita, Rita Martinez. I run the show round here so don't let anyone tell you any other way. You here for the internship?'

Not entirely sure what an internship was I nodded and shook my head and smiled all at the same time, as I was now, after years of blundering into unfamiliar and confusing situations, well practised at doing.

Rita appraised me nonetheless, staring intently at me through her titanium-rimmed glasses, and put a number of ticks and rather more crosses in the boxes of a mental questionnaire. She then turned on her heel and disappeared in a I've-got-a-whole-lot-of things-going-on sort of fashion.

'Hey, now buddy. OK, don't worry about that. Here, now where's that gift I want to give you?' Nelson started to pull open and slam shut the drawers of his large mahogany desk. Finally, after opening one of them for at least a second or third time, he grunted with satisfaction and pulled out a slim black box. Wiping it with the back of his forearm, he handed it across the piles of dusty folders.

'There you go, Randy. That's something to take back to the folks. Little reminder of your time visiting with us? All the clients get one.'

Thanking him I took the box and, sitting back into my seat, lifted the lid. Inside, on deep red-purple silk was a large and shiny magnifying glass. Down the handle ran the inscription 'Chestnut Investigations Inc.'. As I looked back up at Nelson, immobile behind his desk, I was suddenly overcome by a deep fascination for what it was that these people were employed doing in these strange, antiquated offices.

Private detectives!

How many times have I imagined myself as the resolver of great mysteries? As a child I had received, also as a present, a small detective kit which included a plastic magnifying glass so much smaller and less realistic than the one I held now, some plastic noses by way of disguise, and a fingerprint kit. This latter had unfortunately left black smudge marks all over the house and, to my chagrin when I arrived at school the next morning, all over my face.

Many of us, no doubt, at some stage have believed ourselves to have uncovered some crime or injustice, some mystery to be resolved and have, at least in our imaginations, come up with more or less fantastic solutions. Ever since I had taken to writing about the places that I had visited and in which I had lived I had made it my business to become as observant as possible. Perhaps I would be rather well suited to be a private eye, I thought, and laughed quietly to myself. It was certainly very interesting meeting Nelson and being here in his office. I wondered what his colleagues were like. The great man must have read my mind.

Putting a huge glass of water down, he tapped two fingers on his lips.

'Hey, Randy, I want you to meet the rest of the team. Yeah, let's do that. Hey, Makepeace,' he yelled. 'The other guys in the office right now?'

'Oh yeah, everyone here except Delray.' Jack popped his head round the door and his smile twinkled. 'Delray, he's out doing that surveillance on the porn star, remember?'

Porn star?

No!

Surely, I must have misheard him.

Ponster perhaps?

What was a *ponster*?

'Should be back soon. Look, I gotta go. Gotta get on that

building site fraud.' Jack stepped into the room and it took me a couple of seconds to realise that he had changed. Gone were the casual but smart clothes of earlier. The man-about-town look had been replaced. Now he was wearing the dusty jeans and chequered shirt of a construction worker. His hair was greased back, an earring shone in one ear, and on a tanned forearm was a faded tattoo with a special message for 'Mom'. Under that same arm was tucked a hard hat. 'Later, guys. Will be in touch, OK?'

'Bye,' I said.

'Oh yeah, sure, later, Makepeace. Hey, by the way, that buttonhole camera working out OK for you?' remembered Nelson. 'Forgot to ask. I'll be pissed if it isn't. It's top of the range. That's what Jimmy Methis told me.'

'It's sweet. We got some great stuff. Later, guys.'

Nelson grunted something that might have been satisfaction and looked up from a battered file with which he was fiddling.

'Hey, Ernie,' called Nelson, through the open door. 'Hey, why don't you come right on through here one minute? I want you to meet someone.'

In a corner of the room next to Nelson's, tucked away amongst the normal technological paraphernalia of a modern-day office, sat a young, short and stocky Asian-American man. He was staring through thick, black-rimmed glasses with something that resembled devotion at his computer screen.

'Come on, buddy, let's go. Time is money.' Nelson urged him into action.

Ern turned to us, flicking back his centrally parted hair with a metal pen. For someone who I realised later remained resolutely impassive practically all the time, he managed to look slightly annoyed. He half lifted himself out of his seat, before clicking a couple of times on his mouse, and sitting down again. Then with a final inaudible sigh he stood upright and came over to us. He was dressed in a rather fashionable white lab coat.

'Hey, Ernie, I want you to meet a friend of mine, he's from England, you know. Ernie Vinh, this is Randy er . . . Williams. Ernie is our forensic expert.'

'Forensics, really . . .'

Gearing up for a full-on introduction *à l'américaine*, I was about to produce a series of 'how're you doing's and 'just great to see you's and fully expected several 'welcome's and 'how pleased we are to have you here's in return, but Ernie, taking my hand rather begrudgingly, just said 'Hi.' Upon which he turned away, walked back and sat back down at his desk.

Slightly bewildered, I smiled at Nelson who, his hands folded over his sizeable chest, just raised his eyes heavenward and called out to Rita.

'Hey, Rita, why don't you just get Buck in here? He can meet with Randy. You sure gonna be interested in meeting him, Randy. He's an ass, by the way.'

I smiled and nodded and Rita flicked a switch on her desk intercom and issued a short instruction.

While I waited I pulled down two slats in the Venetian blind in what I hoped was the approved fashion and looked out through the silvered eye. Makepeace was just pulling out in a big four-wheel-drive truck, complete with rust and big headlights.

A few minutes later a man appeared in the doorway. It was Buck Burnett. He was dressed as if he was about to go and rescue hostages from a kidnap crisis, which, for all I knew at that moment, he might have been. Entirely in black, he sported a logo-less baseball hat, what appeared to be some kind of flak jacket with endless pockets, and a long leather coat. Little did I know when I shook hands with him that afternoon, my knuckles cracking audibly, how much time I was to spend with Buck. He appeared to be living out some kind of would-be private investigator fantasy. Somewhere between James Bond and the Terminator he had got it horribly wrong. If Buck Burnett was trying much too hard to look like a private eye then it might be said that my next acquaintance, Delray Drummond, a young African-American in his late twenties, was making anything but an attempt to create that impression. Dressed in that ubiquitous uniform of American football shirt, jeans and trainers, Delray bounced up to me when he got back to the office. We were introduced a few minutes after Buck Burnett had bid me farewell by shooting me several times with his fingers and calling me 'kid'. Delray stuck out his hand for a firm yet soft, slightly complicated handshake and smiled broadly at me.

'Yo, bro. How's it doing?'

I conceded that it was doing quite well, thank you very much.

Between them, Nelson and Delray, who seemed to have an easy relationship, told me a little about Delray and what had brought him into the employ of Chestnut Investigations Inc. Born on the 'wrong side of the tracks' (their expression not mine), Delray had attended the local elementary, middle and high schools in East Stoneham, out in the 'hood, where the drop-out rate was something over 70 per cent. Indeed, Delray had been one of only thirty graduates in his final year. This, it seemed, had only spurred him on to make greater efforts and he was now studying criminal justice at Boston University. His path had crossed that of Nelson Mason quite simply because they lived opposite each other in an apartment block in Brookline on the West Side. Delray had a way about him that was immediately charming and when he said he hoped that he and I were going to see much of one another while I was in Boston I wholeheartedly agreed.

Of course, all I really wanted to know about was the porn star.

3

Cabbage, Dumplings and a Little Undercover Surveillance

Although I had been much amused by my encounter with Nelson and his colleagues, and had since spent a certain amount of time wandering around the apartment that I was house-sitting in the South End inspecting objects with my new magnifying glass, I gave it all little further thought. Instead I sat wearily down and fired up my computer.

Some time, not a very long time, later I idly picked up my magnifying glass again and inspected my fingerprints. Just to check that they really were all different.

Taking regular breaks from extended periods of indolence, I had begun to build up a pleasant Bostonian routine for myself. The apartment was over two floors in an old brownstone, and the view from the rooftop terrace took in the whole sweep of the city, elegant in its mix of the old and new. It was a pleasure to sit out there as the summer nights drew shorter and calculate how many words I was going to have to write the next day if I was going to keep to my deadline. If I had stuck to my original timetable a few hundred words before breakfast would have sufficed. Now, if my calculations were right, it looked more like a couple of thousand and that was before I ever got to the rewrites and the general fiddling around sorting it all out. What was most disconcerting was that Chapter Thirteen, a particularly good one, though I say so myself, had simply disappeared into my computer and was resolutely refusing to give itself up however relentless my search. Fortunately, I knew my editor to be a most forgiving person but still it was all beginning to get a bit worrying.

Breakfast was easy. On the corner of East Berkeley and Tremont, in the basement of one of the bow-fronted grandees of apartment blocks, was Jimmy Wang's convenience store. Jimmy, who was actually Jing Hui Wang but not even a poor relation of the famous Boston Wangs, business people and philanthropists who lent their name to theatres and the big YMCA just off Washington Avenue, had just celebrated seventy years on this planet. As he had spent only the first four of these in China and the rest in Boston's South End, it was all the more remarkable that he spoke next to no English, but he was a shop owner par excellence. When I wandered in most mornings he was usually engaged in emptying out another unwieldy packing case from Shanghai, where he had the most resourceful of contacts. Out of the chaos of the shop's contents he always managed to rustle me up something soya-bean-based to get me going for the day before berating his unfortunate son, Jimmy Junior, for his idleness. It was true that Jimmy Junior did not appear to have inherited his father's gift for dynamic enterprise and he was more often than not to be found draped over the railings at the front door of the shop doing his best to impress passing Chinese girls with his smoke rings. His father, repeating mantra-like 'Jimmy Junior no good boy. He kill me. I telling you. He kill me' whilst he wrapped my lychees or rice cakes, cannot have done much for his son's morale and only made his prognostications about his own demise seem that much more likely.

Lunchtime, after a period of keyboard dusting and computer screen cleaning (with marvellous little tissues imported from Shanghai), took a very different gastronomic turn. In order to rearrange my thoughts for an afternoon of concerted writing I would amble along one of the footpaths that make up the Charles River esplanade, avoiding the joggers, who, heads down and earphones on, were a bloody liability. Honestly, you have never seen so many. If they expended half as much time and energy doing something useful then the world would be a distinctly better place. Cutting through West Hill, a small but beautiful Georgian-style square shaped like a keyhole, if such a geometrical image can be sustained, and then under an archway, I would step out onto the brightness and neatness of Charles Street. Here there were any number of Italian delicatessens to pick from but Canuca's Market, who maintained themselves to be freshest by far since 1927, quickly became my firm favourite. The red-awninged supermarket-cum-deli down at the bottom end, not far from the *Cheers* pub, certainly had the most extraordinary selection of Italian delicacies. At first I was transfixed by the dozens of alternatives on the order board but before too long I had thrown caution to the wind over my choice of sandwich for the day – I became almost a popular figure. Certainly no one ever expressed surprise over the eclectic mixtures of fillings that I rattled off to avoid holding up the queue. And there was always a queue at Canuca's.

When it was warm enough I ate on one of the benches in the Public Garden, amongst all the drunks and bums, the poets, the dreamers, the musicians and the fools. Soon I felt quite at home and would greet a few of the regulars with a lofty wave of my pastrami and anchovy light rye super sub with extra salad, Swiss cheese, bacon bits, pickled onion, gherkin, banana and radish, all topped with wasabi and thousand island dressing, then toasted, maybe deep-fried. Or whatever it was that day. If the weather was less accommodating I would wolf my lunch outside one of the three Starbucks coffee shops, along with the office workers who had popped out for a little less than five minutes lest they should miss some vital deal. There we would stand like figures in a Lowry painting, all stooped slightly forward to avoid getting mayo on our ties – or in my case a rather authorial roll necked sweater. Wrapping up the remains of my sandwich and then myself, I would hurry down Commonwealth or Boylston to take shelter in the impressive Boston Public Library on Dartmouth Street where I, more often than not, ran into the same dreamers and drunks and bums that I had met earlier in the park. They have some remarkably comfortable green leather and walnut chairs in the Boston Public Library and occasionally I would sit back in one, eyes closed, and wonder how all these thousands of other authors had managed to finish off their blasted books. I bet they hadn't had to spend hours trying to extricate Chapter Thirteen from the bowels of some computer operating system.

Later, I would wander groggily through Back Bay, over the Massachusetts Turnpike and back into the South End. More often than not I would run into Mrs Walowski, my neighbour, going out or returning to the flat below mine, but in whichever direction she was going it was never without Jackie, a rather absurd black toy poodle. Jackie was named after the former First Lady, of course. She normally dressed in a red halter affair attached around her ribs with matching leash, which would have been useful if an air-sea rescue had been required but on days out in the South End just looked stupid and ostentatious. Secretly, I rather loathed Jackie, but her owner Mrs Walowski was a good sort even if she was, as she described herself, 'zo old'. Due to the pancake make-up, eyeshadow and lipstick that were glued to her sagging but friendly face it was very difficult to give a realistic approximation of her age, but if anything the brightly coloured tights that she wore below rather too short skirts and her extraordinarily imaginative collection of hats gave her a rather youthful air. Mrs Walowski and her husband, both originally from Warsaw, Poland, had both moved to Boston on the latter's retirement from an automobile works in what she described as 'da Mutta Ziti', which I took to mean Detroit. Shortly after they had set up home in what, at the time, had been a run-down working class part of town, almost a no-go area for the 'Polisi', Mr Walowski had moved on to the great assembly line in the sky. With no particular place to go, Mrs Walowski had stayed on, sharing the quite spacious flat and garden with a long line of canine companions, the most recent of which was the dreadful Jackie. She kept herself busy in the local community, attending the Roman Catholic church at the end of the street where they had 'zuch lovely Messes and a priester who is zo young, maybe my grandson!' although, I thought at the time, this she should really have known. She also frequented the church's social club where apparently she was something of a wizard whist player, regularly fleecing the (mainly Korean) old folks. She made up for it by inviting them all over on a regular basis to sample the endless dishes that appeared from her kitchen. More than once I met a group of Asian geriatrics giggling helplessly on the doorstep, gripping each other and the plane trees that lined the street, after a heavy lunchtime session of borscht, dumplings and plum brandy.

'Perhaps it's your common interest in cabbage?' I suggested to Mrs Walowski late one afternoon as she waved off her tottering, red-faced friends. 'You know, the Koreans and the Poles?'

'Ach, no! I have tried that, what they call it zese Korea people? Chim-chi, yes?' She wrinkled her make-up and took a long drag on an ash-laden More cigarette. 'It is *zo* disgusting.'

And that was her final word on the fermented national dish of that particular country.

Generosity of spirit was not, however, something for which you could normally fault Mrs Walowski, and specially prepared dishes were often to be found on the doorstep of my apartment at supper time when I was about to head out to sample the bright lights of Boston. Of course, the city is a walking man's gastronomic delight. From the old Italian trattorias of the North End, serving the finest pasta the wrong side of the Atlantic, to the trendy, wholefoody restaurants of Back Bay and the South End, through the steaming Vietnamese and Korean restaurants of Chinatown and the hissing, spluttering, flaming meat grills and diners of the theatre district, it is a joyful experience. And that is to say nothing, for the time being, of the Union Oyster Bar.

If I was not in the mood to be too adventurous, or more often was feeling wracked with guilt about having done absolutely nothing, zero, zip, nada about my book all day, I contented myself with a burger or a quesadilla and maybe a beer or two at Crazy Joan's Tavern, down on Chandler. Jolene, a Dolly Parton lookalike from Tallahassee who worked behind the bar, took an immediate shine to my accent and I was almost instantaneously one of the crowd.

Quite quickly I worked out an admittedly fairly unproductive routine, but I really did have every intention of getting on with things. So it was with some surprise that when I picked up the telephone after a gruelling afternoon in one of the cinemas just off Copley Plaza, I discovered that it was Nelson.

'Hey, Randy, how're you doing today?' came the inevitable question that makes up part of the whole process of phatic communion so beloved of Americans and which is so worryingly easily learned by foreigners.

'I'm doing pretty good, thanks, Nelson. And how are you doing today?'

'I'm doing good, thanks. So have you been having yourself a good time in Boston? Is Bean Town being good to you?' He chuckled wheezily and then made some none too original allusions to the Boston Tea Party and the American War of Independence that I managed to shrug off, reacting only with a hollow laugh followed by a heavy silence.

'Anyway, look, Randy, I was just calling you to find out how things were going. How are you getting on with that book of yours?'

Again I failed to make any coherent comment in response.

'Sounds good, sounds good,' he said and then changed his tone dramatically. 'Now look, Randy, if you're interested I have a proposition to make you. Why don't you come by my offices tomorrow morning – let's say around ten? I think you might be interested in what I have to say.'

Delighted by the distraction I leapt at his offer with embarrassing alacrity. The sense of guilt was only very slight as I closed the lid on my laptop and watched as the little blue light on the front flickered and gave up.

These days there was a chill in the air, and as I set out through the Theatre District and up Tremont Street I was warmly wrapped in a long overcoat and thick woolly scarf. Making my way up Charles Street between the unkempt Boston Common and the more tended Public Garden I felt myself drawn back into the world that Nelson inhabited. Crossing over Boylston Street I noticed that steam was beginning to rise most authentically from the gratings in the street. This only ever happens in America and it seemed strangely appropriate as I headed towards my mysterious meeting. I don't understand why we can't have a similar system in London. Perhaps it is not steam at all but some special effect involving dry ice designed to create a seductive, cinematic atmosphere in American cities. It certainly works.

Having by now spent a fair amount of time tramping the streets of Boston I had begun to know my way around. It is a relatively confusing city, surrounded, it seems, on all sides by water and meandering rivers that run out into the Atlantic Ocean, and it is a curious experience to cross one bridge to follow the streets of what seems to be a grid-like pattern, only to find yourself crossing back over a river into a completely different part of town.

That afternoon, as the last of the autumn sun shone on the shop fronts of the numerous antiquarian bookshops and antique dealers on Charles Street, I waved briefly at a young woman real-estate agent who had spent an earnest half an hour the day before trying to sell me a condominium. I am still a little uncertain what form one of these takes.

Soon I was making my way up the tree-lined Chestnut Avenue towards Nelson's office. When I arrived outside I looked up and saw the silver private eye glinting in the morning sunshine and thrilled with a certain pleasure. When I knocked on the door below the sign that read 'Chestnut Investigations Inc. Discreet and Confidential', and walked into the reception area, Rita Martinez was there to meet me. She held out her hand and shook me by the fingertips in a rather mechanical fashion but her greeting was friendly and she immediately asked how I was doing on that particular day. Although I told her that I was doing just fine I could not help sensing that there was a certain

official feeling to my visit. It appeared I was not just dropping by for a chat.

Nelson was momentarily unavailable but it was only a
few minutes later that he came bulging out of the narrow
door of the restroom that stood at the far end of Rita's office
space.

We proceeded through some more formulaic salutations
and eventually I found myself sitting again in Nelson's
office as he settled himself, grunting and shuddering, behind
his desk. Nelson spent a few moments shuffling the papers
on his desk as if, in fact, rearranging his thoughts before
he addressed me. This allowed me a little time to inspect
his office, which on my first visit, what with all the toings
and froings of new faces, had remained something of a blur.
The walls were closely covered with framed certificates
pronouncing excellence, competence, service and great
success in any variety of departments. Nearly all the certificates were made out to Nelson, and a surprisingly large
number of them seemed to be signed by him too. Just above
a small glass cabinet filled, and here I smiled, with leather-
bound copies of the complete tales of Sherlock Holmes, an
antiquated pistol, a large magnifying glass and a spy
camera, was a photograph of a scarcely recognisable Nelson
shaking hands with a man that I was fairly convinced had
once been a high-ranking official for the United States
government.

Just as Nelson was about to make a start, Makepeace
suddenly arrived, making apologies for his lateness. I had
seen him a couple of times in town and he had made no
mention of his work or of Nelson, despite my gentle
enquiries, as he was much preoccupied by getting everything ready for his forthcoming hospital visit. His wife, who
was from the Philippines, had two little daughters and as
she did not speak much English, Makepeace was making

arrangements for his mother to stay with them whilst he was recuperating, initially at Massachusetts General Hospital, and then at a rehabilitation centre out near Concord. I watched him grimace as he swung himself into one of the leather chairs next to me and opposite Nelson.

'Now listen, Randy, I like to talk straight. I'm an American. You don't get any bullshit from me.'

Makepeace started to giggle and Nelson gave him a dirty look before carrying on. 'You know what I saw in you, when we first met, you know what I saw?'

'No, I'm not really sure that I do,' I answered nervously.

'I'll tell you what I saw. I saw a young man . . .'

Young man! I was over forty. Just, admittedly, but that surely could not possibly fit into the category of young.

'Yes, I saw a young man full of potential. Full of curiosity. Yeah, filled with a burning desire to find out the truth.'

I could not help but laugh at Nelson's extraordinary over-exaggerations. Even as an educated, thoughtful man, as all those certificates advertised him to be, he could not seem to overcome the American temptation for enormous over-colouring of even the most mundane of issues. Used as I was to the rampant cynicism of an English audience towards all things promotional, I still remained amazed at how fascinated Americans could be with the simplest advertising campaign. Only a couple of days before I had laughed, inwardly, of course, when I had overheard in a bar in the South End two extremely camp young men discussing the latest beauty products to appear on a TV ad campaign. Not only were they extraordinarily credulous about the efficacy of the product but also deeply impressed by the way that it was marketed. I had even heard that there was a competition run for the best TV ad to be aired during the American football annual final. In the USA I am sure that the word hyperbole rhymes with Superbowl.

'Come on, boss. These English guys, they don't like all the talk,' interrupted Makepeace, clearly demonstrating that he had got the measure of my brother at least. 'Just give it to him straight.'

Nelson looked a little irritated again but then appeared to change his mind. 'To be honest with you, Will. I need a guy like you – somebody who is of a certain maturity . . .'

A certain maturity! He was at it again with the soft soap. I laughed and then, quite successfully I think, managed to turn it into a quick clearing of my throat.

'I got this case coming up right now. I kinda need a guy like you to do a little undercover surveillance,' said Nelson as if he was announcing that he needed his car washed.

An undercover surveillance job! Wow, that was incredibly cool, I thought, but with a certain maturity.

'Oh, really! Nice one!' It just slipped out but I quickly rearranged myself. 'Sorry, yes, perhaps you could let me know a little more about the, er . . . nature of this, er . . . undercover surveillance.'

'Well,' Makepeace said, taking up the conversation, 'let's not get too carried away here. What we actually want you to do is just to talk to someone.'

'Just talk to someone?' I felt, to say the least, deflated.

'Let me outline the facts of the case to you,' said Nelson, spreading his hands widely across the desk and reading from an open file. Jack grinned at me but I concentrated on Nelson. I definitely wanted the facts of the case outlined to me.

'A United States citizen, female, is in the process of divorcing from her husband. She is keen to know what overseas possessions he may have kept hidden from her as they will be pertinent to any settlement. She has requested that Chestnut Investigations Inc. look into her husband's financial dealings in both the United States and abroad.

Chestnut Investigations Inc. have so far carried out a number of financial checks which have included several pretext phone calls to the subject and associated financial institutions. As yet these enquiries have not produced any firm evidence to prove the subject's wealth is any greater than that announced to the client's attorneys. Chestnut Investigations Inc. propose an undercover operation to attempt to elicit further information from the suspect in person.'

Nelson looked up from the folder, rather seriously.

'So there we have it.'

'Er, sorry . . . so there we have what?' I asked, muddled. What with subjects and clients and settlements, I was not entirely sure I had understood much of what Nelson had been saying.

'What we are proposing here,' Makepeace attempted to clarify, 'is that the subject, i.e. the husband in the divorce settlement, should be interviewed by a private investigator posing as an innocent party, a casual acquaintance, someone that the subject happens to bump into.'

'Oh?' I replied and finally began to see some method in the muddle. 'So how does that work? Is that er . . . strictly legal?'

'Most certainly, it is legal,' Nelson replied sharply. 'We only do things by the letter of the law in this agency. You'll find plenty of guys out there who'll get up to shady tricks. Not here though. You can be assured of that.'

Just as I, blushing, was about to apologise for having ever doubted the honour of Chestnut Investigations Inc., Makepeace carried on.

'It's what we call a pretext. The investigator, without specifically maintaining that he is any particular individual, actually impersonating anyone, leads the subject to believe that he is anything but a PI. Quite often we do it on the doorstep. Claim to be from a business of some kind, or just a door-to-door salesman. That way we can ascertain whether someone is resident at a particular address or not.'

'Oh, I'm with you. So as long as I don't claim to be, er . . . Arnold Schwarzenegger, it doesn't matter if I lead the subject to believe I'm a bodybuilder?'

'Exactly, but I'm not sure that in your case bodybuilder would be a particularly good cover to choose,' replied Nelson rather seriously and, as far as I was concerned, rather missing the point.

Anyway I wasn't in that bad . . .

'OK, but what I really am not quite sure is why you think that *I* would be of any use to you. I'm really not used to this kind of thing, not like you all are.'

'What the boss failed to tell you just now is that the subject is a British citizen. What he also forgot to tell you is that he attempted to use us as an agency to counter-sue his wife for infidelity. He's met Nelson, been sitting in that seat you're in right now, and he will have seen any number of us come and go. We can't take the risk that he will recognise us if we go in to do the surveillance.'

'The British thing, that's real important.' Nelson now seemed extremely focused on the conversation. 'The moment that the subject finds himself interacting with someone from his own social or geographical sphere, particularly in a foreign location, their guard tends to drop. We have an inherent trust in people whose identity we recognise.'

Trust that is often somewhat misplaced, as my experience – particularly in Africa – had taught me.

'Why would he be in any way suspicious of another travelling businessman from England? A chance encounter at the bar and a chat,' added Jack.

'All we would be asking you to do, Randy, is to just get

yourself in a position where you can have a talk with the guy. See what he's got to say. You don't really have to elicit any information in particular. Just see if you can get him to let slip about any property in the United Kingdom. If he gives the impression that he has some, all you need to find out is a vague location and we can take it from there.'

'Yeah, this guy, he's been resident in the US for the last seven years but he makes frequent trips back to the UK. Tells his soon-to-be ex he stays in hotel accommodation or with his mother. Our client has been over there a few times with him but has never been anywhere but those two locations.'

'She has been aware of payments coming in from the UK but the husband claims these to be simply salary cheques.'

After my initial bewilderment I could now quite clearly see the situation. All of a sudden, I found myself discussing the case as if it were the most normal thing in the world.

'So where would the meet take place, this er . . . chance encounter?'

Makepeace pulled a notebook out of his pocket.

'We have been doing a little bit of what we call pre-surveillance. Keeping an eye on the guy's movements. Finding out if he's got a routine. He is a gentleman of fairly regular habits, you might say. Every day after work, or at least four days a week, he works out at a gym on Tremont and usually heads to the bar of the Four Seasons on Boylston Street for pre-dinner drinks. So, yeah, either in the gym or at the Four Seasons. The gym is your best bet.'

'Oh, not the gym!' I exclaimed, dismayed. 'I'll just hang around in the bar.' I smiled winningly but Nelson shook his head.

'No, you have got to give yourself the widest possible chance of access. Start at the gym and if that doesn't work out you can try again in the hotel bar.'

'Listen,' Jack reassured me, 'I'll be with you all the way

at a distance. I'll give you some pointers as to what to do and say. You'll see, it'll all be over in a matter of moments.'

'Well, what do you think?' Nelson fixed me with what was suddenly a surprisingly piercing stare, his huge features quite animated. 'So you want to give it a go? You do, doncha? Who didn't wanna become a PI sometime in their life? Am I right? Am I right?'

Nelson put on his sincere face again. 'So what do you think, buddy? It'll be great, don't you think?'

So many offers have been made to me over the last ten years.

The answer required of me is either yes or no.

Answer 'No' and the chances are that the opportunity is unlikely to come up again in this lifetime.

Answer 'Yes' (after due reflection, of course) and adventures, occasionally of the hair-raising, occasionally of the unpleasant, but most normally of the fascinating and entertaining nature, have come my way.

I looked at Nelson then at Makepeace.

'Of course I will,' I replied.

Lucky, really. Otherwise this might have made for a bit of a boring book.

4

Just Like Clockwork

The fitting rooms at Filene's Basement were busy as endless items of clothing were tried and either rejected or accepted in the desperate search for a bargain. Filene's Basement in Downtown is something of an institution in Boston. Designer labels, or rather slight seconds thereof, are heaped in great piles in the lower ground floor of a department store building which seems to stretch for several acres. Prices are astonishingly low and of course thousands of people go to fit themselves out there. That anybody should wish to pay the astonishing prices for designer labels in the fashionable boutiques of Newbury Street was astonishing, although those that did were, according to Mrs Walowski, 'poshies'. So that probably explained it.

I found myself in the basement, late the following afternoon, to select my outfits for the upcoming undercover surveillance. I had not brought a suit with me from England and obviously did not own any sportswear. Makepeace and I had already selected my gym kit, although I had rejected the towelling headband out of hand and also anything that involved Lycra. Now, I stepped out of the dressing rooms in my fashionable businessman-around-Boston disguise.

'OK, well I think you got it. Perfect.' Makepeace seemed pleased and I supposed that I was too as I inspected myself in the full-length mirrors when eventually there was a square inch of space amongst the other crowding Narcissi. The light grey suit – smooth woollen jacket and trousers – fitted me as if they had been tailor-made and would have cost a fortune 'new'. The shoes, brown loafers with, I'm sorry to have to admit, tassels, were not the type of footwear I would have normally countenanced but somehow they rather fitted the bill. Only the shirt collar was tight and constricting. It had been eight or nine years since my teaching profession had demanded I wear a tie. The old sensation of being buttoned at the neck made me feel uncomfortable and reminded me of the costumes that I had worn in various theatrical productions whilst at school and university. I knew, however, this was important, reminding me of my new role. Before long I would adapt to these new clothes and they to me.

Putting my original clobber into one of the enormous Filene's Basement plastic bags we left and walked fairly briskly up the hill making our way to some benches by one of the T stops. Makepeace carried my clothes and I, still dressed in my new business outfit, held a holdall of gym kit slung over one shoulder.

Rather as a boxing manager might prepare his boy for a fight Makepeace kept talking me through what I should do.

'Obviously you're not gonna take his photo in with you. You have to memorise him right now. You got it?'

'I think so,' I muttered, and inhaled and exhaled hard. I looked down at the photograph I held in my slightly shaking hand. Something about the man in the picture somehow diminished any of the concerns about what it was that I was about to do. The lines around his mouth and eyes suggested more than a hint of a mean streak. His shaven head gave him a belligerent air. He was definitely a dog who would eat dog with some relish.

'Try to get on equipment near his, preferably opposite.' When he takes a break, you take a break and remember you have to throw yourself into the job. OK? You can't pretend to be lifting weights, running on the machine, doing the floor exercises. You really have to do them.'

'God, really?'

I had forgotten about this bit. I wasn't sure that a gymnasium and I had come into direct contact since plimsolls had elasticated sides.

'Yeah, make sure that you build up a good sweat, use the towel a lot. It'll distract him from taking you in too much. You've got to be like a good magician except almost in reverse. Use your hands so he doesn't look at your face, doesn't even see you. Get it?'

'OK, OK,' I muttered.

Rather like the moments before those same amateur dramatics, before the curtain went up, I just wished that the whole business would get under way. Makepeace seemed to read my thoughts. 'OK, take it easy.' He flashed a look at his watch. 'He should be arriving any time right now. Normally comes straight from work. His office is on the twenty-fourth floor of that block over there.' He pointed at the cold blue reflection of the skyscraper just off Copley Plaza. 'He'll be coming from over there . . . and there he is! Just like clockwork.'

Makepeace snatched the photograph out of my fingers. Now I was disconcerted. The stage manager had taken away my lines before pushing me out into the limelight. 'OK, I'm gonna take you as far as the corner. Then you're on your own.'

Unmistakably, it was our man. In some ways he looked

uglier in the flesh than he had done on the photograph. There was a certain purpose in his stride, a don't-get-in-my-way demeanour, as he turned the corner towards the entrance of the gym. What I hadn't taken into account was the fact that he would be accompanied – in this case by a man of similar build and look, dressed in an almost identical blue suit. What bearing would this have on the operation?

Panicked slightly, I turned to ask Makepeace.

He was gone.

Startled, I looked hurriedly around and only after a minute spotted him on the bench where we had been waiting. Smiling, he waved me off before disappearing behind a newspaper and with a grimace I turned back to the two men just in time to see them disappearing in through the door of the gym. Walking, half skipping, almost running, slowing down and speeding up, I followed them in through the glass doors and into a large hall. The ground-floor lobby of the gym was unfurnished apart from a couple of posters on the wall advertising excruciating-looking physical fitness lessons, and the two men were nowhere to be seen. At the far end was a lift. Glancing up I saw the orange light shift from level one to two. Makepeace had assured me that he had checked the place out. This was the only way in and out and there was no cause for concern. Patiently, I waited, only occasionally muttering 'Come on, come on, come on!' under my breath.

When the lift arrived I hurled myself in but when the doors finally pinged open for me again, although I did not expect to see anybody in the reception area, I ventured out a little timidly. When I saw the two men in earnest conversation with a receptionist I almost jumped back into the lift.

Makepeace had told me not to worry in the slightest if the subject should take notice of me. Indeed, this was rather the point. Nevertheless I could not help feeling mighty conspicuous and right at that moment I felt that I could only have stood out a little more if I had had a Belisha beacon strapped to my head. Sizing up and trying to make sense of the logic of the situation I realised that Makepeace was right and started to make my way towards the desk. Half of me hoped that the men would push off in the direction of the changing area to the right, leaving me room to think, to follow them in my own time, but to my surprise, just as I was about to reach the desk, the two men turned back towards me. The subject was now holding a squash racquet.

'Thank you very much, mate,' he said over his shoulder. 'I knew I left it somewhere. Couldn't remember where.'

He spoke with an accent that I deemed to be Mancunian or similar and the words came out in a series of hoarse grunts. Even so, what he said was strangely anodyne and I couldn't help feeling that it would have been more appropriate if he had muttered a menace about drilling someone through with lead, and waved not a squash racquet but a tommy gun in the direction of the terrified receptionist. Instead, she now cheerfully wished both men a nice day with a little smiling wave as they came back down the corridor towards me. Trying to summon up some of my few acting skills, I walked past them consulting my watch, whistling a few snatches of 'In an English Country Garden', and glanced nonchalantly at the ceiling, before checking my mobile phone for phantom calls. When I reached the desk I turned round and watched them disappear into the lift. Turning to the receptionist I asked her about the membership fees and she pulled out a brochure, smiling. The smile seemed to stop halfway across her face, freeze-framed, as I dashed back to the lift and hit the call button. Her lips only continued on their upward arc as I rushed back to the desk.

'So, sir, as you will see we have a number of different payment methods depending on your intended usage of our facilities.'

Ping!

Snatching the leaflet, I turned back to the startled woman.

'Thanks very much indeed. You've been terribly helpful. Really nice place you've got here. Be back in a . . . uh . . . bit.'

Before I hopped into the lift, I just had time to see the smile deflate as surely as if someone had pulled the plug out of an inflatable toy. Puffing already, I hit the down button so hard I nearly broke my finger.

Bundling out onto the street Buster Keaton style I looked hurriedly left and right. The two men were ambling back up the road towards Tremont and beyond them through the traffic I could see Makepeace sitting on the park bench, seemingly still engrossed in his newspaper. Following at what I deemed to be a safe distance, I watched the two men cut across the corner of the Public Garden, the subject swinging his squash racquet fairly proficiently. Makepeace joined me as I crossed the road, hopping through the home-bound traffic, wondering vaguely if this constituted jaywalking. He looked mildly dazed as I gave him a brief, but, I believed, accurate description of what had happened.

'Well, if you told me that at about a tenth of the speed I might be able to work something out from it,' he laughed.

'Come on, come on, they're getting away!'

Still smiling broadly, Makepeace followed me down the path occasionally putting his hand on my arm when he thought I was about to break into a jog. Some five minutes later the two men arrived at the Four Seasons Hotel and with a slight nod from the top-hatted doorman disappeared inside the shiny exterior.

'OK, all yours. Get in there, order yourself a drink and see how it goes. If you get the chance to catch him on his own, do it. Otherwise, finish your drink and leave. Tomorrow is another day.'

Nodding, I shook his hand for some reason and made for the hotel.

Hanging around in bars is a pastime that I am reasonably, well, very, practised at doing but as I pushed open the door of the Bar Excelsior at the Four Seasons it was with surprisingly little pleasure.

5

Philip Marlowe, Vietnam Vic and the Diner on Highway 33

When I made it back to Nelson's office with Jack, after just a short taxi ride from Boylston up to Charles Street, I was still pumping with adrenaline. Kindly, the other private detectives, all old hands, gathered round in Rita's reception area to listen to my story or, I should say, my report. I started immediately and even I was aware that I was talking rather quickly.

'When I got in there it was pretty quiet, like not a lot of people. The guy, the, er . . . subject was already sitting up at the bar with his friend who was sitting to his right. Well, I couldn't quite believe that there was an empty chair next to him on his left. By the time I had summoned up the courage to go and sit at the bar I was pretty thirsty, I can tell you.' I was rewarded with a small chuckle.

'Of course, when I sat down he was talking to his friend and because his back was to me and I didn't want to make it obvious that I was interested in them, I couldn't hear what it was that he was saying. All I managed to work out was that the other man he was with was American and they appeared to be talking about the exchange rate between the dollar and the pound; anyway, something pretty boring.

Fortunately his friend only stayed for one drink, a Michelob, I think.'

I looked up rather pleased with how observant I had been but nobody else appeared to think it pertinent to my story so I pressed on.

'Well, you won't be surprised to hear that when his friend upped and left I suddenly got into a panic thinking that the subject might well finish his drink and leave. I was thinking about offering to buy him one but luckily, after he had checked the time and given it some thought, he ordered another one himself.'

Delray wanted to know what my opening gambit had been.

'Well, very unimaginatively I let him know that I realised he was English too.'

'Couple of Limeys at the bar,' Buck chuckled. The rest of us ignored him.

'I don't think he much liked me at first,' I explained, without going into a complex explanation of how one Englishman will have made a series of judgements about another almost before, but certainly after, the other has opened his mouth. 'But anyway, I think after a while he warmed to me. I told him a joke, pretty good one, and he seemed to find it funny. It opened up the conversation quite well.'

'What joke was that?' asked Buck enthusiastically.

'Oh, you know, the one about the two statues in the park and God flies over? Do you know that one?'

Everyone shook their heads and Buck pleaded to hear it. I gave them the shortened version and again everybody laughed quite genuinely – everyone that is apart from the deeply disappointed Buck, who didn't get it. Makepeace promised to explain it to him later.

'So then we talk about what we're doing in the States,

you know, like him and me, and I give him the line about coming here to write a book and doing the house-sitting, which was pretty easy because it was all true. Then I asked him what *he* was doing here and he said oh, that he was now a US resident and that he had pretty much given up on the UK and had no immediate intention of going back there.'

'Go on,' said Nelson quite seriously, and I noticed that the atmosphere had changed considerably. Makepeace was taking notes.

'Well, I wasn't quite sure how bullish I should be in my questioning so I told him that I had sold up everything that I owned in England and moved to France some ten years before – which also was quite true. You know, when I went off to the South Pacific?' I added, looking at Makepeace, who nodded in a sort of yes, get on with it kind of way.

'Well, that seemed to give him some food for thought and, just like that, he immediately announced that yes, he did have a house and a couple of rental properties that he was thinking about getting rid of. They had increased in value enormously but were just a headache at that distance. Of course, I was really pleased. Then things started to go a bit pear-shaped.'

Buck's brow wrinkled under his cap. In fact my audience's collective expression was one of profound confusion.

'Pear-shaped, yeah, er . . . Went wrong. Things started to go wrong. For a start, I suddenly discovered that I had left one of the labels attached to the suit, on the right cuff. That was a bit complicated because it meant I had to start drinking with my left hand, which made me look as if I had just undergone some major muscle spasm. I decided to stick my other arm between my legs, which didn't help but was better than holding it behind my back. Then the subject finishes his drink and stands up. Of course I quickly offer him a drink and he says no, he's fine. Picks up his squash racquet.'

'Holy kershmoley!' explained Delray.

'Holy kershmoley, indeed!' I concurred. 'Anyway, most people can be convinced to stay for one more drink can't they? I know I can. No, no, he has things to do. I was on the point of asking him if I could help with them, when thank God, his mobile, er . . . cellphone rang. He answers it. So, I'm waving at the waiter like I'm drowning and fortunately the guy . . . subject, gets into his call and I'm trying to fish my wallet out of my left-hand inner pocket with my left hand and it gets stuck. The hand, I mean. Well, both.'

Rita mimed trying the same manoeuvre.

'Anyway . . . luckily he turns away and I quickly get my hand out from between my legs and pull my other hand out of my pocket – if you see what I mean – and finally get hold of my wallet. God knows what the waiter thought but he just managed to plonk down two drinks on the bar at the moment the subject snaps his phone closed! Luckily he has forgotten that he wasn't having another one but he is looking a bit preoccupied. Don't know what about. "So," I asked nonchalantly, "whereabouts are your flats?" His apartments. "Oh, them," he says, and takes a big sip of his drink. Then he just starts to talk. Apparently a couple of the places he owns are in a town just north of Manchester in a place called Boroughford and his main residence, he kindly told me, believe it or not, is in a block of flats, I mean apartments, opposite the Manchester Metropolitan Hotel.'

On that, mildly triumphant, note I stopped talking and looked up to see the reaction of the audience. Very pleasingly they all nodded thoughtfully and muttered *well dones* under their breath. It was very gratifying.

'Hey, sounds like you did good, my brother,' said Delray and grabbed my hand as if he was about to embark on an impromptu arm-wrestle, and the others agreed.

After the rest had gone Nelson asked me if I had enjoyed the experience.

'Nerve wracking at the beginning,' I told him, 'but once I realised that the worst he was likely to do was not answer my questions I relaxed and began to think about the best way to tease information from him. You know, since I've been doing this writing business, going out and getting a story, I seem to have got a lot better at that sort of thing: how to ask the right sort of question, not to ask too many leading questions but also not ask questions that block the person you're talking to into a corner. By the end of it, I was bloody loving it, as we might say in England!'

'Hey,' said Nelson, 'Makepeace was telling me about your books. I was just checking them out on the Internet. I'm what you would call a book kind of guy myself.' He gestured expansively at the glass-fronted cabinet stocked with the Sherlock Holmes collections and numerous other titles.

I told him that I had already admired his bookshelves and he was very pleased.

'Hey, if you like books and you're still interested in this PI business then maybe I've got something here that would interest you.'

Nelson lumbered to his feet and shuffled to the book-case, a brass key tiny in his hand. 'Pull up a chair,' he said, and for the next couple of hours we pored over his volumes and talked detective business.

'You're really getting a taste for it, aren't you?' asked Nelson, after I had gone back over the day and he had explained to me the next steps that they would take to build up the case on the subject.

'Yes, I find it fascinating.' I surprised myself by how wholeheartedly I agreed with him.

'Well, while you're Stateside we're sure to have some more cases you can get involved in. We'll call. Yeah, we'll call. Now, this Dashiell Hammett, *The Thin Man*, picked it up in a small store up in Washington State, great little place. Been up there sorting out a false identity on a triple homicide. It's a first edition but you'll see its been rebound in buckskin. Whaddya think of that . . . Course I couldn't let you take that one. Oh, heck, you can borrow it if you want.'

So it was, in the early evening, I found myself emerging from the Chestnut Investigations Inc. offices clutching two plastic bags from a local liquor store that had been conveniently found in one of Nelson's desk drawers and had been filled with important reading matter. Making my way back to the South End on foot, for it was a fine autumnal evening, I now possessed a small library and, it appeared, a new job.

When I got back to the apartment I found Mrs Walowski struggling with Jackie on a lead, her travel pooper scooper, a bag of shopping from Jimmy's Convenience Store and the keys to the front door. She was grateful to me for opening up for her and invited me into her apartment to sample some caraway seed cakes that she had baked and some particularly vicious aquavit that had arrived in the post from Poland for her that very morning. I didn't want to be long because I intended to head out to Crazy Joan's bar and restaurant to celebrate my day's experience and probably tell Jolene and the others there all about it. In fact, as I was talking to Mrs Walowski, I thought I might as well tell her about it too. Unfortunately she did not react with quite the enthusiasm that I was hoping for. Instead she sat down heavily and threw her hands up in the air simultaneously

'No good you young boy, no good you become *polisi*,' she wailed.

However hard I attempted to explain that I was not going to become '*polisi*' and that private investigation was a much nobler calling, she was having none of it. Failing to adequately pronounce Sherlock Holmes in Polish, I left my neighbour still shaking her head and muttering '*no polisi, no polisi*' as I went up the stairs, making good my escape.

Jolene and the crowd down at Crazy Joan's were a much more malleable audience and when I had finished explaining to them my heroics of earlier in the day more beers were ordered. People momentarily stopped playing cards and darts and pool and discussed any number of private investigation anecdotes that they had heard over the years.

'Y'all want to talk to Vietnam Vic over there. He got plenty of stories to tell you. Probably knows a few about private detectives too, I shouldn't doubt it. You just wanna ask him. Go on, go right ahead, Randy.'

Wandering across the bar, I wondered how Jolene, too, had got my name so badly wrong. How difficult was it, I thought again. It was not as if I had introduced myself as Randy.

Had I?

This awful thought kept my mind off why I had spent much of the time on my previous visits to Crazy Joan's avoiding Vietnam Vic. Of course, it was for the simple reason that he looked utterly deranged. His face was surprisingly soft, lined and mournful, and his stubble and long hair kept back by a bandanna made him look older than perhaps he really was. But it was his eyes that suggested his retreat from the world. Deep brown, they were seeing somewhere a long way distant from where we were now, seeing something much more intense. He preferred to sit on his own at the heel of the bar and drink copiously, not that the alcohol ever seemed to have much of an undue effect on him.

Perhaps the real reason that I thought he was crazy was that I was sure that if I had been in Vietnam, which presumably he had been, I would definitely have not remained sane. He also reminded me of a tramp I had once lived next door to in a lodging house on the fringes of a rancid coastal town in Australia. *He* had been completely nuts. His madness may have had something to do with his diet, which consisted solely of raw red onions, eaten in the manner of an apple and washed down with copious quantities of methylated spirits. On all but one occasion that I had stayed in the hostel I had successfully resisted his invitations to dine with him.

Some days I feel more gung-ho than others and that particular evening at Crazy Joan's was such a day. Finishing my drink, I went up and sat next to Vietnam Vic.

'You been hanging around with some of them private detectives then, have you?' he asked without delay, as if the word had got around the whole bar as soon as I had walked in. Of course, I have got quite a loud voice.

Not sure of the answer that would please, I announced that I had been.

Vietnam Vic looked at me expressionlessly.

'Some of them good. Some of them bad. Like the VC.'

The Viet Cong? I wasn't sure that it was quite the same thing but said nothing.

'You wanna hear a story? About a private eye and a friend of mine back along when we came home from 'Nam?'

'Sure,' I replied, rather authentically, and settled into the comfortable bar stool as two icy Buds slid down the zinc top of the bar.

'Well, we got back to the US in seventy-one. Just finished our last tour of duty, there was about ten of us leaving the demob camp at the same time. Not far from here. Fort Jones on the way down to Rhode Island. Day we left I never heard or saw from any of those guys again. Not that we weren't buddies. We were. Maybe we guessed if we forgot about each other we could forget about the whole goddamn mess.'

I was concerned by the direction that this conversation was heading.

'Must have been two years maybe more after we got discharged, I'm working as a mechanic in New York City down on the Lower West Side. Didn't like the work much but I was good at it and I was trying to get myself back on my feet. One day this guy comes in. Pretty normal-looking guy. Seems he's looking for me. Says he wants to talk to me. I says talk if that's what you want but don't expect no answers. Unless I'm good and ready.

'So the guy asks me when's the last time I heard from Johnny McCarthy. I say who wants to know. He was one of us ten guys, you see. I said I didn't see anything more of him after that day we all left Fort Jones. Didn't know where he went. Didn't know if he got a job, or a woman or a house or nothing. Didn't even know if he was still alive. Guy leaves. I didn't think no more of it. I'm trying to get my life together.'

Vietnam Vic stopped talking and took a suck on the bottle of Bud in front of him. For a moment I thought that this might be the end of the story. Just as I was about to talk about the weather he started up again.

It had been another six months later and he had moved out to New Jersey right on the edge of town, almost out in the boondocks. Driving home one day from work, he stopped by a diner, right out in the middle of nowhere, big parking lot, bright lights, nothing much all around. He gets

out of his pickup and heads inside. When he sits down he
looks at the menu and when he looks up for the waiter he
sees that the man sitting on the table one over from him is
the private dick who was looking for Johnny McCarthy.

'Mind if I join you?' he asks the PI.

'No, sure, buddy,' the guy replies.

'So did you ever find old Johnny?' asks Vietnam Vic.

Johnny had got a big family. His mother and two sisters
lived in a grand old mansion in upstate Vermont. When
they found out he was out of the army they pleaded with
him to return. Wise nineteenth-century investments on
the part of one of Johnny's forefathers meant that none
of the McCarthys would need to work again. He could
relax, go hunting, have his friends around. Maybe travel
some, go to Europe, get the whole mess out of his head.
But Johnny refused. He refused to return to Vermont. He
refused to have anything further to do with his family
and he refused to have anything further to do with the
McCarthy millions. A few days before the private detective had come looking for Vietnam Vic, the old lady
McCarthy had died. She'd left twelve million dollars to
be divided between her three children: two older daughters and Johnny. Legally obliged to try and track him
down, the McCarthys' attorney had employed the private
detective. It hadn't been difficult to keep track of Johnny's
movements. He had drifted from job to job, become a
loner but no trouble to anyone. His was one of countless
cases of young men unable to fit back into Civvy Street
after their war experiences. He worked a while and then
moved on, worked a while and then moved on, staying
in boarding houses, camping in the summer. He was
working in a timber yard when the PI tracked him down.
Over a coffee and leaning on a bandsaw in a dusty shed
the private investigator revealed to Johnny that he had

just inherited four million dollars. All he needed to do was sign for it and the money was his. Could even be done at a local attorney's office.

There had been a silence between the two for a little while and then Johnny shook his head wearily.

'Don't want no part of it.'

He had looked at the private detective and shaken his head again. The private detective, as his job obliged him to do, took the information back to the two sisters, who readily, almost cheerfully, agreed that their brother clearly wanted no share of the inheritance and therefore presumably it would only be right and proper if they divided it neatly between the two of them: fifty-fifty. The private detective, shocked by this reaction, took it upon himself to track Johnny down again. Finding him now working further up country he explained that Johnny had until the fourth of July to sign, otherwise his sisters could legally divide his third between them. Johnny nodded but still maintained that he had no interest in the money at all. The private investigator, one of the good guys, was baffled and although he respected Johnny's decision wanted to give it a last shot.

'Look, I'll be in the diner on Highway 33 between six and eight in the evening on Friday week, the twenty-sixth. If you change your mind you'll find me there and I can help you sort the financial arrangements out.'

Johnny nodded and, pushing the sweat-banded cowboy hat down on his head, bid him farewell.

When that Friday came around the PI sat down in a booth in the diner on Highway 33 at six o'clock sharp, ordered a coffee and waited.

At half past six there was no one.

At seven no one.

Seven thirty, still no one.

Then at seven forty-five an old pickup pulled into the

parking lot and deposited a dishevelled figure. It was Johnny. He ambled his way over to the diner, pushed open the squeaking glass door and sat down in front of the private investigator.

'So, you changed your mind?' asked the PI.

There was a long pause. Silence between the two men.

'No, sir, I didn't change my mind. I don't want no part of their lousy money. No part of their lousy world.'

'So why did you come back? You didn't have to.'

'Just thought it was right and proper to thank you, sir. You thought 'bout me. You didn't have to do that. You didn't have to find me again. You went beyond the line of duty and I sure appreciate that. Not many people around these days who would do that. Good night.'

With that Johnny picked up his hat, put it back on his head and strode slowly but purposefully back out of the door.

The private investigator had always wondered whether the man who had delivered Johnny to the diner and drove him away again realised that he was sitting next to a man who had just turned down four million dollars.

When I returned later to the empty flat it struck me for the first time, quite out of the blue, that it might well be unwise to get involved with the Chestnut Investigations Inc. crowd. I knew nothing about these people, next to nothing about what they did, next to nothing about the risks involved. Perhaps it would be wiser to avoid further contact. I could make some excuses to Makepeace – after all I had to get on with this flaming book.

Reminded, I dragged my laptop onto the kitchen table with a sigh, in the process pushing the books that Nelson had lent me to one side. Before I started work I ought really to arrange them, I thought, and because I am very good at doing practically anything that does not involve getting down to it, I started to pull them from the plastic bags. Within a few moments I felt a new surge of interest and excitement bubble up inside me again.

The books could be divided into two seperate categories: training textbooks and private investigator fiction. Putting the manuals aside for the time being, their bland covers and wordy titles not interesting me as much as the colourful paperbacks, I flicked through the selection of detective novels I had been given. Some of the names were familiar to me – Holmes, of course, featured heavily, as did a number of other British detectives. Inspector Morse had been well thumbed, as had Lord Peter Wimsey, and it seemed that Nelson also had a certain fascination for the Belgian egg-headed detective Hercule Poirot, Agatha Christie's cerebral creation. Perhaps slightly less so for Miss Marple, who only featured once in the undeniably brilliant *Sleeping Murder*. Unsuccessfully, I tried to imagine Nelson in St Mary Mead. There were, however, a number of other titles and authors that I did not recognise. These were predominantly American. Nearly all the books had lurid sleeves featuring, delightfully, damsels in distress and *femmes fatales*, cars that still had running boards and, most dominantly, men in hats with notebooks and pencils and possibly revolvers stuck in the pockets of their long gaberdine coats. Most of the copies seemed to be in almost pristine condition, a sign perhaps that they had never been read or, more likely, that they had been held in great veneration. A certain Rex Stout had created the character of Nero Wolfe, a PI whose corpulence and immobility bore an uncanny resemblance to Nelson Mason. Mickey Spillane's alter ego Mike Hammer was too brutal for me and even Dashiell Hammett's Sam Spade had a wholly unacceptable talent of stumbling upon bloody corpses – two dozen in one book alone, the cover proudly announced.

Somebody called Robert B. Parker had created a detective by the name of Spenser. Spenser, it appeared to my interest, had worked, as much as it is possible to work if you do not really exist, on the streets of Boston – or, as I noticed, was written on the back of one of the books, the 'mean streets' of Boston.

What was I getting into?

But it was Philip Marlowe who really caught my attention; Raymond Chandler's character was a man of extraordinary class. 'A good enough man for any world' I saw from the cover of *The Simple Art of Murder*, he was fearless and had a tongue that could wither baddies at a hundred yards. Some of his one-liners were unforgettable and I practised a few of them in the mirror in the hall of the apartment lit only by the silver light of the street. Unfortunately I did not have the correct type of hat or gaberdine mac and had to make do with a dressing gown and a woman's straw boater with an elasticated chinstrap and decorated with plastic flowers that I found in a cupboard and which, I decided afterwards, could well have been left by Mrs Walowski, when she came to visit my hosts, her tenants.

'Trouble is my business . . .' I muttered and wished I had the *cojones* of Marlowe (or even Spenser's sidekick Hawk, who was about seven foot tall and bashed people's heads together with the same gusto as a cymbalist on the last night of the Proms).

Marlowe was forever taking lead without complaint, rescuing blondes from dire danger and generally doing the right thing in an ugly world. I knew then, and it is not always the case in a reading career, that I was going to enjoy the adventures of my fellow investigator of the truth. I cocked the hat down further over one eye and withdrew the two fingers that I was using as a Colt .38 Special from the pocket of my dressing gown and pointed them at the mirror.

'Go ahead, punk, make my day.'

Or was that someone different?

Putting the straw hat down, I reached for a copy of Raymond Chandler's first full-length novel *The Big Sleep* and opened it at the preface, written by an academic from a university in an American town much better known for its rodeos. Soon quite absorbed by his assessment of Marlowe's character, I realised that the fictional detective and I really had quite a lot in common. Obviously there were differences, but the similarities were striking, particularly the fact that we were both just over six foot tall and in our late thirties to early forties.

Philip Marlowe has a straight nose and a jaw of iron and is capable of throwing a hard punch. He is an intellectual of sorts, amusing himself by replaying tough chess matches. He is deeply attractive to women even though he smokes and drinks. He is a romantic hero with a tough-guy mouth. His talk makes him a cynic but his actions make him an idealist. Fearlessly, he walks the meanest of streets in his search for the truth. In the process he is likely to be punched, manhandled, drugged, locked up, shot at or even knocked unconscious but his self-deprecating humour acts as a foil to these injuries. Before long, he has picked himself up, dusted himself down and is off to the next adventure.

Raymond Chandler had himself pronounced his requirements for the ultimate truth seeker:

'Down these mean streets a man must go who is not himself mean, who is neither tarnished nor afraid. The detective in this kind of story must be such a man. He is the hero; he is everything. He must be a complete man and a common man and yet an unusual man. He must be, to use a rather weathered phrase, a man of honour, by instinct, by inevitability, without

thought of it, and certainly without saying it. He must
be the best man in his world and a good enough man
for any world.'

Marlowe was certainly all of these things and yes, I
thought, as I glanced up at my reflection in the window pane,
there were certainly definite comparisons to be made . . .

Anyway, enough of the fiction for the time being.

The training manuals were thick and serious but once I
began to consult them I found them, if anything, less believ-
able than the novels. Although it was clear that the purpose
of these textbooks was educational, I soon found myself
quietly gurgling with astonishment. My eyes widened as I
moved from one title to the next. They seemed to cover just
about any aspect of criminal investigation. I was astonished
and absorbed: 'Cold Case Investigations', 'Practical Homicide Investigation', 'Little Black Book Three', 'Art of
Investigative Interviewing', 'Process of Investigation',
'Secrets of Successful Process Serving', 'Successful Personal
Injury Investigation', 'Death Investigations Handbook',
'Forensics for Dummies', 'The Evidence Collection Field
Guide'. Slipped in between these last two was even an old
back copy of *PI Magazine*. It was way out of date but
remained nonetheless useful, its articles covering all manner
of subjects: 'Effective Interviewing and Interrogation Skills
in Fraud Investigations', or 'Automotive Product Liability
Claims'. Apparently franchising was the newest PI trend.

The book that Nelson had most carefully drawn my attention to in his office I came to last. It was a comparatively
slim tome and was entitled *Uncovering Reasonable Doubt –
The Component Method* and written by a certain Brandon
A. Perron. I flicked it open and cast my eye down the
list of contents. Once I had wondered what was involved
in a 'purview' I moved on to Chapter Two entitled *The*

Search for Truth: Critical Thinking for the Criminal Defence Investigator. I started to read and at four thirty in the morning, having been absorbed for nearly six hours and feeling strung out on too much coffee and cigarettes, I staggered for bed. But by then I was conversant with any range of topics that any serious private investigator would need to tackle. How to investigate case reviews and analysis, write an investigative journal, perform an initial defendant interview, examine and inspect a crime scene, how to investigate the alleged victim and witnesses, and the report of investigation and testifying. I had also dipped into how to investigate domestic violence crimes and felt myself to be relatively well informed about the drug war.

Struggling in the half dawn to shuck my clothes and kick off my shoes, I grinned at the twinkling skyline. How utterly ridiculous it all was. Something straight out of the movies. I was too old, and tired, for all this cops and robbers stuff. Who did I think I was? Starsky or Hutch? That said, the section on cocaine smuggling had really been very interesting.

Well, if I was to be here for the next four months I couldn't write all the time, could I? I had worked out how many words I need to write per day and although it was admittedly rather larger than it had been the last time I had made the calculation, I was sure I could keep to it with a couple of energetic hours put in from, let's say, six to eight in the morning. That would leave me the whole day to embark on private investigations. Good plan, I thought, as I looked down from the window and watched a sheriff's car cruise by. Imperceptibly, on an unheard command, it gathered pace and its siren started up its long thin wail as the lights on the roof began to flash red, white and blue.

6

Rimbaud, First Blood

E ven after another morning of flipping through the textbooks and dipping in and out of some of the detective
stories (the six to eight book-writing routine was definitely
going to begin the next day), I could not help but think that
this whole private investigation business was something
much more closely related to fiction than to reality. This
impression was not much changed after my attendance,
two days later, at a seminar at the Public Defender's Office
which took place in a glass skyscraper on Summer Street
and Kingston just in between the Financial District and
Chinatown. Nelson had arranged for me to attend as a
special visitor to, as he put it, give me a taster and had
rung me with the details. The title of the seminar, given by
Nelson himself, was the outlandish-sounding 'Investigation
of a Homicide Scene – Blood Spatter and DNA Traces'.
When I stepped out of the elevator on the sixteenth floor
and made my way down a noiseless thickly carpeted
corridor I found myself entering a large lecture hall, down
one side of which was laid out a number of folding tables
covered in white cloths and loaded with all different types
of foodstuffs. The forty- or fifty-odd people in attendance

– of all shapes and sizes – had congregated for the main part around the cookie and doughnut section of the buffet. Buck Burnett stepped away from the crowd – out of which he could not have stuck more if he had tried, dressed as he was in his trademark SWAT team outfit – and came over to greet me. He was friendly and smiled underneath his toothbrush moustache. On the other hand he could not resist his extraordinarily irritating habit of calling me Limey every other sentence (that said there wasn't much between it and being called Randy) and introducing me as such to a number of the other people present. Delray Drummond was there too, giving the boss support. His open face and his generally cheerful disposition immediately made up for the annoyance caused by Buck.

He asked me whether I had found the Public Defender's building easily and if I knew my way around town. I told him that I had begun to get a better understanding of the layout of the city. Whereabouts did he live from here, then? He pointed across the park out west to the red-brick apartment blocks the other side of Fenway.

'I got myself an apartment now, just this year. It's right over that way. Hey, you know, it's like a little more convenient with the ladies. You know what I mean?'

I thought I did. I was not sure that I could remember.

'But before that, when I lived with my mom and Leroy, we were way out that way back in East Stoneham.'

He waved his hand out further round to the south.

'Leroy . . . ?'

Delray did not seem to take umbrage at the leading question.

'Oh, yeah, Leroy, he's my twin brother. Actually he's my kid brother, by twenty minutes. He's a pretty neat guy.' Delray grinned at me with an affirmative nod as if to reinforce the idea in his own mind. He looked away and then back at me, as if sizing me up. 'Actually, we kinda worry about him. He has had a whole load of trouble. Mom and me, we don't like the guys that he hangs with. They got a real bad reputation. One of those things. Never know which way it's gonna go. Know what I mean?'

When he paused I looked him in the eye and could see the concern. Sympathetically, I smiled at him and we turned back to the room and to the seminar ready for the appearance of Nelson – by video-link, of course, as he now rarely left his office apart from to go home or accept one or two lunch invitations at some of Boston's better addresses.

The class was attended by a number of people who hoped to carve careers for themselves as public defence investigators. These students, once qualified, would be employed by the state government to work on behalf of defendants in criminal cases. Working for the public defence attorneys, it would be the work of these people to discover if there had been any miscarriage of justice or indeed any way of uncovering reasonable doubt that their client was guilty as charged. Although, prior to my arrival, I was not really certain about the type of person who would be most suited to this job – important as it clearly was – I was surprised by the huge variety of individuals who had appeared at the seminar. Some were clearly of the Buck Burnett persuasion, there simply for the kicks, hoping that this training would allow them to pursue some exciting, action-packed and above all admirable lifestyle. Their eyes squinting with intimations of shrewdness, they held facial expressions of such seriousness that it must have hurt. Perhaps they were capable of putting up with the pain because their bodies were so clearly highly tuned, at no doubt considerable cost, in one of the plethora of gymnasiums that I had discovered dotted around the city.

Also amongst Nelson's audience were a selection of people who clearly were there to do good. The one noticeable piece of gear that singled each of them out from the rest was an extraordinarily capacious shoulder bag containing enormous amounts of equipment. This particular group spent much of the rest of the evening rummaging.

Although all age ranges were represented, I was most taken aback by the number of people present who must have been at least into the early years of their retirements. Almost without exception women, they were neatly, demurely dressed, most wearing skirts, tights, sensible shoes and half-moon glasses over which they could peer perceptively at anything that should come their way. Sitting as they did grouped together, handbags on their knees, they gave the impression to the passer-by looking in through the window of the lecture hall that they might have congregated for a Miss Marple lookalike competition.

Whichever category these would-be defenders of the truth came from, before long they were sitting in an orderly fashion in the ranks of seating ready for the show to begin. Even those most eager to profit from the endless supply of free doughnuts and cookies paused as the lights dimmed. Out of a greenish glow appeared the enormous features of Nelson Mason. As he came into focus he looked not a little like some animation that might have been created by the Wizard of Oz. Then I remembered that of course Nelson was almost as large in reality as this huge projection that looked down on the bedazzled audience.

'Fellow truth seekers, in your work as public defenders,' he boomed in a much amplified voice not at all his own, 'some of the most difficult cases you will have to face are those of homicide. Every day in this country people are the victims of the most brutal, brutal murders. Nearly 80 people die every day just from gunshot wounds. There will have been agony, terror, violence, blood, gore and more.'

All this he explained in the tone of a film announcer luring customers to the movies.

'When you are called upon to assist at the scene of a murder, expect to be assaulted on all sides by the outcome of human evil. Not only will you be forced to look at objects of the most awful horror but you will also encounter odours that are beyond description.'

Just when you thought it was safe to go back in the water . . .

The audience sat frozen in their seats by excitement. Even the bag-wielding brigade paused for a moment between a bite of doughnut and another rummage, so utterly thrilled were they by the prospect of these terrible and violent scenes. Nelson, after he had explained the exercises that they were expected to accomplish, faded from the screen with a knowing wink, to be replaced by a series of photographs so gruesome in nature that they might have appeared in a promotional manual for the London Dungeon. On each occasion as a picture flashed up a question typed itself across the bottom of the screen. The audience were expected to jot their answers onto a multiple-choice sheet. After a little while they were unable to contain themselves any longer and turned to one another to excitedly discuss their answers in a pub quiz atmosphere. Everyone was almost certain that they knew the correct answer, but they weren't really quite sure . . .

Somehow, the story behind these photographs, the real history of these horrible crimes, just disappeared and everything turned into some sort of grotesque game.

But then I have found that much in America resembles

a game. Violence is dealt with at some sort of televisual distance. Lives ruined, lengthy prison sentences and even death – cruel homicide or state provided – is a fate that belongs to somebody else. The brutal side of American life, which is served up to one and all through endless chattering television screens, is a daily diet rich in horror. Everyone believes themselves to be inviolable, untouchable. Terrible things happen but never too close to home, only to other distant people. The frisson that I initially, guiltily, felt turned to numbness and the numbness to revulsion. Everyone is sullied by this proxy horror. Along with a loss of innocence surely comes a loss of a sense of guilt on the part of the perpetrators. Nothing really matters any more if it doesn't happen to me.

My impression of unreality was not lifted when, as I was making my way out of the auditorium for a beer with Buck and Delray, a voice boomed from behind me.

'Hey, Randy!'

I turned and there, huge and illuminated, was Nelson. 'How are you fixed in the morning? Pop by the office? Say ten?'

'Sure, no problem, Nelson,' I replied, and not until I was speeding earthward in the lift realised that it was only in a mad world that a man would talk to a screen.

Just as I was pulling on my coat, Delray asked me whether I might like to go and have a drink with him. Pleased by this friendly gesture, I happily accepted.

As we made our way down Charles Street the lights in the false gas lamps twinkled an attractive orange and I wondered whether these too were not part of film-set Boston, which, along with the steam rising from the manhole covers, were all laid on to entice the tourist and improve his or her 'vacation experience'. Soon we were heading out between the Common and the Public Garden. Initially, of course, our conversation, between near strangers, was of a very inconsequential nature.

Soon, though, Delray summoned up courage to ask me a bit about where I came from and what life in Europe was like. Although I was slightly taken aback by the relatively little he knew about the 'Old Continent', as opposed to that which I, by exposure, knew about the United States, I was at least impressed by his desire to find out. He had quite a good understanding of British democracy and even some knowledge about the political system, having taken a class on the subject, but surprisingly, or not perhaps, he was most intrigued to find out about our royal family.

'That Lady Di, whadda ya call her, Princess of Wales, she was one serious little . . .' I wondered how it was that Delray Drummond would finish off the sentence and considered a number of suitably Marlowean options myself but I was never to find out because just at that moment he changed the topic of conversation.

'This is a pretty interesting kinda joint. German, you know. Maybe we could go in here?'

The 'joint' in question was an old-fashioned restaurant with a half-timbered front. Near the corner of Tremont and Stuart, it stood in stark contrast to the concrete and glass around it. Across its front read its name in gothic script and it maintained itself to be the second-oldest existing eating establishment in Boston. We pushed open the door and made our way through an already busy lobby into the bar. Behind it, laid out in great simplicity, was a spacious dining room of bare boards and white linen tablecloths. Black and white photographs agreeably presented the history of the restaurant to its still-steady clientele.

'You wanna sit up front here or are we going to get a table?' Delray asked. We took two seats at the heel of the bar and he ordered some beer. I could not help observing as I glanced at the other customers, buried in newspapers or chatting vociferously, that my new friend's face was the only African-American one amongst them. I also could not help being aware that they had noticed this too. Only Delray himself remained, purposely as he later described it to me, oblivious to this. I knew what it was like to be of one particular racial origin when all around you are of quite another. In India and in Africa it had initially been uncomfortable, but afterwards quite normal given the ethnic make-up of the local population. Here in America, however, the exercise of asking yourself what somebody else was doing on your patch seemed to be a daily one, undertaken with at least a degree of suspicion and, at worst, a degree of dislike.

Delray knew this but he was determined to exercise his citizen's rights and go where he wished, do as he chose. It was, after all, the land of the free.

'So Delray, umm, about this porn . . .'

'Drummond is a Scottish name, isn't it?' he asked, interrupting me very annoyingly. After we had taken our first sips and set our shapely glasses down, I agreed that I thought it was.

'But in my case, it's not just a Scottish name is it? Drummond, that was my family's slave name,' he explained without any seeming rancour.

'Was it?' I asked, attempting, probably unsuccessfully, to express curiosity without being intrusive.

'But, now y'know, Drummond that's *my* name. It's *my* name now. *I* am the owner of it now.'

Delray had researched his ancestors in the archives of his university library and also in the annals of the Black Heritage Foundation. Here he had traced his roots back to Jamaica, and before that, although he could not be sure because 'they didn't bother to record the names of the

Negroes that went onto the slave ships, cos too many of them died', he thought that his family originally came from Ghana.

So it was with a degree of cultural confusion that I discussed the migration of slaves with this American man whilst we sipped our European beer and waited for the steaming boiled potatoes and frankfurter sausages that were served up in a gleaming mound alongside the sauerkraut by a woman whose own family hailed from Hanoi in Vietnam.

After a couple more glasses of something rather sickly and slightly fizzy, brewed by monks in the Low Countries, Delray told me more; more about his home life, his upbringing, his mother, of whom he was immensely proud, and rather less about his father who he had last seen when he was seven. Leroy, his brother, also came up in conversation but only in passing. I wanted to know more about this brother, whether he too had broken the mould and left the housing projects, where they had been brought up, the crime, the drugs, and the unemployment. But Delray skipped on and over this topic of conversation and soon we were discussing his career at Chestnut Investigations Inc. and about his hopes for the future, his plans to set up his own private investigation firm himself.

'Kinda useful, me being an African-American and all. There ain't so many of us guys around in this line of business. No shortage of clients where I grew up,' he added rather ruefully.

Shortly after my arrival at Chestnut Investigations Inc. the next day, I realised that the real reason Nelson wished me to visit him was so that he could ask my opinion of his presentation of the night before. When he had discovered that I was a teacher he was genuinely interested, seeing

himself, as he did, as a purveyor of information, someone
from whom great truths could be learnt. When I first arrived
Delray Drummond and Rita Martinez were seated in front
of the great man's desk and he was giving them the benefit
of some of his past cases. Unfortunately I arrived in the
middle of one of these and, after the normal round of 'Hey,
Randy, how're ya doing's, when he picked up where he
had left off I was unable to follow the story.

Instead I contented myself with inspecting the pictures
on the walls of Buck Burnett's office. Most of these seemed
to be of some type of military hardware ranging from F111
jets to a particularly impressive collection of Colt pistols.
All of them American icons.

Somehow, the society of the United States seemed to be
constructed on a foundation of great household names –
people or objects or enterprises, all of them success stories,
all playing their part as the building blocks of a nation. They
make up the American heritage. There is a King (of rock 'n'
roll) and a Queen (of pop) even a Prince. Carriages are
produced by Corvette, Cadillac and Pontiac, trusty steeds by
Harley Davidson. Palaces and castles of glass and steel,
built as monuments to power and the dollar, tower towards
the sky, protecting the wealth of the nation. Barely older
than the last century, legends, living or otherwise, have
come to shape the past of the land. They have the same
resonances as George Washington or Abe Lincoln and, rolling
off the tongue, they are all quintessentially American: the
Alamo, Barbie, Jimmy Dean, John Wayne, the Model T Ford,
Hendrix, Las Vegas, Marilyn Monroe, KFC, Peanuts, Route
66, Superman, Viagra, Wal-Mart, Oprah . . . all make up the
history of the country as surely as Cromwell, Dickens,
Marmite, Shakespeare and umpteen monarchs make up the
fabric of the United Kingdom. The Golden Arches have
become America's Stonehenge.

Just as I was about to leaf through one of Buck's back copies of *Hand Guns in America* to find a particularly interesting-looking story entitled 'Tissue Damage and the Hollow Head .45', I sensed some movement from the cubicle at the far end of the room. Slowly I approached and peered over the top to see the oval pimply face of Ernie Vinh, Chestnut Inc.'s forensic expert, to whom I had briefly and almost wordlessly been introduced on my first visit to the offices. Looking back up at me through a pair of sturdy and studious-looking glasses, he tried on a smile.

'Hello, Ern. How are you today? Do you remember me?'

'Hello, hi, hi, hi, hi,' was all that Ern could come up with by way of conversational gambit before he turned back to his glimmering computer screen and gulped another mouthful of candy from a large glass bowl on his desk.

'Yes, well, hi,' I agreed as I peered more closely at his screen. What seemed at first to be an indistinguishable mush turned out to be a photograph of a human hand that appeared to have been flattened by some sort of rolling stock but was still vaguely connected to its owner's arm. Ern was industriously, and I have to say enthusiastically, measuring how much spread there had been. Tottering back to Nelson's office I found the team much enthused by the great man's latest anecdote.

'Hey, that is so totally awesome. You mean, you found it was him just because of some kind of aftershave he was wearing?' asked Delray incredulously. 'Holy kershmoley!'

'Yes, it's what's known as sensory recognition,' announced Nelson, sagely. 'Not going to be the piece of prima facie evidence you would be looking for but when I put the information to the client he was able to confirm what I had said. Just went back to the guy and he blabbed like a baby. So, sure it can be useful.'

Although slightly doubtful of the veracity of the story, I

was interested to notice that Delray was furiously noting all that Nelson said in a notebook. This gullibility was certainly a component of the American National Character, I thought from my comfortable but unkindly English, deeply cynical perspective. It was all telling tall stories in the playground, or rather the schoolyard.

Finally Rita and Delray returned to their business in hand and Nelson invited me in with a wave of a giant hand.

'Randy, hey buddy. Sorry to keep you.' He went on with no further preamble, 'Think I might have your first official case. You interested? Yes? Cool. Can you get yourself to Cambridge by ten thirty this morning? I want you to meet Buck out there. He'll explain everything when you hook up.' He gave me Buck's cellphone number and instructions about how to use the public transport system to get myself to West Cambridge, one of the smarter suburbs of Boston. In fact I had already regularly travelled on the Massachusetts Bay Transportation Authority – known as the 'T' – which was as efficient as it was sterile.

I hope that that morning I was able to preserve some of my normal sangfroid and Nelson was unable to notice that, although I was sitting, I was hopping from one foot to the other in excitement about the prospects of getting out there on the street. A real gumshoe.

A Limey gumshoe.

'Can I, Nelson, er, could I just ask? Could you let me know what kind of case this is that we will be er . . . working on?'

'It could be anything,' Nelson replied jokingly but very unhelpfully. 'No, kidding. Well, I don't really want to spoil the surprise but let's just say that here, at Chestnut Investigations, it's what we call an MPC case.'

Trying not to run, I left the office, waved briefly at Rita, pulled the glass door open and hurried down the narrow flights of dusty stairs, out into the street and off to the nearest T station at the top end of Charles Street.

Most of the commuters had dissipated by the time I stepped out at Cambridge and turned right into an attractive tree-lined avenue of clapboard houses of varying sizes, decorated in several attractive pastel shades.

There was no need to ring Buck on his cellphone as I had no problem at all locating him. His vehicle stood out in the street rather as an asteroid might have done had it landed overnight. Buck was at the wheel of an enormous SUV – a sports utility vehicle – and was assembling the equipment that he believed necessary for our investigations. A metal torch about two foot long hung from his belt and he was carefully folding a pair of leather gloves one into the other before tucking them into the side pocket of his bomber jacket. A small can of Mace, some sort of incapacitating spray, was clipped to his side along with a large holster. It was empty; empty only because Buck was now in the process of slotting some enormous-looking bullets into a silver revolver that must have been almost as long as my forearm.

'Hey, Limey, how did you find me so quick?' Buck smiled at me from behind a pair of mirrored shades which I could just see under the peak of his baseball cap that was pulled down low over his face. 'Just got to get tooled up,' he went on without waiting for a reply. 'You got everything you need?'

As I had no idea what it was that I would need I only had my camera, which hung round my neck, and a tourist map of Boston. I nodded assertively, however, as if I, too, was completely 'tooled up'.

'OK then, buddy, let's go get the bad guys!'

Buck had jumped out of the cab of his vehicle as if landing by parachute and slammed and locked the door.

'So the boss tell you that we got an MPC here?' he asked as he made his way across the quiet residential road as if he was crossing Baghdad High Street.

'Yes, an MPC . . .' I simply did not have the guts to ask.

Pulling the hem of his jacket at least partially over his gun in its holster, Buck set off down the pavement. As I followed my brain whirred, at no great speed, trying to find a solution to the letters MPC. I wondered whether there could be any connection with MCP – male chauvinist pig.

Male pig chauvinist?

It didn't sound very likely.

Anyway, surely they didn't go hunting them down. Half the country would end up behind bars.

As it was, a few hundred yards down the road this conundrum was answered. Up some wooden steps we climbed onto the veranda of one of the smaller houses in the row. Pretty in its way, the house was in need of some redecoration, the peeling paint around the window sills giving it more the impression of a seaside beach hut than a grand residence in this smart part of town. The porch was greatly overgrown by plants, in hefty earthenware pots, which turned and twisted and climbed in amongst one another creating a screen of greenery that disguised the house from the outside world. An ancient but smart-looking bell, of the sort you see in Greek villages, hung outside the front door and Buck, in no way backward in coming forward, rung it as if he was announcing an armistice. The noise, not surprisingly, brought an immediate reaction – the sound of something collapsing and a short female shriek. Buck looked at me and unbelievably his hand crept to his waist. Just as he was about to lower his shoulder and smash the door down with his fairly significant bodily weight, it opened of its own accord.

Standing in front of us, weaving slightly, unsteady on

her feet, stood a woman dressed in an enormous floating garment that started at her considerable cleavage and finished somewhere around floor level. Her arms were held wide apart, the looping sleeves of her dress hanging down low. On her head she wore a turban which was slightly awry but nevertheless matched her lipstick perfectly. Down the woman's entire front was a huge splash of blood.

Appalled, I stopped breathing until I recognised that the blood was entirely the wrong colour – much too orange – and smelt very strongly of paint.

'Good day to you, ma'am,' said Buck. 'Er, is there something wrong? What's that?' He pointed in a rather obtrusive way.

'Oh, you don't wanna worry about that. The paint pot slipped just as I was finishing off one of my pictures for my exhibition, you know. Yeah, like I say, don't worry about that. You guys the dicks, right?

We nodded as I realised that this was the first time I had been so described, at least in this context.

'Hey, am I pleased to see you guys. Nelson said you would be right over this morning. You just have to find my Rimbaud. He went missing yesterday right after that goddamn son-of-a-bitch dog walker took his leash off in the memorial garden, which she knows she's not allowed to do. Poor little Rimbaud, he just got all confused. It's not surprising he ran off. I mean, who could blame him? Sacked the goddamned dog walker. She won't see a buck from me. But Rimbaud hasn't come back.'

The woman then began to wail in the most unbecoming fashion and even burly Buck Burnett looked a little disconcerted.

'OK, er . . . Mrs Kreutzer, why don't you just try and calm down a bit. Take some deep breaths or somethin'. Let's go inside shall we?'

Just before Mrs Kreutzer had appeared at the door I had reached the conclusion with a flash of excitement that MPC must stand for missing person's case. Now, with a jolt not dissimilar to a lift suddenly in free fall, I came back down to earth clutching the realisation that we were in fact pursuing a missing pet – a goddamn mutt as the vernacular might have it.

Such was my disappointment that I barely took in the extraordinary surroundings in which Mrs Kreutzer and the missing Rimbaud lived. The whole place was a clutter and jumble of bric-a-brac, clothes, kitchenware and miles of books, most of which seemed to address the naked human form in any number of more or less erotic guises. Canvases were stacked all around the room, all in a state, it would seem, of work in progress.

'Take a seat, take a seat,' suggested Mrs Kreutzer as she leant an arm against an archway and her head against that arm. As there was clearly nowhere to sit we remained standing and Buck began his interview. He had clearly learnt the technique carefully and had a checklist from which he worked.

Quickly we discovered Rimbaud was Mrs Kreutzer's most dearly loved possession, no, really more friend and sometime adviser, spiritual and emotional, apparently. She handed us one of several dozen photographs of this adorable pet. Somewhat to my surprise, after the praise that had been heaped upon its little, slightly bumpy and mildly distorted head, I discovered when I saw the picture of a splay-legged, buggy-eyed creature that Rimbaud belonged very clearly to the canine category of pooch rather than pedigree.

This did not stop Buck, however, from drawing the wholly, as far as I could see, illogical, or at least unproven, conclusion that we were dealing with a petnapping. As a result, he insisted on referring to the dog as the 'victim' and for the rest of the interview I was to have the utmost difficulty in restraining my laughter. This problem was only intensified when Buck asked Mrs Kreutzer, almost his first question, in fact, why she had named her dog after the character in a particularly violent Vietnam movie.

'*Rambo: First Blood* – that is a seminal movie, Mrs Kreutzer. Sly is at the top of his physical form. Wouldn't you agree?'

'No, oh, not him, not after that awful man – all muscles and machine guns. Awful garbage that kind of thing. My darling is called after Rimbaud – the French metaphysical poet.' And here she applied a monstrously caricatural French accent. 'You know, *Le Bateau Ivre* – The Drunken Boat?'

Buck clearly didn't.

'You see, my darling little boy, he, too, has such a wonderful imagination.'

We followed Buck's list of procedures to the letter, including questions about Rimbaud's last known whereabouts. Any particular personal habits and routines? Did Mrs Kreutzer believe that Rimbaud had any personal enemies?

Oh, no never. Who could have wanted to harm such a wonderful creature?

'So, what did you make of the client?' asked Buck as he polished his reflective sunglasses after we had bid farewell to Mrs Kreutzer, stepped back through the jungle porch down the steps and had walked back along the street to Buck's surveillance vehicle.

'Barking. Probably more barking than her surrealist dog!' I replied cheerfully.

Buck looked a little confused and at a loss for words. Then something struck him. He stopped.

'Did you hear what she said back there? I just

remembered. Jeez. What she said. *Rambo: First Blood* is garbage! *First Blood* is garbage. Jeez. She wants to see some garbage she should go see a movie like, you know, like one with Jean-Claude Van Damme . . . Yeah.'

He climbed into the cab and flicked the ignition.

'He's one of the French guys too, ain't he?'

7

Shooting It Out

After Buck and I had picked up a couple of half-gallon cups of coffee from a 'Drive Thru' a few hundred yards from Mrs K's, consumed about a third of them and ditched the rest, we walked into the garden of her next door neighbour. Buck again did make some efforts to hide his gun, ensuring that it was only just visible. He had told me a couple of days previously that he was very proud to have recently received a permit to, as he called it, 'carry concealed', which meant that he was able to hide his gun under his clothing. For some reason this appeared to be more difficult to achieve than simply a licence to wander down the street looking like Wild Bill Hickok. As he was clearly a firearms enthusiast I asked him what I thought to be a reasonably pertinent question as we looked up at the closed blinds of the neighbour's house.

'So why, exactly, do you have such a big gun? Wouldn't it be easier to have something like, er, a bit more discreet? Get one that was a bit more comfortable.' The gun that he was carrying at that moment would surely result in him having some significant hip problems in later life.

Buck did not appear to worry about any future ailments

and patted his hip comfortably. 'You know what, Limey, this baby packs a serious punch. I'm not gonna mess with any of those pea-shooters. Shoot a guy with a .22, it'll go straight through him and he'll keep on coming. You'll just make him mad.'

'Oh I see . . .'

Utterly bemused and amazed as I was, this was all I could think of to say.

Getting no answer at the next door neighbour's we headed on to the next house on that side of the street. In common with many of the houses in this area (with the exception of Mrs Kreutzer's) this was a smart, broad-fronted, wooden affair painted in a delicate light blue. 'Fairview'. Although anyone peering through the peephole in the front door would have got a fairly nasty shock on seeing Buck standing there with his hat pulled firmly down over his mirrored sunglasses. So it was perhaps surprising that the door opened and a small man in a vest and braces looked up at us.

'Can I help you, gentlemen?' he asked, blinking up at us a couple of times through thick, rather smeary spectacles.

'We sure hope so,' replied Buck, flicking a card out of his top pocket with irritating ease. 'I am a private investigator and this here is my . . .' He cleared his throat before he added, 'This here is my partner.'

'Oh, is that right? A couple of private dicks, huh?' The man's tone changed rapidly. 'Why don't you guys get some real work then? I don't like you guys snooping. That's no kinda man's job.'

For a nasty moment I thought he was going to spit on his own doormat.

Slam!

Buck flushed deeply under his sunglasses and I could see his fists clenching uncontrollably. 'Did you hear that guy? I can't even believe it.' He made as if to knock, or rather hammer on the door again, but I suggested in a casual, conversational kind of way that perhaps we would be better advised to try one of the other addresses.

The next house was a much larger affair and from the piles of plastic toys and jumbled bicycles it was clearly a family home. When again we climbed the steps and knocked on the door, Buck pronounced with some pleasure that this was proper gumshoe work. Of course, Marlowe was always pounding the streets in search of evidence that would free the innocent or condemn the guilty. Rapping on doors, he never knew what diorama of human existence he would find when finally they were opened. Nor, of course did he know who might appear framed in the doorway: might be a lush, or a blonde, a mobster, maybe a stoolie, a stiff, a palooka or even another snooper. On one slightly bizarre occasion he had been greeted by a gay Mexican male nurse with homicidal tendencies. More often than not, Marlowe's steady hand slowly crept towards the trusty service revolver in his mackintosh pocket. Even for me it was beginning to become a well worn, rather pleasing procedure, although on this case I didn't believe we were going to be much in danger.

Young voices thrilled inside with the excitement of trying to be the first to the front door handle. Buck and I took a few steps back, sensibly so, as we would have been taken out at the knees by a number of small human cannonballs that came hurtling out of the door. Nine little boys and girls stopped suddenly and stared up at us. One of the shyer little boys ducked behind the shoulder of his friend and only occasionally peered up to see if Buck hadn't yet gone away. But Buck most certainly hadn't. Plucking another of his cards from his pocket he handed it to a bemused eight-year-old with a pony tail and then reaching into his attaché case made out of something that was probably Kevlar, he pulled out a picture of Rimbaud.

'Now, I want you guys to look real close at this photograph. I want each and every one of you to look really closely and tell me whether any of you guys have seen this dog before.'

Automatically nine arms reached for the air, even that of the little boy hiding behind his friend, eager to make a positive ID.

'OK, you guys, so when did you last see this dog?'

'We have seen it every day for like ages,' said one of the boys. 'That's Rimbaud. That's Mrs Kreutzer's dog.'

'Rimbaud was a French poet of the nineteenth century,' announced a slight, pudding-bowled girl with a degree of solemnity that did not foretell any future career as a life and soul of parties. 'He produced his entire work by the age . . .'

'Yes, yes, I think we knew that, thank you,' interrupted Buck. 'OK, you guys, now I want you to listen real good. Any of you see this dog any time soon then you can ring my number right there on that card.'

Eager faces leant forward to read the details.

Just as we were stepping back down the stairs a woman drying her hands on a towel that was tucked into the string of her apron came to the door smiling. When she saw us both she stopped and looked slightly concerned.

'Oh, I thought you were my mother.'

'No, ma'am!' said Buck, surprised at this confusion of identity and sticking the photograph out again. 'We are not. Can you make a positive identification of this animal? We are investigating the suspicious circumstances surrounding its disappearance. Do you have anything you would like to tell us about? Any information that could prove useful?'

'Oh, that funny-looking thing. No, I don't think I do have

anything to say except it comes past here with the dog walker most mornings and most afternoons. They both look bored as anything but I guess it's what they're getting paid for.'

'So would you know where this dog walker, er, she lives then?'

'Oh yeah, sure, that's Mary. She lives right along there.' The mother, scooping up one of the children, stepped out onto the porch and pointed at a small house on the corner of the street.

'So you know that Mary, do you?' asked Buck. 'What kind of person is she then?'

'Oh, she is just a wonderful person. She's so kind to the children and she just loves those animals.' The woman paused briefly and then looked back at us. 'Why do you need to know? She didn't do anything wrong, did she?'

'Oh no,' replied Buck sarcastically. 'She just went and lost one of the dogs she was given charge of.' This last crime seemed to equate, in his mind at least, to a recently uncovered genocide. 'I think we better have a word with this here Mary,' he said, stepping backwards down the steps. 'We are mighty obliged to you, ma'am. There may be something in it for you once we clear this mess up. You sure going to be hearing from us again. You can be certain of that.'

'Oh, right. Well, you have a good day now.' The woman turned and ushered her brood back in through the door. As they went in she turned and gave us a little wave. 'OK, well maybe see you guys around some time.'

I smiled at her apologetically but the woman didn't seem to find anything odd and smiled pleasantly back.

'So what kind of reward are you going to be able to give her then? I hadn't heard that there was a reward for this,' I asked Buck when we out of earshot.

'Oh, no, there's no reward. That was just bull. You have to spin these guys a few lines. Make them believe they're important. But we're only interested in the victim. These guys they're just collateral,' announced Buck as he climbed back onto the driver's seat of his SUV.

'Oh,' came my increasingly standard response to one of Buck's statements. 'So, what do you think we should do? Maybe we should go and get the dog walker's, er, Mary's version of events?'

'Heck, no,' replied Buck brusquely. 'I already got a bad feeling about that one. I think she's right up to her neck in it.'

'Oh.'

'Just kind of lost the dog. I don't buy that one. No, this one has got a stake-out written all over it.'

'Stake-out?' I asked innocently.

'Yeah, we're coming back tonight and we're going to sit and watch that house until we see some action. You got me?'

'I got you,' I replied, gamely.

'Yeah, that mutt gotta being kept against its will in there before the handover goes off,' he replied, grinning with self-assurance. 'Stands to reason if the dog went in there. Yeah, stands to reason if the dog went in there it's gotta come out. If she's going to hand it over for the dough, stands to reason she's gonna do it at night.'

Nobody, apart from Buck had, as far as I knew, suggested that the dog was in the house or indeed that there had been any purposeful abduction but he looked in no mood to be questioned, so for once I chose to keep my counsel.

Sitting in the front seats of Buck's huge car, we gazed down the street towards a sign that read 'Bowl Heaven Billiards and Bowling Club'.

Perhaps it was the sign that gave Buck the idea.

'So, Limey, you like guns, right?'

'Well, I wouldn't have said that I *liked* guns . . .'

'Hey, now we got some time to kill, how's about we go down to my club? You'll like it down there. It ain't so far away. Guess it'll give you a chance to see what real Americans are all about. Not like the pussies who live round here.'

'Well, that sounds very nice . . .'

Pushing an ignition button on the dashboard, Buck pulled out into the lunchtime traffic and we were soon on our way out of town. Direction Marlboro County, as far as I could see. Before long, by American standards, about forty minutes later, we turned off the highway and headed off into open countryside dotted with the occasional attractive farmstead. This was almost a shock to me after the bustle of Boston and the teeming freeways: a world almost un-tarmacked. Here, for the first time was the place that Gertrude Stein was perhaps speaking of when she explained that what makes America is that there is more space where nobody is than where anybody is. For now.

There was something deeply restful about the view laid out before us as we drove further out into the country. The gentle roll of the hills was of a pastoral beauty that made one think of a calmer, more peaceful, era. Waving grass pastures dappled dark grey and the deepest green as clouds in fast-forward slithered across the sky. Wistfully, I thought of travelling these country lanes with a small horse and trap, rolling past the wild flowers in the hedgerows that reminded me so much of the West Country of England where I had spent many years. My wanderings would be accompanied by a soundtrack of wild birds and clip-clopping hooves and my own tuneless whistle. Instead, now, we were hermetically sealed from the outside in air-conditioned cool and the only sounds to be heard were the low purr of the seven-litre engine of the SUV and an immensely irritating series of peeps and broken commands from a GPS system that was mounted on the dashboard. As Buck drove he seemed almost entirely oblivious to his surroundings, but busied himself like an airline pilot with any number of buttons, dials and sensors. Occasionally, he consulted something that looked, to me, mightily like a radar.

'Wonder how many of my buddies are gonna be at the club right now?'

I wondered instead how many buddies Buck possessed in the first place. The grim conclusion that I reached was that the only people to become Buck's buddies were unfortunately almost certainly going to be people who were very much like Buck himself. I steeled myself for my introduction to the club.

Before very long we found ourselves turning into a hamlet. The houses had clearly all been designed and constructed at the same time: a new model village built on a horseshoe grid with private fences and gates leading off to large bungalows shaded by ancient trees. The whole place seemed carefully, almost sterilely, groomed. Every few hundred yards or so there was some reminder, in the burly form of a uniformed person, of the fairly hefty security presence in this rich rural retreat.

With a smooth movement of the wheel Buck turned the vehicle up one of the secret driveways. As we headed up amongst some beech trees whose leaves were already beginning to turn golden reddish brown I glimpsed a sign, black letters on a white board, that read 'County Rod and Gun Club'. The lane took us winding through more woodland and alongside a large lake before pulling out onto a sweeping circular drive. On the far side was a large, low log cabin constructed from smoothed tree trunks and sporting an authentic, stained corrugated roof and a wonky smokestack. The driveway was all but full of cars and pickups, and on the tailgates of most of these sat one or more men deep in conversations with cans of beer cradled in the crooks of their arms.

'Oh yes, the good old boys. They're all here. You gonna meet great guys here, Limey. You're gonna be pretty impressed. Oh, yeah.'

When eventually we pulled up Buck slid from the front seat with some alacrity and, shaking the hands of a few passers-by muttering 'Hey, buddy, how ya doing, hey', moved around to the trunk. This he swung open as a magician might open a box of tricks.

'Look what I've got!' he seemed to be saying.

And what he had got was astonishing.

Once he had worked open a complicated combination lock he flicked two switches, and three sides of a wooden cabinet, perhaps four foot by four, swung down as the lid slowly rose as if on hydraulics. Ensconced in specially moulded foam were, and I counted them, twenty-three different handguns of varying sizes. A tiny single-shot anti-quated pistol that would have fitted easily into the palm of my hand looked ridiculous alongside something that looked too heavy to lift and made what Buck had hanging on his hip look almost inoffensive.

'Just carrying half my collection today. No point in running around with all of them. There's a whole lot of cash gone into these babies. I think I have fifty-three right now.'

Before long a number of men had collected around the boot of Buck's car and had engaged him in lively conversation. The stereotyped photofit of a typical Buck buddy was quite wrong. These men differed widely in age and background. Some looked as if they were regularly employed in some manual capacity but others wore expensive leisurewear and looked as if they were rarely to be found doing anything more arduous than a round of golf.

The one thing I was soon to discover, however, that they did all have in common was an unshakeable, implacable, really quite disconcerting belief in the power and the importance of the gun.

Before I knew what was happening I had been taken aside by a small rather cheerful little man in a shiny shirt and a pair of what I would have thought were uncomfortably tight jeans. He was an optician in a small town not far from Concord and he wanted to take me through the history of small arms manufacture in the United States of America as recorded on grimy educational pictures that hung over the bar in the clubroom. Wildly patriotic, he would have nothing to do with Beretta or SIG or the widely reputed and renowned Heckler & Koch. Instead he was a devotee of those good old names Smith & Wesson, Colt and Winchester.

The man, whose name was 'Curly' Curtly, quickly warmed to his task of instructing me in all things ballistic. Within minutes I had been walked into the main club dining room and seated at one end of the long table. Curtly suggested I might like to learn how to strip apart a relatively straightforward-looking pistol and then with maximum rapidity reassemble it.

'Course, when you get a bit of practice you can do this blindfold,' said Curly Curtly. 'Sometimes, you know, when I get back in from work I just ask my wife to put a bandage across my eyes and I just work through my collection, strip 'em down, reassemble and onto the next.'

'Oh, so what does your wife make of that?'

'Well, she gets kinda irritated. If I'm not quick enough she gets real impatient, because after I've done 'em all once over, it's my go to put the blindfold on her and then she gets to strip 'em all down. Sometimes we time it. Or get a few friends over – have a competition. Kinda fun.'

'So why have you got all this different ammunition, er . . . ammo, er . . . bullets, you know?' I interrupted as I was pretty sure I didn't want to hear much more about Curtly's domestic arrangements. 'Do they have er . . . different uses?'

'Affirmative, you got that one totally correct. All the same calibre, yeah? But see these ones here? These ones are steel ones, they're the cheapest you can get – I just use them for target practice. I'll be showing you that in just a minute. These ones here, they're lead and I tend to use them for solid targets, you know, like beer cans and bricks and things? Don't ricochet so bad. And these babies here, you see the hollowed-out ones with the copper heads; they're the ones that I use when I'm carrying insurance. So anyway—'

'Sorry, what did you say?' I couldn't believe my delighted ears.

'Oh I'm sorry. Yeah, carrying insurance, that's the same as packing heat, you know . . . You betcha. If I'm driving through the 'hood, I'll be packing heat.'

I really needed to write it all down.

'So anyway, take today. You'll see I've got the .38 strapped to my ankle and under my arm here, this is a .50 but they both pack the same whack as the one on my hip, you know what I mean? These copper hollow heads, they're the best for all kind of one-on-one action.'

'Oh, I see. So what's so good about them, then?' I had an awful feeling that I knew the answer to this one.

'Well, it's really all about tissue damage. You put one of these into a guy it's likely gonna come straight out through the other side. But you put one of these babies into a guy at twenty yards and there's gonna be one small hole at the front and there's gonna be one mighty big one at the back. He's going to stop right where you shot him.'

Curly Curtly reached into his pocket and pulled out a bottle of nose spray which he squirted delicately into either nostril before rubbing his nose gently with a small and rather effete handkerchief and sniffing a few times.

'Ooh, this furniture polish they use now in the club house, it just does terrible things with my allergies. I'm really gonna have to talk to the president about that. I can't never shoot straight if my nose is streaming like this. You know what I mean?' Curly Curtly sniffed again and rubbed his nose before continuing soberly.

'But you know, a lot of great marksmen, they have had their demons to deal with. Bonnie and Clyde, you know them for sure. Well that Clyde Barrow I heard say he had a wheat allergy. So if he ever was going to raid a bank he had to lay off the bread for like a week before.'

Curly Curtly seemed immensely pleased with this snippet of information. He gazed down lovingly at the collection of unbelievably carefully engineered pieces of weaponry and they gleamed back malevolently at him.

'You wanna shoot some of these babies?' he asked. 'That's the real fun part. Come on down and we'll let you have a go with them.'

Before I could answer he ushered me down a few steps into the cellar.

As I passed him, Buck was heavily engrossed in conversation with some of his friends, snapping, clicking, adjusting, tweaking and aiming one of his handguns all the while.

The basement was divided into two halves. One side, protected by thick perspex, had been converted into a viewing lounge, with two rows of old velvet cinema seats and, strangely, a multicoloured fifties jukebox. In the other half of the room was the firing range itself. Men wearing large orange earmuffs giving them the allure of weird, rabid praying mantises, were occupying seven or eight booths and were firing bullets, semi-incessantly, at the far end wall, on which was affixed a number of round bullseye targets. From the other side of the soundproofing the noise being created was deadened to a series of pops, rather like the noise made by an elderly moped, but once we passed through the thick plastic door into the range itself the noise was suddenly deafening. Curly handed me my own pair of bulging earmuffs which I donned immediately with no time for sartorial concern. Within a few minutes a booth was freed up and after the man had wound his target back towards him on a system of pulleys, snatched it from the clothes peg with which it was attached, sworn briefly under his breath and binned it in a crumpled ball, he smiled at us and wished us better luck than he had had.

'OK, so here is what I want you to do, Randy,' shouted Curly into my muffled ear. 'You're going to feel your hand tighten around the grip. You're a righty, correct?'

Righty? Umm . . . Oh, yes.

'Affirmative,' I replied.

Affirmative!

'OK, so you got your right hand nice and tight around the grip. Now you're gonna wrap the fingers of your left hand over the fingers of your right hand but you're not gonna bring your thumb round the back of your right hand one. If you do it'll shatter when the gun fires. Instead you press one thumb alongside the other. OK?'

'Like this, do you mean?' The gun fitted snugly, comfortably, warmly in my fist. My thumbs slid comfortably, warmly, one next to the other as if they had been so designed. With a sudden surge of concern I realised that it actually felt pretty good.

'OK, good, you're just gonna get used to that for a little while, feel the gun in your hand, feel the weight. OK, put

the gun down. Pick the gun up. Let's see you do that a few
times. OK, put it down again. Try and pick it up a bit quicker
now.'

How soon it became almost second nature to snatch up
this weapon and point it down the range with my hands
slipping so easily and correctly into place!

'OK, let's get you a target.' As Curly rummaged in a
cardboard box under the counter he muttered something
which I didn't hear.

'Sorry,' I said lifting one muff away, 'I didn't quite catch
that.'

I was immediately half deafened by a volley of shots
from the booth next door to me and hurriedly clamped the
ear defender back into place. I attempted to lip-read my
way through the rest of the conversation

'I said Massachusetts is getting so legalised, you know,
much too much regulation. They say now you can't even
shoot photographic images. It just has to be an outline
target. You know, like silhouette.'

'Oh.'

'Yeah, before we used to like shooting at photographs of
people. More realistic and a hell of a lot more fun. 9/11 it
was Osama bin Laden. Just recently we had that Saddam
Hussein. And, you know, some guys, if they're pissed with
someone, they just like to shoot pictures of them. Might be
their wife. Girlfriend. Boss. You know, there's any variety.
We had a really good firm making those targets up for us.
But now it's against the law.'

'Oh, that's a shame, isn't it?'

'Darn right it is. Here we go. This will have to do.'

Curly unfurled a roll of paper which, once spread out
and weighted at the bottom, transpired to be quite unlike
the bullseye targets I had seen the others shoot earlier. A
number of sloping lines delineated the outline of a human

body on a six foot by two foot piece of paper. Clipping it up onto the clothes peg Curly wound it back to the far wall but the various different target areas were still easily visible.

'Now we don't want you being any kind of pussy now, do we?' asked Curly.

'Absolutely not.'

'That's what we want to hear, soldier,' Curly replied eagerly, a slight glaze descending over his eyes. 'OK, at this distance we're not gonna mess around with body shots at all. Just go for the head and throat don't you think?'

'Absolutely. Splendid idea.'

'OK, I'm just gonna ask you to squeeze off six shots right out of this Colt .45. The one you just been practising with. It's great. It'll kick plenty but you'll soon get on top of it.'

I took the gun again, now loaded, and it seemed to weigh strangely more than the sum total of its bullets.

I raised it into the firing position.

As Curly nodded his encouragement, I slowly squeezed the trigger. The effect was electrifying; the gun sending a charge through my whole body, forcing me to pull the trigger again.

And again.

And again.

And again.

And again until there were no more explosions, just a click on an empty chamber. Slowly, almost regretfully, I lowered the gun back down to the counter as the last smoke of the cordite cleared through the powerful extractor fans in the roof.

'OK, Randy, let's see how you did.' Curly had already begun to wind the target back. In silence we studied the results.

Five shots out of six had disappeared into the target

directly above and between the eyes, burying themselves deep in the cortex of the brain. The sixth shot would have smashed the jaw completely away from the face.

I wanted to cheer.

Or cry.

8

A Pretty Neat Kind of Place

B uck Burnett had much enjoyed his afternoon at the club.
It confirmed to him, and to me, for the umpteenth time,
that his fellow club members were indeed 'good old boys'.
In particular he had enjoyed experimenting with something
that he described as a semi-automatic SIG but was, in fact,
what I would have called a machine gun.

'Slightly tricky on the permit side,' he admitted. 'But you
know, it's the right of every citizen to carry arms . . .'

Quickly I attempted to nip his proposed exposé on this
subject in the bud. After two, nearly three, hours at the Rod
and Gun Club I had had enough of weapons for, well,
possibly a lifetime.

Only a few days earlier, as I had been breakfasting on
Jimmy Wang's soggy doughnuts and an enormous plastic
cup of not very real Colombian coffee and soya milk, my
attention had been drawn to the endlessly squabbling television set on the wall of the kitchen. It was tuned to the
only channel that was not likely to reduce me to a gibbering
wreck within half an hour, the others consisting, as they
did, of the same lengthy loop of advertisements, interspersed with snippets of comedy re-runs.

That particular morning the breaking news had been about a boy from Chicago who had used a firearm to shoot his half-sister, his mother, his grandmother and his step-father before blowing his own youthful brains out. This particularly murderous rampage had been spectacularly facilitated by his use of an Uzi machine gun. Normally, this fully automatic is not widely available. Fortunately for the lad, he had been able to purchase it on the Internet. Heart-breaking murders of this nature caused by gunshot wounds are daily occurrences in the United States. Everyone looks on helplessly and, in passing, listens to the wailing and watches the wringing of hands. It might almost be worth becoming a florist.

Somehow, in fiction, firearms are simply accoutrements necessary to provide metallic colour to the scenes. Although their presence, their omnipresence, is not exactly benign in the pages of detective fiction, they do not possess the malevo-lence of the weapons that I had manipulated earlier in the day. Marlowe is always 'taking lead' but these are never injuries that cannot be remedied by the application of a handkerchief, preferably lacy and feminine, and a couple of large slugs of whiskey, straight from the bottle.

Sure, droppers are always pulling out bean-shooters and burning powder. Most of the goons are heeled, the flatties too. But, hey, if the lug that gets knocked off is a junkie, then the streets gotta be a cleaner kind of place. You're on a confidential lay you got expect a dose of lead poisoning now and again. Blow one down, blip off, bop a guy, you gotta expect the brunos or the bulls gonna be coming right after you and they sure as hell gonna be packing. Be your chance to see some Chicago lightning right up close.

Gun battles, maimings and shootings have a cosy kind of feel when contained within the pages of a book. Perhaps it should not be so. My afternoon at the gun and rod club, the smell of cordite still on my fingers, had proved, beyond reasonable doubt, that the reality was very different.

'Course, it's not guns that kill people, it's people that kill people,' Buck had told me not once but five times. I had counted.

It did strike me, however, that the sorry task that the tragic young man from Illinois had set himself would have been remarkably more difficult to accomplish had he only had the contents of a kitchen drawer at his disposal.

'So, this stake-out?' I asked, pronouncing the word stake-out as I might have done 'moonwalk'. 'What exactly does it involve?'

'What's that? Oh, you mean in the Kreutzer case? The canine disappearance?'

'Yes, er, that one . . .'

'Oh, well it's pretty standard moving surveillance. We set up outside this dog walker broad's place . . .'

'Excuse me, did you just say broad?' I couldn't help ask but Buck ignored me.

'Yeah, so we set up outside the house and then we sit it out. You gonna be a private investigator, you gotta get pretty used to the stake-out. Could be few minutes before we see some action, could be plenty of hours. You experienced like me, you just go with the wait.'

'So, what do you do while you're waiting?'

'Nothing, dude.'

Dude!

But then I supposed dude was better than Limey.

'Nothing must distract you from the subject's house. You gotta check your surveillance equipment is operational but otherwise you have no distractions, you understand, no distractions.'

'No, no, no distractions, absolutely not. Not a book or the radio or anything? No, OK . . .'

'You're just going to check that your walkie-talkies are fully charged and in working order. I might scope out her place with my night-sight, get a closer view. No, buddy, after that you just wait.'

'So, what if she doesn't come out? What if she just stays in her house all night? Like just goes to bed?'

'Well, you just sit it out.'

'What all night?'

'If that's what it takes.'

This did not sound in any way my kind of fun.

'What about food?'

'Pack everything you need.'

'What about the loo, er . . . looroom . . . er, bathroom, you know, little boy's room?'

'Make sure you go before the job. Otherwise take an empty orange juice carton.'

'God, really!' I said and promptly forgot the only piece of good advice Buck ever gave me.

Buck had been cogitating when a few minutes later he spoke again. 'Course, it'll hot up if the pooch gets picked up from her place. Then we'll have no choice, we'll just sit on the guy's ass and tail him till we see where he's taking the mutt. Only way.'

'Then what . . . ?'

'Well, if we see the animal, then we have to call it in. Get the cops involved. Probably unearth a major dog nabbing ring. Yeah, could be a big one.'

'So . . . you wouldn't, you know,' I glanced nervously at one of his guns that now gleamed on the dashboard. 'You wouldn't, like try and get in there? Try to get the dog back yourself.'

'Well, you know, Limey, if this was just a one-man surveillance, you know, just me and them, yeah, probably I'd just go in there, but what with you being so inexperienced I wouldn't like to risk it.'

'No . . . Oh good! I mean, yes, that's right, very sensible approach.' Somewhat relieved I settled back into my seat and we drove back to the offices in Beacon Hill in near silence. This was not unpleasurable.

Just as we were checking the battery packs on the walkie-talkies and video camera surveillance equipment that we were going to be taking down to the stake-out, Nelson called for me through the door of the office.

'Hey, Will. Could you come in here and sit in on this one, please.'

'Go ahead, buddy, I can handle this,' said Buck as he plugged a battery charger into the wall.

'Will, I want you to meet Susie,' Nelson said as I had entered and waved at Makepeace who was sitting the other side of the room. 'Susie, Will is one of our investigators. He's over here on secondment from the UK, but we're not gonna hold that against him!' Nelson gave one of his wheezy laughs.

Neither Susie nor I joined in as I sat down next to a woman probably of much my own age. I have to be careful when I consider how old people are because initially it is now my reaction to consider them to be a decade or so older than I am. When the truth is out, more often than not I discover them to be some years my junior.

There was something that I found slightly dislikeable about Susie which had nothing to do with her extraordinary appearance. Her hair, which was of a golden brown not her own, was yanked brutally, painfully from her brow up to the top of her head where it swung loose as a pony-tail. This effect, combined with some budget cosmetic surgery – her mouth had the lips of a botoxed goldfish – reminded me surprisingly, shockingly, of one of those shrunken heads of tropical South American provenance.

Later I was to think that in some ways it was a shame
her lips too had not been sewn together. Or is that a little
too unkind?

Susie was presentable enough, very smartly dressed, with
the figure of someone who makes sure they pay the membership of their gym on a regular basis and get value for money.
But something around the corners of her bloated mouth
and her onyx eyes made me feel somehow that her heart
was small, that she felt life had been unfair to her and that
now she was going to get even.

'Susie, if it's OK with you, I'm just going to give Will
some of the background to this one. He is totally used to
this kind of case so you don't have to worry about that.'

Smiling at Susie I gave the best impression that I could
of knowing all about these kinds of cases, or indeed of even
knowing what this case was about.

'Will, Susie has reason to believe, and sadly in this day
and age we come across this kind of problem a lot, she thinks
that her husband is probably being unfaithful to her. In this
case he has announced that he is going to head off for a week
on his annual golfing holiday. Although he has been on this
holiday over several consecutive years, as I understand it,
Susie says she has always thought this pretty phoney. I think
you said that normally his golf clubs don't ever come out of
the closet from one end of the year to the next.'

'Too right, the lazy son-of-a-bitch. He don't even walk
to the convenience store. You're not going to tell me he's
going to walk like five miles round a golf course. You gotta
be kidding me,' was Susie's considered response.

'OK, Susie, now we need some extra information from
you. Will, can you take some notes, please?'

'Sure,' I answered promptly and patted my person in
several unlikely places in search of a pen and paper. Pointing
with one of his numerous chins and winking for a

millisecond, Nelson pointed to a pad and pencil that were miraculously positioned on the corner of his desk nearest to me.

'OK, Susie. So we have a photograph here of your husband. His name is John, is that correct? And he is forty-two years old and six foot two, weighs 200 pounds, dark hair, wearing a beard at the moment. Blue eyes, likes to dress casual.'

I could never work out how many pounds there were to a stone let alone 'do the math' to try and convert people's weight into kilograms but it looked to me as if 200 pounds was on the hefty side – not the Nelson Mason size – but nevertheless heavily built.

'That is correct,' replied Susie crisply and prodded at the corner of her mouth, dabbing at thick lipstick.

Nelson then ran through a number of other details about her husband including his make of car, his place of work and his 'intimates'.

'So, do you know who your husband is going golfing with?'

'I have no idea. He said some people from work. Anyway that's what I'm paying you people for. I believe they are heading up to Maine. Right up there somewhere near Bar Harbour, some place around there.'

'OK.' Nelson finished making some jottings of his own. 'What time do you imagine he'll be leaving your place? This is in like two days? On Tuesday, if I am correct?'

'Yeah, he said like seven thirty in the morning or something.'

'OK, well you can be confident that we'll have a guy on him for the duration of that whole week. Make sure we get our best on the case. Makepeace, who you know – he'll be on it. Hey, probably get Randy here on it as well.'

This last comment took a couple of seconds to sink in

and when it did it was like being hit hard in the middle of the head with the baseball bat that hung in a glass cabinet just above Susie's head. Still, I did my best to raise what I believed to be a winning smile and aimed it in Susie's direction. There was no, absolutely no, reaction.

When Nelson had finally gathered all the information that he needed he ushered Susie from his office, as much as it is possible to usher anybody whilst seated immovably behind a desk.

'Yeah, you just need to see Rita on your way out, please, Susie. She's gonna tell you all the financial details. We need to get the billing sorted out right now. Sorry about that, but you know – it's the American way.'

'What, what er . . . was that all about then?' I asked and kicked myself for the tentative, nervous tone to my voice.

Just as Nelson was about to explain all to me, there was a peremptory knock on the door and Buck stuck his head into the office.

'Hey, Limey, let's do this thing. Just going to do the stake-out on the Kreutzer case, boss,' he added for the benefit of Nelson.

'Go get 'em, guys,' muttered Nelson absent-mindedly as he started to open and close the drawers of his desk again.

It was coming up to six o'clock and dusk when we rounded the corner of the street and headed down towards the dog walker's house. As we did so we inevitably passed by Mrs Kreutzer's place.

'OK, lady, we're gonna get your dog back. You better believe it.' Buck beat his breast twice. He slowed as we passed the client's house and as we did so through the foliage of her pot plant collection we glimpsed the figure of Mrs Kreutzer. There was something strange about her comportment, I thought, only very briefly. Buck, to my surprise, must have had the same thought because suddenly we screeched to a halt and he ground the gear stick of the large vehicle none too gently into reverse. In video rewind we found ourselves passing Mrs Kreutzer's house in reverse. As we came alongside the steps to the porch she turned, blinking, as I wound my window down at Buck's none too polite request.

'Oh, hello, boys,' Mrs K shrilled. 'How are you today? Give them a wave, Rimbaud, give them a nice wave.' And with that she picked up one of the front paws of the dog she held in her arms and waggled it in our direction. The dog, who was undeniably Rimbaud, was impressive in his lack of interest. With scant attention to parking regulations Buck got out of the car and almost ran to the bottom of the steps. Unwillingly I followed him.

'Hey, Mrs Kreutzer, did you just ring in to the office then? You know like when we were on our way here? I didn't get a call on my cellphone.'

'No, dear, why? Oh, no, well you see it was just this afternoon I was doing some clearing up around here. You can see it kind of needs it. Then just as I was thinking about having one of my herbal teas, then guess what?'

'No, I really don't think I can,' replied Buck about as sarcastically as was humanly possible. Mrs Kreutzer didn't seem to mind in her state of euphoria.

'It was just like a miracle! There I was and who should I see just coming right on up the street towards me?'

'Don't, it's too much for me,' muttered Buck.

'And here he is – just as right as rain – my little Rimbaud!'

But Buck wasn't listening. He was already headed for the car and I quickly realised I had no choice but to follow.

The expletives that emanated from Buck's mouth after we had climbed back into the SUV clearly have no place here but suffice it to say that he made his dissatisfaction clear all the way to Beacon Hill.

When our services no longer appeared to be required

back at Chestnut Investigations Inc., Buck, who actually lived out the north side of Cambridge, offered to drive me back down to the South End. He didn't mind, he just loved riding around in his 'Caddy'. As the day had been eventful, I was pleased not to have recourse to the public transport system however effective it might be, so I thanked him and accepted.

'Say what, you want me to introduce you to a pretty neat kind of place in your neighbourhood?'

Buck was, he told me, loving the power of the 7.5 under the bonnet as we purred down Washington a few minutes later.

Silhouettes, the 'pretty neat kind of place' in question, was in fact to be found in a rather gloomy and rubbish-strewn side street on the edge of Chinatown. From the outside it was not possible to tell what kind of establishment Silhouettes was, but it was fairly easy to guess. Above the entrance the outline of a curvaceous female figure, some fifteen feet tall, flashed red and yellow neon in the early evening light as she leant herself against a long, metal pole that was clearly not being utilised for any kind of construction purpose,

Buck pushed open the door and immediately warmly shook an enormous bouncer by the hand, calling him buddy as we made our way down some steps. On a raised level some yards from a brightly lit stage was a very large bar area with high tables and stools. Although it was early the club was already full of patrons. Serving them most efficiently were two or three dozen young women dressed only in micro knickers and high-heeled shoes. The customers were, without exception, men and, almost without exception, fully clothed. This, considering the corpulence of most of them, was incontestably a good thing.

Buck suggested bourbon.

I hate bourbon but Buck had already disappeared as a crowd of hostesses descended upon me. I smiled nervously at the first girl to drape herself over one of my arms. She was blonde and tanned and had great blue eyes that gave her a permanent air of surprise.

'Hey there, my name's Candy.'

Before long I discovered that all the girls had similar soubriquets : Pearl, Sugar, Flower, Petal, Peaches or Blossom.

'How about you, honey?' asked Candy, and purred slightly and embarrassingly.

'I'm Randy.'

This was of course not at all what I had meant to say but Candy did not react. Anyway, as is my habit, I began to babble badly in an attempt to cover my blunder with an avalanche of words.

'Actually, my name's Will, I'm from England, actually,' I announced finally, as if this was some sort of excuse.

'England, is that right?' muttered Candy absent-mindedly as she lightly scratched one naked breast. 'Hey, Kelly, guy over here says he's from England!'

Kelly who was, at that moment, really quite busy tucking dollar bills into her G-string came over and shook my hand coyly. She was quite as pretty as Candy but in no way as vacuous. She smiled up at me and enquired whereabouts I was from in the United Kingdom. After I told her she announced that she was keen to go to England herself and was making arrangements to get there for the following September.

'Oh, I see, will you be going over there to work? Doing this sort of thing . . .' I trailed off and looked out over the stage-cum-dance floor that was now positively wriggling with naked flesh.

'Oh no, this isn't my job, no. No, I'm studying right here

in Boston, Sprites University, majoring in Chinese economics, and I'm hoping to do a postgraduate year over at your university in Bristol. Do you know it?'

'Oh, I see, yes, I do, great.' Kelly was really very easy to talk to, I thought, as I noticed the diamond gleaming in her navel. 'So you only do this . . .'

'Oh, this?' With two elegant hands, she pointed at her outfit or rather lack of it. 'Oh, no, I just do this to pay my way through school. This job would be way too boring for me. You know, I do the pole dancing, that's easy with my training in gymnastics. Like when I was a little girl, that's what I did. Maybe I'll do a little bit of lap.' She paused for a minute, thinking. 'Yeah, I'll do a few lap dances but I don't do no private work like those girls over there.'

She pointed to the left-hand side of the club where young women were writhing, with a degree of grace it might be said, on top of a number of perspiring, middle-aged men. Unfortunately, I could see amongst the crowd what looked remarkably like Buck Burnett's black baseball cap. Two brown breasts saved me from having to see the expression on his face.

Despite the intimacy of the physical relations between the two parties involved in the private work, this was clearly just a transaction; there was no eye contact.

'So what do you think of that Tony Blair, then?' My attention was drawn away and back to Kelly, who was still standing in front of me, holding a drinks tray elegantly on three fingertips, and who was still wearing practically nothing

'Sorry? What did you say? It's the music. I thought you said Tony Blair, ha, ha. Oh! You did say Tony Blair? You mean Tony Blair, Tony Blair, the Prime Minister?'

Kelly was too sweet to have attempted a sarcastic

response but yes, agreed that she did indeed mean Tony Blair the Prime Minister.

Before I had a chance to give her the benefit of my opinion, or rather my several opinions, of Mr Blair, Kelly, quite unexpectedly, gave me her own. In brief, because her views were long and lengthy, she thought that he was at best a kow-towing, boot-licking, poodle of the American President (who incidentally, Kelly thought, was a 'prize dick'). Above and beyond that she thought Blair was also an arrogant, thoughtless murderer. I paraphrase.

When eventually she finished giving her opinion and put back on her high-heeled shoe, the bottom of which she had been inspecting, I was really incapable of saying anything much in response apart from 'I agree.'

'You do?' She clapped her hands together and wiggled her bottom delightedly and delightfully. Catching the large clock over the entrance out of the corner of one lustrous eye, she excused herself and headed towards the stage for her six thirty pole dance.

'So you met Kelly, did you?' said a voice that was at once familiar and strange. Turning round, to my surprise I found myself shaking hands with Vietnam Vic.

'I didn't know you hung out at Silhouettes? Sure glad to see you. Thought you were going to show at Crazy Joan's.'

'No, I don't come here . . . Never. I mean a friend brought me along . . .'

Over his shoulder, I could still see Buck Burnett bobbing in the background.

'Guess you kind of like it here though?' asked Vic as he ordered a Wild Turkey and Coke from a nice, friendly person called Bambi.

'Well, yes,' I wondered aloud. 'Can't quite remember when I was last in a . . . well . . . "such an establishment" shall we say.'

Vietnam Vic laughed and ordered us another two bourbons before I could stop him. Now I think about it there had been one occasion when a friend and I had taken a fatefully wrong turn in the back streets of Montmartre but that is quite another story, which obviously there is no room for here.

'Somehow this place seems OK.' Lots of people were laughing, and on the surface it was until Vietnam Vic scratched that veneer off for me.

'You see that one over there?' He pointed at a skinny woman with metallic red hair. 'She got a crack problem that costs her five hundred bucks a week. That one over there she got four kids. Only twenty-two years old. They make some money these girls, depending what they're willing to do. And quite a few of them they do more than they'd want. Why? Cos they gotta pay the club a hundred and fifty bucks per session before they make a dime.'

'But they're not doing it, you know, against their will?'

'Only in the same way that everyone who is only doing it for the money is working against their will.'

'So why do you come down here then?' I laughed and then stopped when Vic leant towards me, a serious look on his face

'Oh, because this is where we have the meetings. I told you about our group, right? All about setting up war protests putting pressure on the government to get our boys out of Iraq. That Kelly you were talking to, she's a member of the group so it's kinda handy for her. She can work and meet all at the same time.'

This was baffling.

'So, Kelly is working as a stripper to pay her way through college and at the same time she is an active war protester?'

'That is correct.'

'And you have your meetings here so Kelly can strip after college?'

'No,' Vietnam Vic said and leant closer towards me. 'Real reason we meet here is because we reckon what with the music and the kind of venue we got, the Feds are never gonna be able to get in on our conversations.'

'The Feds?'

'Yes, you know, the FBI.'

That night, when I was walking back up the stairs with a parcel of Chinese food that, despite its appearance in the 'Meals for One' section of the menu, appeared to weigh four or five pounds and was surely enough for a large family who had invited their neighbours over, I could not help thinking about the meeting with Susie earlier in the day. Part of me was repulsed by the pursuance of somebody who presumably was entirely unaware that he was being followed. There seemed to be something almost unclean about the activity. Then again, if indeed this man, her husband John, was cheating on her, presumably she had the right to know. In any case I was sure this was how Marlowe would argue the situation. More surprising than this was Susie's decision to employ a private detective to have him followed. Perhaps she was pushed to this measure in desperation. So in love with him, so besotted by him and possessed naively of a belief in the happy-ever-after of matrimony, she could not live with the incertitude. Somehow, though, after my short meeting with her this did not ring true. Perhaps then she had some alternative agenda, I mused as I dipped into a bucket of extremely tasty Szechwan prawn noodle. Who knew what it might be? Perhaps as the case unfolded it would become apparent.

Later, feeling wholly unwell, I sat in front of the colossal television after my colossal supper, seven eighths of which remained uneaten. I had yet to decide whether to throw it away or put it in the refrigerator and throw it away in a few days' time.

Presumably Nelson had been joking about my role in this whole history, I thought as I flicked channels on the TV in an inane slideshow.

Whatever the outcome, whatever my role in this affair, whatever the outcome and truth of John's golfing holiday, I mused when I woke up at three o'clock in the morning with monosodium glutamate flashing through my system, whatever happened, it was all strangely satisfactory.

At eleven o'clock the next day when I appeared at the offices of Chestnut Investigations Inc. as I had been instructed, I found the offices all but devoid of activity apart from Rita Martinez, who was seated at her desk typing at the speed of an intercity train clicketty-clacking over the rails.

'Hey, Randy, how are you doing?' she asked with something that resembled interest and possessed a certain amount of warmth.

'Hey, Rita, how're you doin'?'

Now I could do the whole American 'meeting and greeting' thing with ease.

'I'm good and you?'

'Good, and you.'

'Yeah, good. Hey, now listen, we just got to wait for Buck to get back. He just went out to deliver some subpoenas. Whole load today. Big insurance case coming up. He shouldn't be too long, then you and me we can get going.'

Wrong-footed momentarily by spending too long wondering what serving a subpoena involved, I missed my chance to ask Rita what we were going off to do. By the time I collected myself she was already rattling away again on her keyboard and would accept no interruption. And so it was that before long Buck returned looking gloomy. This lowering of his spirits was quickly revealed when he removed his sunglasses in front of the mirror in the reception area and touched gingerly at a swelling black eye.

'Goddamn subpoenas!' he muttered without further elucidation and disappeared off into his office. Here he was able to tend to himself in perfect isolation as it transpired that that morning Ernie Vinh had headed off to the forensics lab that carried out private testing for the agency. He needed to pick up some results and discuss all matters of scientific interest with his friends who worked there. I had seen Ern a few times since our non-conversation and our relationship had advanced not at all.

'OK, let's get going,' ordered Rita Martinez as she jounced her bunch of keys up and down in one hand and flipped her cellphone open and closed with the other.

'Well, I was just wondering . . .' Although never normally timid, I did find Rita Martinez fairly alarming. 'Yes, I was just wondering, you know, what exactly we're going to do.'

'That's so typical of Nelson. He never explains anything too good.'

And nor it appeared did Rita. Climbing into her small but seemingly turbocharged minute Japanese sports car we set out in the direction of the North End.

'No, no, I'm kidding with you. Nelson says we have to get you some wheels.'

'Wheels? What for?'

'We are going to pick you up a surveillance vehicle. If you are going to be on the surveillance you'll need wheels, won't you? We got a guy we work with in the North End. We did him some favours with some missing automobiles a while back. He just loves to give us a good price.'

'A surveillance vehicle?'

'Yeah, here we go.'

In amongst some semi-derelict buildings in a plot that had recently been cleared stood a number of vehicles of all makes and sizes and of all vintages. In the middle stood a Portakabin from which a second-hand car salesman appeared. He looked and sounded, despite variants of accent, like every other second-hand car salesman I have ever met anywhere in the world.

'Hey, you guys. Hey, how are you doing, Rita? You look just even greater every time I see you.'

I don't know why he bothered. Rita looked anything but impressed.

'We just need to pick up some kind of surveillance vehicle for Randy here.'

'Hello,' I said.

After a fifteen-minute exposé of the man's interest in British sports cars, which I somehow knew I was going to get, we turned our attention to the vehicles in his lot.

'So, Randy, what floats your boat?' he asked metaphorically, if entirely inappropriately.

There was one particularly attractive red soft top number made by, I think, Pontiac but as I decided that it probably said much too much about me psychologically, I didn't bother to mention it. On the other hand, and goodness knows what this did say about me, I was also much taken by a grey fin-tailed, low-slung car that must have been twelve feet wide, well, at least six, and possible three times as long. I walked over to it admiringly.

'Hey, you like the Olds'? She's a beauty, ain't she? Built in sixty-five. She's got a 7.2 and she'll top out at 120 no problem. Look at that back seat. Great for the drive-in, wouldn't you say?'

Initially I failed to understand the allusion and then when I did I started to laugh. Then I spotted Rita's rather stern gaze and stopped.

'Don't waste our time, Jimmy. Driving around in that he'll stick out more than that Buck Burnett and that great big jokemobile he insists on using. If I told him to lose it once I told him a thousand times. Boy, is that guy an ass.

Jeez. No, what Randy here needs is something inconspic-uous. Thought about some kind of SUV but I think just your regular sedan just as long as it's white or brown or maybe even grey.' She turned to me. 'White and brown. We find those work the best. You got so many of them around and nobody looks at white now, do they?'

When it came to selecting surveillance vehicles I was more than happy to bow to Rita's superior knowledge and finally we ended up choosing a light grey Dodge Stingray that was plenty fast enough and in its own little way pretty good-looking.

'OK,' said Rita as we said farewell to Jimmy and one another outside the car lot. 'You're gonna get yourself to the offices some time tomorrow, yeah? Nelson can go through the pre-surveillance briefing with you.'

Pulling into the mid-afternoon traffic at the wheel of the Dodge Stingray, sliding on my shades and grooving to some Otis on the radio, I smiled. Fairly soon, of course, as happens in all the best dreams, I was going to wake up.

9

Going South

Not since the seconds ticking down to the start of a one-day cricket international between England and India at the Wankhede Stadium in Mumbai had I experienced an atmosphere of such feverish excitement as there was that early September evening at Fenway Park. The noise of the crowd and the music booming out over the public announcement system was amplified tenfold by the comparatively intimate surroundings and gave me to fear greatly for the stability of the one-hundred-year-old, green-painted, wooden stadium that is home to the Boston Red Sox, probably or possibly, depending on your partisanship, the most famous baseball team in the world. Thank goodness they were not squaring up to meet their arch nemesis the New York Yankees on that occasion because then, surely, the arena would have collapsed in on itself like a house in a Charlie Chaplin movie.

Makepeace and his wife Irene and their two pretty but bashful daughters had met me outside the stadium under fluttering flags, each of which proclaimed a year that the Red Sox had won the World Series. They were only a little late and I just had time to wonder who it was that had

devised this term 'World Series'. To my fairly certain knowledge, that particular competition only involved teams from
the United States and the odd Canadian outfit who had
wandered over the border by mistake. This surely didn't
constitute a contest of a global nature? Or perhaps in the
mind of certain American baseball fans it did?

Jack, I noticed, was limping badly when we shook hands
and as we climbed the historic steps I asked him how his
knee was.

'Oh, I got to tell you something about that.'

Before he could go on we were out into the open and
the weak sunshine, looking down onto the almost unnat-
urally green diamond of the baseball pitch and a huge wave
of razzmatazz engulfed us. Both Makepeace and I were
much too sensible to try to explain baseball or cricket to
one another and I contented myself with cheering wildly
at the right moments and eating an enormous number of
hot dogs, some with chilli, some without. Even after I had
had to have a break in the middle of the seventh, I successfully managed to not think for one minute about the
provenance of the meat therein. The game seemed to go on
interminably and I found myself watching the innings tick
by. This was of little use to me as I had no idea how many
there should be in total and thought it rude to ask, however
nonchalantly, when the proceedings were to come to a halt.
Still, it was undoubtedly an honour to find myself in the
stadium where all the baseball greats that I had ever heard
of had played. On this very field had performed the famous
Babe Ruth . . . and . . . well . . . yes, Babe Ruth had been here.
Borrowing the programme from Irene, I leafed through it
in an effort to recognise a few names . . .

The Red Sox won, so only when the party was over,
and it really was quite a party, did we try and make our
way through the throng. Wading away, I called over to

Makepeace in a voice loud enough to reach him over the
noise of a band made up of people who I believe to be
called Majorettes. They made a right old racket, and whatever your cultural perspective, they looked quite absurd.

'So, what were you going to tell me?'

'Oh, yeah, about the knee. It's pretty much gone south.'
Makepeace grimaced and I forewent asking him in which
other directions it could have gone. 'Yeah, so the doc tells
me I got an operation all fixed up for the end of next week.'

'Ouch, but still that's good news, I guess, that you've got
a date. Presumably you'll be out again pretty quick.'

'Quick as I can. I got to do a load of rehab, though. Won't
earn a dime until I'm back in action. We'll just be surviving
on Irene's salary until I'm up and running again.'

'Oh, yes, that's not good news,' I said rather hopelessly.

'Yeah, it'll be a bit tough and the worst thing is I won't
be able to come on that surveillance with you.'

'Oh, yes, oh no, that'll be a shame,' I replied quite
sincerely. 'I wonder who I'll get to do it with then?'

'Oh don't even worry about that. Nelson will sort something out for you, you can be sure about that.'

When, on the Monday after the game, I made my way over
in the direction of Nelson's offices from the South End, the
traffic was abysmal. A light rain was swishing along
Tremont Avenue and everything glittered in the lights of
the cars. Even though it was only early afternoon, the streets
were gloomy and unwelcoming. To make matters worse
there was not a single space on any of the steep climbing
streets that criss-crossed the top of Beacon Hill. Instead I was
forced to park behind the Holiday Inn on Cambridge Street
and tiptoe my way across the traffic accompanied as usual
by seemingly dozens of doctors, nurses and other medical
professionals, waving umbrellas like a demented forest on

the move, as they made their way from Massachusetts General Hospital to goodness knows where. I was always amazed that they left work, to shop, to have coffee or to head home, still dressed in their hospital uniforms, their face masks hanging around their necks and their funny little caps still tied onto the top of their heads. Whenever I passed them I surreptitiously looked out for any traces of blood. On one occasion, definitely, I saw a man sitting on a bench just outside the Harvard Cocktail Bar reading the newspaper still wearing his surgical gloves.

When, at a later date, I mulled over with Nelson the possible reasons for this phenomenon, as detectives tend to do, we came up with a number of unlikely reasons: extortionate hospital laundry bills, perhaps, lack of changing facilities, or simple time constraints. We decided eventually that these people just felt pretty good letting everybody see them dressed this way, letting them know which profession they pursued. Surely a simple, but easily legible, badge would have sufficed. 'I am a Doctor – oh, yes!' It would certainly have been a great deal more hygienic.

When I finally made my way up Chestnut Avenue and negotiated the anything but even brick pavements, buckled and warped as they were by the roots of the aforementioned trees, I found Buck Burnett standing just inside the porch smoking a large cigar.

'Hello, Buck,' I greeted him tentatively. I had been a little nervous of him ever since his reaction to the Kreutzer/Rimbaud debacle. Now his manner was much changed although this did nothing to reassure me.

'Hey, partner, how's it going? How're you doing, buddy? Good to see you.'

'Oh yes, how're you doing?'

Buck hurled what must have been at least two thirds of his cigar onto the street where it hissed out in a swirl of smoke. Coughing heartily, he leant against the door of the building and ushered me in.

Nelson was in expansive mood at the pre-surveillance meeting that I now attended. 'Hey, Randy, how are you doing? I think you're going to like this one. Since we seen Susie, Rita and me, we've been to do what we call a PPS, a pre-pre-surveillance. It just involves driving by the premises of the subject's workplace or home to check out where we're going to start the surveillance – what we call the stake-out.'

Stake-out!

This was great.

'By the way, you're happy if we refer to John as the subject, yeah? When we talk about the person being followed, we tend not to use their Christian or family name. Stops it getting too personal. There are a number of different expressions used in the industry. Some PIs say victim, some use suspect, others the target but we stick with subject. Hope that's good with you?'

I agreed heartily that it was absolutely good with me and smiled broadly at everyone.

'That's great. OK, so Rita and me, we've checked out the place. Looks pretty straightforward. Rita, stick up those photos on the board, please. OK, I explained to you about this one? Makepeace is off the case, as I think you know? Shame, he's one of the best we got. So now you're going to be travelling with Buck. Sorry about the change of plan.'

And he really sounded as if he meant it.

'Yes, that's fine,' I said as cheerfully as I could but I felt doubly disappointed at this news as I had much been looking forward to driving my new car, the Dodge Stingray, and felt that I had probably spent as much time as was humanly possible in close-car proximity with Buck. Fortunately, my dismay was short-lived.

'That's great, OK. So, you will be car A, Buck, and you Randy, you'll be car B. Everything OK with the Dodge?'

'A-OK,' I replied. I had definitely heard someone say this somewhere. I just hoped it hadn't been in an episode of *Happy Days*.

'Good. So, let's have a look at these photos.'

Rita flicked them up onto some magical magnetic-type board where they stuck. They were remarkably good, clear, black and white pictures taken of a street from either end.

'So, Randy, you're going to pull in here. We have a bit of luck. There is an empty dwelling just right here. Go halfway up into the driveway. You should get pretty good cover from this mailbox.' He tapped his pen on the photograph to demonstrate the exact place. 'OK now Buck, he's going to be right here further up the street. That OK with you, Buck?'

'Yes, sir. That'll be just fine, sir,' he replied as if he was on a parade ground – and quite a large one at that.

'Oh, by the way, Buck, you're not going to be taking that big SUV of yours.'

'Yes sir, that was my intention.'

'No, Buck, that was not a question. You will *not* be taking the SUV. I had Rita fill up the Nissan Cherry with gas and it's kitted out, serviced and all, ready for your trip.'

I glanced carefully over at Buck. Even though he was hidden under his cap peak, I could tell he was poleaxed.

For some moments all he could mutter under his breath was, 'Not the Cherry! Oh, man, oh, man. The Cherry.'

'Good thing about this stake-out. The subject's gonna be leaving his house at seven thirty.' Nelson Mason carried on cruelly ignoring Buck Burnett's anguish. 'Why is that a good time for him to leave his house, Randy?'

'Er . . . because he will be getting a good start on the road?' It sounded ridiculously early.

'No, tomorrow being a Tuesday there's going to be plenty of other people all going to work around then so they're all going to be leaving their place at the same time. We don't need him coming out onto the road and all of a sudden he sees two other guys light up their headlights. There should be plenty of traffic and that'll give you good cover.'

'Ohhh, right . . .'

'OK, let's give you the equipment you need. You will be in permanent walkie-talkie contact with Buck, Randy. Don't forget to recharge your walkie-talkies at all times when you're in your vehicle. If you lose radio contact move over to cellphones.'

Walkie-talkies!

Roger!

'You will need your laptops. Take these with you too.' He flicked two CDs over the table to us. 'Put that in your machine, you'll have GPS directions for the whole of the US. It's gonna come in useful if you get lost but Buck should be able to talk you in.'

'Sure thing,' murmured Buck, his head still down. 'Sure thing. Nissan Cherry, oh, man.'

'OK, what else do we need you to know, Randy? Remember, it doesn't matter so much if the subject sees you. There's plenty of people travelling the coast this time of year but what he doesn't wanna do is keep on seeing you. So if you feel you've been spotted then you're gonna let Buck take over for a while and then maybe you can switch back in later on.'

That seemed reasonably straightforward.

'If he pulls up at a private residence, see if you can work out whether there is an alternative exit, otherwise pull in where you have visual on the gate and sit tight. If you need to do any snooping let Buck do it.'

Certainly, I'd let Buck do it. For a moment I felt a vague sense of camaraderie come over me but it didn't last.

'I don't care if it takes an hour or five hours or ten hours or if you're there the whole night. Remember, that's the work of a private investigator. You gotta put in the hours.'

The glamour of the whole adventure was only mildly tarnished by the thought of staying up all night in the car and once I had got my walkie-talkie and been given a crash course in how to operate it, I hurried back to the car and made my way directly to Crazy Joan's. I knew that I needed to get to bed early but I could not help installing myself at the bar for an hour or two and regaling Jolene and Vietnam Vic – it being Monday the bar was all but deserted – with an outline of my forthcoming adventure. Jolene laughed and called me a 'crazy Brit' which in the euphoria of the moment I did not mind at all. Vietnam Vic was a little more circumspect.

'So, it don't bother you none following this guy around?'

'Er . . .' It was not as if I hadn't already given this some thought but the excitement factor had, as sometimes happens, forced it to the back of my mind. 'Well, if he isn't doing anything wrong, why would he worry?'

'So, if you weren't doing anything "wrong", you wouldn't mind someone following you around?'

'Well . . . it all depends . . .' Although I knew it didn't.

'All getting a bit like a police state, if you ask me. Everybody spying on everybody else. You ever read *1984*? Should've done. It's by one of your guys.'

I told him that I had, with some enthusiasm.

'So, you must know what I mean? Where are all our freedoms going? You with your Houses of Parliament and us with our Founding Fathers. True, you're a two-bit PI, that don't matter squat. What you've got to worry about is the government. They're the people you need to fight against.'

A long silence ensued, during which Jolene brought over the hamburger I had ordered and I did my unsatisfactory best to eat it with some level of decorum. Just as I was wondering whether I should try and retrieve a piece of dill pickle that, through some mechanics that I did not understand, had escaped my grasp and landed amongst the bottles of spirits the other side of the bar, Vietnam Vic spoke again.

'So was you for the war or not?'

'What, you mean the war in Iraq?' I asked, then pulled myself up short suddenly, thinking that perhaps he was harking back to Vietnam about which I knew next to nothing.

'Sure I mean the war in Iraq. You know any other war going on around here?'

Whether I did or I didn't, Vietnam Vic, unknowingly, had opened up a part of me that more often than not, due mainly to a terrible sense of helplessness, I had kept quite carefully under wraps. For a period of a couple of months after the invasion by the Coalition Forces – they could hardly have called themselves the Allies, as this might have denoted some international consensus – had invaded Iraq in 2003, I had felt physically sick every time I opened the paper or switched on the television or radio and heard the weasel words of the American and British governments. What upset me most about the action, carried out not because America and Britain should but because they could – surely never a good enough reason – was not the comprehensive misunderstanding of international politics, the lessons not learnt from history, the lies, the ineptitude, the self-aggrandisement. All this we might have come to expect from people whose only driving force was their ego and their – the word made my skin crawl – 'legacy'. What upset me most was the painful knowledge, drawn from my travels down many a dismal and dusty road, on foot and not in a cavalcade of limousines, that the individuals who made up the populace of Iraq were not numbers to be counted, or not as the case may be. They were instead individual fragile components of human society who had either been destroyed or had been made to suffer the most dreadful physical and emotional pain. They would not walk away, retire or go off to write their memoirs. They would suffer – forever.

Probably Vietnam Vic was somewhat taken aback when I put this to him with some vehemence. Up until then I think he had considered me something of a fey curiosity but now his eyes gleamed with comprehension and agreement.

'You're right on my wavelength, Randy. Right on my wavelength. You hear that, Jolene? Freakin' A, brother!'

Even my amused admiration of this last turn of phrase would not cheer me up now. Sliding off my bar stool, I told Vietnam Vic that I would think about his invitation to meet some of his war protester friends on my return. I will admit that I was slightly mollified by the news that Kelly was included in that number. But anyway I had better head off. Early start and all that.

Despite a couple of BCs – bourbon and cranberry – a revolting but effective Jolene speciality that I had been practising making at home and which I had consumed with vigour while I attempted to pack a bag, that night was a remarkably sleepless one. Thinking again about the whole Iraq issue depressed me enormously. It made me want to move to a different planet. I had already, to all intents and purposes, left Britain by way of some pitifully useless protest and now as I gazed into the reddy-brown, mud and blood liquid in my glass, I glimpsed the extraordinary irony of my presence now in the country that was governed by the very people who had wreaked such carnage. To my annoyance but also, I admit, slight relief, any thoughts about the terrible human suffering taking place in the Middle East were eclipsed now as I also imagined any number of cata-strophic outcomes of my forthcoming trip.

Admittedly the 'subject' John, whose picture I had seen at the office and which I had committed to memory, had looked a benign enough sort of character. But he was big. What would happen if he accused me of following him? Things could get nasty. I tossed and turned a little more and fell into a hapless slumber in which I dreamt of roles reversed. No longer was I the pursuer but the pursued, the hunter hunted. Visions of the bulging John hunched at the wheel of an unimagined vehicle, scarlet in the face, roaring up the freeway on my tail, woke me, my brow damp, much, much too early.

Despite my sleep deprivation, I was soon bouncing around the apartment like a nervous jelly bean well before the sun had risen over the Mystic River. Casting my eye around for a last time, I pulled the door to the apartment closed and tiptoed down the stairs in order not to disturb the elderly Mrs Walowski or, worse, the awful Jackie sleeping below. Out in the street all was remarkably quiet and I had no trouble at all pulling out of the small parking lot and taking the two left turns around the block to get myself onto Commonwealth Avenue and off in the direc-tion of the genteel suburb of Brookline where John, I mean, the subject, lived with his wife, the terrifying Susie. I am not often out on the streets of any city at half-past four in the morning and, on the occasions that I have been, I have had the greatest difficulty doing anything but trying to get myself home.

So, this drive through early morning Boston was quite a revelation. There seemed to be a whole different world living under the moon, and all along the road in the base-ments of apartment block buildings down cold, concrete steps glowed the neon lights of twenty-four-hour convenience stores. Jimmy Wang was already stacking boxes of little-known Oriental vegetables from the back of his van, all the while delivering instructions to a bleary-eyed Jimmy Junior to little effect. Around the snack bars and coffee houses lurked, or rather huddled from what was already beginning to be a cool autumn, crowds of homeless people. Not just the Gentlemen of the Road, their faces battered by the elements and the booze, but young people, middle-aged people, women and even to my utter astonishment teenagers and children. This was in horrific contrast to the world in the hustle and bustle of daytime, big city, money machine, cosmopolitan, metropolitan Boston.

My couple of months or so had given me, on balance, a very positive opinion of Boston. I had enjoyed the ballet and the cinemas, the galleries, the restaurants, the parks and the shops but these scenes were now a disheartening shock.

My laptop had whirred and clicked, located a satellite and then found the address that I was making my way towards. It peeped politely at every turn. It had found planning my route in no way extraordinary. One of the beauties of driving in America is the grid road system. Even 'ancient cities' like Boston are laid out in a pattern and are remarkably easy to negotiate despite the occasional surprising one-way system. So soon, almost sooner than I would have liked, I found myself heading the car slowly down the street where the subject lived. With surprising ease I found the uninhabited house that Nelson had referred to and with a couple of clicks of the gear shift reversed the Dodge Stingray effortlessly up into the empty driveway and turned off the ignition. Just a last light puff of grey exhaust, that soon evaporated in the breeze, gave signal of my hidden presence.

Marlowe was at his best on a stake-out. A Thermos of

coffee and a sixpack of doughnuts would see him through a whole night's surveillance. It was the loner in him that made it so easy. Just Marlowe, the subject and the night. As the engine of the Dodge Stingray ticked hotly I pondered the concept of an all-night stake-out. The prospect was insufferably dull. Half an hour here, half an hour there, that I could handle as long as these brief periods were interspersed with the odd car chase, regular meals and plenty of contact with the offices of Chestnut Investigations Inc.

Sliding down a little in my seat, I peered out of the driver's window. As Nelson had foreseen, although most of my vehicle was out of sight I had a clear view of the street underneath the tin loaf-shaped letterbox down the street. Just as I recognised the form of Buck Burnett through my binoculars, looking thoroughly outsized in his tiny Nissan Cherry, my walkie-talkie crackled and it was he.

'Hey, buddy. How's it doing this fine morning?'

'Oh, hello . . . buddy. Er, how's it doing?'

'Yeah, good. So how're you feeling on your first live surveillance case? Pretty excited, huh?'

'Well . . .' I had not really had time to think about it so nervous had I been about not finding the place or arriving late. I checked how I felt. And Buck was right – I did feel excited. My pulse was heightened and somehow my nerves and senses were more alert than they had been in the weeks I had spent trudging the streets of Boston and avoiding getting on with my book. Pushing that particular memory hastily to the back of my mind I told Buck that I was indeed pretty excited.

'Yes, my Limey friend. That's what it's all about. It's the thrill of the chase. It's primorvial, my friend. You've gotta love it.'

Although I had to swallow hard, and smooth away the

broad grin on my face with one hand before I pressed the talk button on my radio, I somehow in a strange way had to agree with him.

Primorvial it most certainly was.

Unfortunately, Buck, as I should have realised right from the start, was, as far as his walkie-talkie was concerned, a prattler. There was nothing he liked more than telling me his every movement and initially, when I was not used to the scene or how to use the walkie-talkie, I found myself most disconcerted.

'Hey, partner, I am just going to retune,' he informed me as we sat there in the breaking dawn of another New England morning.

'Oh, no, don't do that. How will I be able to keep in touch with you if you do that?' I snapped a nervous finger off the communication key.

'Hey, don't worry, buddy, I don't mean the walkie-talkie, I mean the other radio.' This piece of information helped in no way at all until I heard down the airwaves some reggae music flip to country and western via a few bars of Stravinsky and realised that he was referring to his car stereo.

'Thanks, buddy,' I said back down the radio and then remembered that it was he, Buck, who had told me that nothing should distract the PI on a stake-out. There really wasn't much point in reminding him of this.

'Ten-four,' responded Buck.

'Sorry?'

'Ten-four,' replied Buck again.

'Yes, but what does that mean, ten-four?'

'Oh, I dunno, it's just a thing we say when we're on the walkie-talkie.'

'Oh.'

As time went on, however, I grew more used to ignoring

anything but his more direct requests and just found it comforting that he was still in contact.

Whatever was going on in the house hidden behind the trees where the subject lived, this 'golfing holiday' was getting off to a slow start.

Seven thirty, his estimated time of departure, his ETD, as Buck liked to call it, came and went. By eight o'clock I was getting a bit bored and wondering whether I would give Buck a call and ask him what we should do next.

Lights were coming on in the surrounding households and before long I could hear the clunks of front doors closing and the whirr of engines starting and bit by bit the daily commute commenced. All over the city people were climbing into their cars and making their way to their places of work, the routine for some of maybe thirty years. All except, of course, the subject. He did not appear to be going anywhere. What on earth could he be doing? Perhaps we had got the wrong day, perhaps we had got the wrong address. Any number of things could have gone wrong but still I resisted the temptation of reaching for the walkie-talkie and contacting Buck. Of course, I knew I was a 'rookie'. I just did not want to have to be told so by Buck.

With a total lack of anything happening, of any 'action', I began to slip off into a daydream about what delights the rest of New England might proffer. Not once, of course, has the reality of any destination been anything like that which I imagined it to be. This is not to say that the real experi-ence has always been necessarily more aesthetically pleasing, more exciting, than the picture I have built up beforehand. Very often the experience was more uncom-fortable, more dangerous, even simply more boring than I had envisaged. Without exception, however, the picture in my mind's eye was always crude, amorphous and colour-less compared with the essence of physically being somewhere, of experiencing life with all my five senses. It was the difference between watching the Derby on the television from the comfort of your armchair and riding the winner yourself. Still it was fun just imagining . . .

Closing my eyes gently I envisaged the rugged forests and endless beaches of the New England about which I had heard so much. Kennedy lookalikes and the famous Maine lobsters, arm-in-arm gripping mugs of clam chowder, roamed around my mind just as . . . the walkie-talkie squeaked and squawked. Initially I could not make out what it was that Buck was saying but suddenly the word 'subject' floated clear of the white noise.

'Here he comes,' Buck said in hushed tones.

As I peered under the mailbox I saw the front end of a grey car stop momentarily and then pull out towards the road.

Yes, the right model.

Holy kershmoley!

The adventure was about to begin.

Looking left and right, the driver stared straight at me or at least straight down the road towards where I was parked. It was him. It was the subject. It was John. As I slid a little down in my seat, Susie came out dressed in a flimsy, silky dressing gown, her arms folded across her chest against the cold. She most certainly did not look any better first thing in the morning. Whatever the words that she spoke to her husband as he departed, they did not appear to be ones of any particular warmth. There was no kiss, no touch. As he pulled out, she glanced both ways down the road but to my delight she did not appear to spot me or Buck, even though it was for us that she must have been looking. I counted to ten as I had been instructed and allowed another car to pass in front of me before I pulled out and started to follow the subject's car.

Oh, crikey! The chase really was on!

As we were now performing something known as a 'box' formation, Buck, after he had seen which way the subject intended to travel, had pulled out in front of him. Now, with Buck in front, on these single-lane roads, at least he could not take off at high speed. If he were to turn off left or right, either Buck would see his indicator and turn ahead of him or he could cut across on the next block whilst I would keep on the subject's tail ensuring that I had 'visual' at all times. Buck could then work around to pull out in front of him a little further on. Somehow, now, I felt vaguely more relaxed as, although I had absolutely no idea where I was going, it didn't really matter. As long as I had the subject in my sights I was doing my job. Unfortunately, everything did seem to bother Buck and he squawked incessantly down the radio.

Strange it was, I agreed, that someone who had claimed to his wife that he would be heading north to New Hampshire, then on to Maine, as far, nearly, as the Canadian border, had quite clearly just got onto US 1 South. US 1 – Route 1 – is that extraordinary road that travels from the Florida Keys all the way up through to Canada running almost straight north to south and, of course, south to north. Either he had made a great mistake or indeed, as Buck put it, 'something was definitely going down'. Soon we were heading out through Quincy and on to Weymouth, a resort on the coast.

Buck was still out at the front of the subject's car and I, finding myself neatly tucked in behind a truck containing several thousand gallons of super-sweet fizzy drink, managed to keep an eye on it by occasionally pulling out into the outside lane just until I could spot the rear driver's side light. There seemed no great sense of urgency and the US's low speed limits – here, fifty-five miles per hour on what would be called in Europe a motorway – meant that we were more pottering than zooming.

After about half an hour I saw the subject's indicator light begin to wink as he moved over to pull off the highway following the signs for Hingham. Buck had had enough time to see that this manoeuvre was taking place and so our strange cortège pulled out simultaneously onto the side road. Nervous now that the subject would have a clear look at me, I pulled down the sun visor slightly so only my chin and throat were visible. Unfortunately this also meant that my own ability to clearly see the road was somewhat diminished. Consequently I slowed down some more hoping that Buck would still have visual in his rear-view, which I was thrilled to realise was just exactly the right expression. I was still feeling pretty pleased with myself when, a few seconds later, Buck squawked that the subject was heading into a gas station. He was going to follow him onto the forecourt and wanted me to cover the far exit.

This manoeuvre turned out to be relatively easy because instead of heading into the service station by the pumps, I needed only to drive on to the next intersection and turn right, the gas station being as it was on the corner of a block. Pulling over just past the exit, I turned around slightly in my seat. From here, if the subject pulled out of the parking lot and carried on down to the right, I would have no problem picking up the surveillance. If instead he pulled out and turned left onto this big wide road I would only have to make a looping U-turn to be able to follow him.

As I turned off my engine I could see the subject climb out of his car and walk quite casually into the service station. He was dressed in jeans and a loose white shirt and wore sunglasses for no more suspicious reason than the sun was shining brightly. He was probably just stocking up with provisions for the long journey ahead but of course this did not explain why he should be so off his chosen route. To my astonishment, just as I was making a few deductions, I saw Buck coming round the side of the Nissan Cherry. He was crouching down as if he was inspecting for scratches along the side of his car. Several people carrying paper bags of groceries towards their cars looked at him quite mystified and before I knew what had happened he had slipped into the shop and was making his way, again with a curious crouching gait, around large displays of various beers, remaining all the while behind the subject, who had picked up some bottles of water and a large box of chocolates and was making his way to the queue at the counter. Buck moved swiftly over to the newspaper section and picked up the first magazine he could lay his hands on. Even at my distance and despite the reflection of the glass front of the store I could see that he was now pretending to be totally captivated by an article in *Sewing and Knitting Monthly*. As the man moved into the queue Buck abandoned his reading matter and queued up behind him. The subject paid for his purchases and started to make for the door, upon which Buck promptly made to follow him. When the woman at the counter asked him what it was that he wished to buy, he half-turned back, waving his arm in her direction in a 'don't hassle me' fashion before stepping up the pace after the subject. By the time they arrived outside our man had clearly noticed Buck, who turned away and started to whistle in an extraordinarily guilty fashion. Realising that he had been noticed, he 'dove' into his car and, lying almost flat on the seats, grappled for the walkie-talkie to tell me he was going to be taking 'evasive action'. This, it appeared, involved reversing smartly into a Chevy on the other side of the parking lot. This resulted in a tinkling of reflector glass and the wailing of the other car's alarm. Appalled, I was convinced that the subject would now go over to him and demand explanations. Instead he just looked in amazement at this scene, shook his head, put his groceries in the boot of his car, checked his watch and walked around to the driver's seat.

'You gotta get on him, Limey, you hear me?' Buck sounded as if he was calling me from the burning tail of a Lancaster bomber. 'He's your man, OK, don't lose him. I'll catch up with you just as soon as I can. You go get him!'

I was not at all sure that it was my job to 'go get him' but I had to think quickly as the subject pulled out onto the street and passed alongside me. Lifting my arm up to lean my elbow on the window sill I successfully covered my face. Through the windows of the cars parked in front of me I could see him pulling slowly on down the street. The Dodge Stingray started with refreshing and relieving ease. Only having a second to glance back at Buck, who was now surrounded by an ever increasing crowd of people more or less amused or irritated by the chaos that he had caused, I pulled out into the traffic.

I was on my own.

10

Loud and Clear

Before long the subject had settled down to an easy speed – the speed of a man going on a golfing holiday perhaps? We were now passing through some pretty, near perfect, American suburbs heading towards the direction of the ocean. I was almost beginning to enjoy the ride, my mind wandering slightly from the matter in hand. Possibly, had we carried on much further, I might have completely forgotten the reasons for which I now found myself driving through the coastal town of Hingham.

Just as I was retuning the radio I suddenly glimpsed out of the corner of my eye the left-hand indicator of the car in front. The subject was actually driving the car one ahead of that but when the car in front of me went to turn left crossing over the stream of traffic I immediately saw that the subject's car was now indicating to turn right and within a second of me having a clear view of it, it did. I slowed right back and only turned the corner after the car was some fifty to one hundred yards on down the road. Quite quickly after it came back into view the car turned abruptly off the street and into the forecourt of a substantial-looking bungalow. Desperately trying to remember what

Nelson had suggested I should do in these circumstances, scrabbling for the surveillance manual that had slipped down the side of the passenger seat, I pulled in behind a parked car. Although I could see straight through the windscreen of the vehicle, I was quite carefully hidden from view if anybody should stick their head out of the gateway.

At that moment everything started ringing and squawking all at once. My walkie-talkie sssssssshhhhhhhed loudly and eventually Buck became audible announcing that he was 'losing me'. This he repeated on a number of occasions until my mobile phone started to ring. I flicked it open and saw that Nelson was calling.

'Hey, Randy. How're you doing?'

'Fine, fine. Hang on!' I fumbled with the buttons on the walkie-talkie and pressed the one to speak.

'Buck, can you just shut up for a minute, I'm trying to talk to Nelson,' I said abruptly and then felt guilty at being so rude. Well, quite guilty. Miraculously his radio fell completely silent.

'Sorry, Nelson. Sorry. We've had a bit of a . . .'

'Yeah, Buck told me. Did I ever tell you he is an ass? I can't believe him. OK, Randy, now stay calm. Don't worry about it. We can still save this surveillance.'

I certainly hoped so. The responsibility of my situation and a certain sense of loneliness came weighing in heavily upon me.

'So where exactly are you now?' Nelson's tone was soothing.

I craned my head back and just managed to glimpse the address of the street on the neat black and white signpost.

'I'm on Monterey and Vincent Street. John, I mean the guy, the man, the um . . . subject, he's just gone into a . . . a private residence.'

Despite my attack of the nerves I was quietly pleased with the 'private residence' bit.

'Oh, OK, Randy, don't panic. This is what I want you to do. Just listen to me carefully.' Nelson could be quite soothing when he tried. 'You're going to get out of your car, you're going to wear your sunglasses and a hat over your eyes. Just carry your map like you were doing some tourist visiting. I want you to walk down to the end of the street. Have a good look inside the gate. If you see any action or any tags you just let me know.'

'OK, ten-four. Roger. Over. Er . . . over and out . . . No, wait, wait. Nelson. What are tags? You did say . . .'

'Oh,' he laughed. 'Licence plates?'

'Oh fine, OK. Thanks. Four-ten. Over and out. Bye . . . see you, then.'

I snapped my cellphone shut and, preparing myself, opened the driver's door and stepped out, closing it quietly. I did not lock the car lest I needed to get back into it in a hurry. All I needed now, of course, was for someone to steal it.

Acting impressively innocently, I made my way down the sidewalk. The house that the subject had pulled into was just coming up on my left-hand side. Keeping my head straight ahead, I managed to swivel my eyeballs and glance through the gates, this strange manoeuvre hidden behind my sunglasses.

Sure enough, in the yard in front of the house was the subject's car parked alongside something called an Oldsmobile Sedan. Without slowing down too much, I managed to memorise the number plate. Thanking my lucky stars that American state 'tags' are generally only a few digits and letters long, I made my way down to the end of the street. Just as I turned the corner I whipped a pencil out of my pocket and wrote them down on the corner of the map.

Then, equally nonchalantly, I made my way back down towards the car. There was still no sign of anybody and a minute or so later I reported back to Nelson.

'OK, let's have that tag number. I'm going to get a friend of mine to run a check on it. I can get back to you pretty soon.' I gave it to him and waited, the nervous tension rising up in me again. Two minutes later a beep-beep, beep-beep signalled his return call.

'OK, he's at his mother's place. No need to worry. Probably where the chocolates were going. Just sit tight. You're just going to return to normal procedure. Sit tight in the car and just follow the normal surveillance procedure when he comes out. Do you read me?'

'Loud and clear,' I replied, now more relaxed. I had forgotten about people reading each other.

About forty-five minutes later the subject pulled out of the driveway alone. As he turned left and away from me he waved cheerfully back towards the house. Letting off the handbrake with a sigh of relief I pulled out and followed.

Soon we were back on US 1 and when we hit the junction of Interstate 93 he started to head westbound and climb up and around the conurbation of Boston. We had completed almost a 180-degree circumvention of the city and found ourselves back on US 1 heading north. This was more like his plan.

Hours passed and he appeared to have no desire to stop. This, of course, was when I learned that he had a bladder lined with stainless steel and I had the curious sensation that I might well indeed burst.

On we drove, on and on. Until, of course, as if without any premeditation, he pulled off the highway and into a very normal-looking motel. Unsure what to do I drove on a little while and then pulled over and disappeared precipitately behind some large metal rubbish bins. Reappearing a little later, a weight off my mind, I rang Nelson. He explained that I should check that the subject was indeed booked in to stay and then find myself a room, preferably on a different floor, but with a view of the parking lot.

When I arrived at the motel the subject had unpacked his bags and was clambering up a wooden set of stairs to the first floor. I watched him return and heave out an enormous bag of golf clubs from the boot of his car before finally locking it.

With as much self-assurance as I could muster I made my way into the reception of the motel and asked for a room.

'Hey, I guess you're from the UK, is that correct?' a helpful, kindly but rather overly-jovial man enquired as he handed me some simple paperwork.

'Yes, that's right,' I muttered, and felt embarrassed that I was not being more chatty but I had too much on my mind to hear at length about some relations of his – well, of his wife – called Brown, he thought. Couldn't remember where they lived but the UK was kind of a small place, wasn't it, with all those little cottages? Did I know them?

No, I bloody didn't.

'OK, here you go. This is room 212. It's on the second floor. You just take the stairs over there.'

'Oh, on the second floor did you say? Oh, no, I really need something on the ground floor, er, the first floor. I wonder if you could do anything for me there? It's just that I . . .' Here I grappled around for an excuse. 'It's just that I have a very bad hip. Ow, yes. Very bad. Much worse after all the driving. Can't cope with the stairs, you know.'

Once I had taken hold of the keys of a ground-floor room and had managed to bat off any further attempted questions from the man behind the reception desk, probably about the Queen, I darted out of the side door. Under normal

circumstances I am extremely happy to engage in inconsequential chit-chat with strangers but on this occasion I was
convinced that while I chewed the cud with him the subject
would be loading his bags back into his car and making
good his escape.

So it was with some relief that I saw the grey car still
sitting in the same bay, its engine ticking hotly. Unlike any
of the other cars mine was reversed into its bay and it stood
out horrendously from the crowd. Deciding, however, that
it would be more conspicuous to move it, I walked around
under the covered walkway and, popping open the boot,
grabbed my bag and went into my allotted room. Through
the window and its net curtains I had a clear view of the
subject's car but this did nothing to calm my nerves. Sitting
on the bed nearest the window I peered out as I rang Nelson
on my cellphone. I imagined him sitting Buddha-like behind
his great desk in the cramped office as we spoke and he
reassured me. There was nothing to worry about. This was
normal procedure.

Well, it might be for him.

All I needed to do was keep an eye on the car and if he
should leave without his bags then there was little to worry
about as he would eventually return. I would still need to
follow him to find out whether he was going to meet up
with anybody. The chances were, Nelson thought, he would
probably go out for something to eat and then head back
to the motel.

Calmed only slightly, I propped myself up on some
pillows on the capacious bed, giving myself a clear view
of the car park, and wondered what to do next. I had a
guide book for New England but it was of only minimal
interest as I had no idea where my journey would next take
me. Finally I picked it up anyway and leafed through it
listlessly.

As I kept a weather eye out for any movement outside I read more about New England's role in the War of Independence and its current position in American political life. For some reason, but surely not a partisan one, I had been particularly badly taught about the reasons for the American Revolution, that is to say the American War of Independence. I read on. American colonists, who had made the country, this New England, their own, felt that they had no, and perhaps needed no, representation in the parliament at Westminster, on the other side of the 'pond', and the phrase 'no taxation without representation' became increasingly popular in many American circles.

As a result, they began to boycott British goods and took a notably dim view of the price they were being asked to pay for their tea. On December 16th 1773, a group of renegade colonists, calling themselves the Sons of Liberty, disguised themselves as Mohawk Indians, which involved, I imagine, little more than a quick trip to the barber's, headed down towards Griffins Wharf in Boston and boarded three clippers: the *Dartmouth*, the *Beaver* and the *Eleanor*. Working through the night they managed to tip ninety thousand pounds – forty-five tonnes – of tea worth an estimated ten thousand pounds into the drink. For weeks afterwards the waters around Boston were a deep, Typhoo brown. Understandably extremely annoyed about this wanton waste, the British started to get rather heavy-handed and headed off to Lexington and Concord, where they intended to confiscate arms and arrest a few revolutionaries. It was the first fight of the American revolutionary war. The guns fired on the bridge at Concord were the 'shots that were heard around the world'.

Just as I was beginning to move on to a rather dense chapter about native American civil rights my eyelids began to droop. Snapping myself upright I spent a few minutes making a cup of coffee from endless different little packets. It was disgusting but I drank it anyway. Under no circumstances should I doze off. The effects of the caffeine were minimal. Picking up my guide book, I sat back down on the bed. A few minutes later I fell fast asleep.

Waking some unknown time later, I was much disorientated. The motel bedroom was now in darkness, only a small amount of neon light shining through the window. Feeling giddy and sick, but above all immensely tired, I jumped up. For what seemed like long minutes I tried to work out where on earth I was and what I was doing there. Had I missed an important job interview? Clunk by clunk everything dropped into place and my body suddenly ran cold with sweat and my extremities tingled as I realised my great mistake. With no pretence at subtlety I pulled apart the net curtain and pushed my nose to the window.

The subject's car was gone.

Checking my watch I hunted around for my keys and only after I had located them did I think to turn on the lights, which I hurriedly turned off again as I shot out of the door. I checked my watch again, not having taken the information in the first time, and discovered that it was now nearly six thirty p.m. There was no movement in the parking lot and I stood for a few minutes at a complete loss as to what to do. My first instinct was to get into the car but the realisation was slow that I had no particular place to go. Instead I walked down towards the reception past the dark windows of the empty motel rooms. Thinking hard I opened the door of the little cabin and walked in to find the same man behind the counter. He looked up and smiled fully, perhaps hoping that I had had a change of heart and was now returned to engage him in lively conversation.

He asked whether I was comfortable. I wasn't particularly.

I needed to know where the subject had gone. Still I could not think of what question to ask without raising his suspicions.

'So, hello, I'm feeling a bit . . . a bit hungry. Yes, starving in fact. Would you have any ideas where I might find something to eat?'

'Yeah, sure, you have a diner just right here on the next block. Maisie's.' The man pulled out a map of the area and started to draw a line marking my route that only served to heighten my sense of urgency. 'It's not too expensive and you can get pretty good food there. Yes, we recommend it to all our customers. You might even get some fish and chips!'

Ignoring the mockest cockney accent since Dick van Dyke, I pressed on.

'Oh, you recommend it to all your customers? Have you recommended it to many this evening?'

The man looked a little surprised at the question but replied cheerfully enough that he had. I didn't think I could ask him to be any more specific.

Stepping outside again I had everything firmly crossed. But why, if Maisie's was only on the next block, why had the subject taken his car to get there? Was he meeting someone? Did he have his bags packed or was he returning to the motel – perhaps with company? I climbed into my car and drove the sixty or so yards to Maisie's, a brightly lit, cheerful-looking establishment. The very first car I recognised in the parking lot was the grey sedan. Heaving a huge sigh of relief, I realised that I would not have to ring Nelson and admit my terrible failure. How quickly I had forgotten the moral dilemma I had had about this surveillance job! Now I was just concentrated on not losing the trail.

The easiest thing to do now would be just to sit tight.

But no, I needed to know whether he was in the

restaurant on his own or not. I wondered whether I should try and peep through the windows but they were strung with little red and white checked curtains and anyway perhaps it would have caused some surprise to see a stranger in the night peering in. Instead I pulled my baseball cap down firmly looking no more strange than many of the cool dudes I had seen walking about. Pushing the door open I attempted to scan the room as quickly as possible, praying that I would not immediately make eye contact with the subject. He was not there. Peering back through the glass door of the restaurant into the night I checked the tag of the car I had seen. It was a match. As I turned back to double-check I was greeted with the smiling face of a young waitress.

'Will it just be you dining tonight, sir?' she asked politely.

'Yes, no, well I was just looking for a friend. No, I wasn't, no, no. No, actually I'll have a table for one, please.' Out of the corner of my eye I had spotted some booths designed for two people and pointed over in that direction.

'Sure, just follow me.'

As I made my way over to the booth I cast my eyes around again. Still I could not pick him out of the crowded room.

'Remember, even if there are no counter-surveillance measures taken you have to be ready for any changes in the subject's appearance,' Nelson had told me in the pre-surveillance briefing. No reason why the subject should not change his clothes for reasons no more suspicious than personal hygiene.

'Changes in appearance,' I muttered as I sat down, then smiled up at her. 'Yeah, look for changes in appearance . . .'

'Sorry, sir? Hey, do I know you? You sure look kind of familiar.'

'No, no, no. Sorry I'm . . .' I didn't really know how to

finish off the sentence short of announcing that I was in
the process of going quite mad.

'Oh, that's OK. Coffee, tea, or do you just want a regular
soda?'

She left me alone a while with my menu but it was difficult to concentrate. Pretending as cleverly as I could to be
looking at the forty or so different types of hamburger, I
cast my eye over the room again. My vantage point was
good. Nearly all of me was hidden from direct gaze. Peeking
back I checked out the twenty or so tables, discounting,
probably quite wrongly, any that seated more than two
people. Only as I cast my eyes back down to the table did
I realise that I had failed to take in the dozen or so figures
sitting with their backs to me at the bar. They were of
differing sizes ranging from ample medium to extremely
large. So far I had not seen the subject from the rear but as
I looked closer I thought I saw something familiar about
one of the individuals. Just at that moment he very thoughtfully dropped his paper napkin on the floor and I realised
that it was my man.

All of a sudden I had quite an appetite. Having neither
eaten nor even drunk much all that day I set about a large
meal as I watched the subject enjoy his. Fortunately the rest
of the evening passed off without incident and I made my
way back to my room two or three minutes after the subject
had turned back into the parking lot.

Television and film are really the perfect media for
displaying the activities of a private investigator on surveillance. Neither the audience, the actors or the film crew have,
due to the miracles of editing, to put up with the relentless
tedium of sitting and waiting, or in the case of the following
day, driving and waiting.

The next day consisted of a lot of driving. Just driving,
in fact. Driving and switching radio stations. There are

thousands of them on the American airwaves and each is more tedious – or irritating – than the last. They only become bearable when thrown into contrast by the endless advertising breaks, which intersperse them at astonishingly frequent intervals. Finally, we arrived in the small seaside town of Kennebunkport.

We carried on through the smart downtown area and followed the coast past impressive-looking motor yachts moored in the marina and out on past a disused fairground. A side road took us off out into wooded countryside and I sat back keeping one winding corner between me and the other car. Relaxing, I suddenly realised I was enjoying the ride. So this was the life of a private investigator. All expenses paid and a trip through beautiful country. I really had a lot to thank Nelson for. What was more, it appeared that I was something of a natural as far as this surveillance business was concerned. The sun pattered down through the already golden-brown foliage of the trees that overhung the narrow road. Delightful, I thought as I turned the corner, fully expecting to see my subject going around the next. But then he was gone.

He had disappeared.

11

Atlantic View

Rounding the next corner and then the next, I realised that something had gone horribly wrong. Ahead of me stretched a long straight piece of road perhaps half a mile long.

There was no sign of the car.

Slowing to a halt I suddenly realised that I did not enjoy this private detection business at all. It was extremely stressful. The boredom was nothing to the terrible worry when something went wrong. Oh, how I had enjoyed the hours of gentle miles clicking away, thinking my thoughts and biding my time. Now my heart was thumping horribly and I almost turned on the radio again for a bit of soft rock comfort.

Not knowing what to do, I experienced much the same sensation that I had when once I had found myself in a small boat in a storm on the English Channel. It had been impossible to decide whether to go forward to my destination or back to the picturesque port and its little pub from whence I had come. How I wished I was sitting there now. Paralysed momentarily by indecision I felt quite dazed. Almost in automatic mode I put the car in reverse and, there being nowhere to turn around, zoomed back down the road, the transmission whining all the way at the same pitch as my brain. Glancing about left and right I looked for any possible hiding place for the car. Did this mean that he thought that he was being followed? Was this what Nelson described as a counter-surveillance manoeuvre to throw me off his trail?

Surely not.

He had no idea that anyone had the intention of having him followed.

Did he?

Why would he?

Just as I believed that I must have gone back far too far, I suddenly noticed to my left a small lane that cut back sharply from the road and that was only just wide enough for single traffic. I stopped and wondered what to do. If I headed on down the lane, what would I do if I found him coming back towards me? There would be no escape. But I had to know where he had gone. Perhaps he would keep on this track until he came out on another completely different road and then I would have lost him completely.

Slowly, as that was all the lane would allow me, I nosed down the track. A few hundred yards further on I could make out, in the late afternoon sun, the form of a huge red building surrounded by wooded parkland. As it came more clearly into view I realised that it was a strange neo-gothic castle, something out of a horror movie. Just there, off the lane, was an entrance bordered by two sloping stone walls. On one of these was a sign in gilt letters on ocean-blue gloss paint. It read 'Sevenoaks Sanatorium and Nursing Home'. Slowing down beside it, I smiled.

A nurse! He was having an affair with a nurse.

Ha, ha! It all seemed a little corny.

For only a few weeks of the year?

And out here?

At that moment, however, I did not really have too much time to ponder the true nature of his visit. I urgently needed to find myself somewhere to hide. Pulling on further down the lane, to my relief I discovered that the lane ended only in a large hedge. There was just enough room to back up and turn around.

Finally I accomplished a twenty-five-point turn with the assistance of the Dodge Stingray's extraordinarily light power steering. Pulling the car in close I could see that there would be no possible way that anybody would notice my presence as they pulled back out onto the road unless, of course, they were looking for me.

I sweated lightly.

For at least half an hour no traffic pulled in or out of the gates and I began to wonder whether perhaps he had checked in for some kind of rest cure. Having met Susie, albeit only briefly, this solution would not have surprised me.

After about three quarters of an hour a green low-sided van pulled out piled with clippings and dead branches. As it drew away I realised that I could see the face of the driver quite clearly in the wing mirror.

I settled in for a long stake-out. That was after all the life of a private eye.

Soon I was battling against heavy eyelids.

Short naps always provide the most vivid of dreams and the one that I had now, when my eyes closed fully, must have been one of the most vibrant of all. Somehow I had got myself onto the set of *Dr Strangelove* and was sitting at the great dark command table. I was joined there by Saddam Hussein, Tony Blair, and George W. Bush. George W. had a machine gun mounted on the table in front of him, and occasionally, with the assistance of Buck Burnett, who fed him the bullets, he took aim at countless civilians that trooped across a cinema screen; whenever he fired the people fell down and the blood dripped onto the metal floor. Vietnam Vic was seated next to me in a wheelchair but no word that he spoke, even though he was shouting at the top of his voice, could be heard over the sound of the chattering gunfire. Just as it seemed as if the machine gun was going to be turned on us Kelly, dressed only in a pair of high heels, rode into the room on a white charger, bearing a Stars and Stripes on a long pole.

Unfortunately, just as she scooped me up, my cellphone rang. It was Nelson.

'Hi, Randy, how're you doing?'

'Hey, Nelson . . .' I repeated back to him the normal social niceties.

'I'm good, good. Just checking in to find out how it's going,' he asked cheerfully, but in hindsight I fancy that he thought the real reason for my silence was that I had something to hide.

'Sorry, Nelson, just been on the road all day and didn't find the right moment to catch up with you.'

'No problem, buddy. Can you give me your location?'

Checking my laptop, I did as carefully as I could and explained to him the present situation. He hummed and, annoyingly, did not have any particular conclusions to draw.

'Jury's out on this one,' was all that he could remark. We paused for a while to think.

'Hey, Randy, you used to be a high school teacher, didn't you?'

I had forgotten in an earlier conversation he had expressed some interest in my former career. I agreed that I had.

'So you know what makes these youngsters tick, correct?'

'Well, sometimes I used to think I did.'

'Well you are going to be my man. I have a case right now opening up involving a teenager.'

'What is that all about?'

'Oh, it's a homicide.'

'What, you mean . . . you mean a murder?'

'Well, maybe what you might describe as unlawful killing. Hey, I'll catch up with you later, Randy, OK. Keep me updated, OK?'

Then, as Americans do without a second's thought and in total contrast to their greetings, he cut me off. I have never met anyone in the United States who has to ask your name even once after a first introduction. Nor have I met anyone who will not claim to be always available to assist you in any way whatsoever, even if they are not. Chasing the buck, paying the bills, is all-important. No matter what, you must show the world that you are indispensable and at the same time impressively gainfully employed. You don't have time to say goodbye at the end of a telephone call because you are already onto the next thing. Soon after arrival I had noticed that most of the mobile phones were of the folding variety, popular perhaps because they could be closed with an attractively dynamic snap. And, now, I gotta get going. I'm busy and, look at me, I'm succeeding.

Sitting back in my car seat I suddenly felt a thrill of excitement again. Now I was seriously enjoying this private investigation business. I wondered what this new case could possibly involve. My imagination seemed to thunder away in front of me and I could barely keep focused on my present surroundings.

Some time later a large refrigerated lorry arrived, announcing its provenance from a food wholesalers. I was pleased to notice that the driver, even though he glanced down the lane, did not appear to register my presence.

Again it was just a matter of sitting tight and waiting.

After the truck had disappeared I relaxed back in my seat and wondered whether it was wise to open up the bottle of water that I had bought in haste from the vending machine at the motel. I inspected its rather narrow neck. It was warm now but I was beginning to feel dehydrated. Just as I was unscrewing the cap, the nose of a small white van appeared at the entrance to the sanatorium.

As it pulled out I could see that the back had been specially modified and rose high above the ground. When I was able to see its entirety I realised it was a van into which a disabled person could drive on their electric wheel-chair. One of the patients going off for an appointment or just to the shops, I assumed.

Just as I was about to cast my eyes down again to my drinking bottle, the driver leant across the passenger seat to check that the way was clear.

It was him! It was the subject!

I couldn't believe my eyes.

What on earth was he doing with this disabled person's vehicle? Had he stolen it? Was he moonlighting this job? Neither deduction was at all satisfactory. First, his own car was still somewhere in the grounds of the sanatorium. Second, he was unlikely to be moonlighting for a few weeks a year. So what the hell was he up to? Although the van had now turned the corner and I could no longer see the driver I was convinced, absolutely convinced that it was he.

Somehow, subconsciously, we become used to recognising not only people's physical traits but also their little characteristics: the way that they hold themselves, sit or stand, an inclination of the head, a gait. So it was, when I was teaching, that I could recognise one of my students at a distance which was far too great to be able to see their physical or facial features. I often used to have a little bet with myself that if I saw one of them engaged in some minor wrongdoing I would be able to call out their name before I was ever able to clearly see who it was.

Dropping the bottle into the passenger's footwell, I switched on the engine and put the car into drive even before I really considered what was going to happen next.

The van set off up the road and turned and turned again until it was heading back in the direction of Kennebunkport. The subject was heading south again but on these strange coastal promontories it was only possible to return to US 1 by heading back into the main built-up area and then taking the link road back onto the main highway. He could be going anywhere. Once the van was ahead of me – and now I had little choice but to remain at what I believed a safe distance behind him, there being no other vehicles on the road – I could see that there was a bulky automated wheelchair in the back of it. To the side of the heightened back rest I could see the form of a head slumped to one side and moving fairly freely with the motion of the vehicle. Increasingly astonished I rang Nelson, fumbling with my cellphone in order to scroll through to his number.

Perhaps there was something slightly excitable in my voice when he answered because he urged me to calm down.

'It's OK. Just keep on with them and you'll soon see what the outcome is. After all, buddy, isn't that half the excitement? It's the suspense, that's the thing that keeps us going. It's the mystery, isn't it?'

I certainly agreed that it was and, as I did so, I could feel my pulse racing. My hands were slippery on the steering wheel.

What on earth could be going on here?

What was this secret assignation?

Sure enough, the van carried slowly on through downtown

Kennebunkport and followed the signs that indicated US 1. Fortunately, due to the nature of the vehicle, the subject was travelling at only a very reasonable speed. Soon I began to relax and now with the increased traffic began to tuck myself in behind vehicles and tried to remember the modus operandi that Nelson had taught me.

Soon we were back out on the highway heading north, and thanks to the high sides of the van I was able to keep the vehicle in easy line of view. Somehow, once we headed out onto major roads like this the surveillance became that much easier. I had got this licked!

Dense forests fringed either side of the road now and a wonderfully clear light shone over distant hills and out to the glimmer of the ocean to my right. We had just passed all the signs for Portland and showed no sign of slowing up when the subject began once again to indicate.

Pulling slowly into the exit lane behind him using a small grocery truck as cover, I followed him off the busy thorough-fare and out into the country. Although still heading north we were inexorably being drawn further and further to the coast and before long the road actually broke out onto an ocean corniche. Momentarily I was distracted from my task as I gazed at the waves breaking onto what seemed like an endless beach.

Twenty minutes after we had hit the ocean road we came to a curving left-hand bend around which was laid out an extensive car park. This was a popular sightseeing spot and I could see why as I looked up and down the coast at wonderful wooden houses built out on lonely promon-tories, slightly hazy in the ocean mist. Gulls squawked and swooped over seaweedy rocks that were occasionally spat-tered with golden sand thrown up by the breaking, bursting, thundering surf.

The van pulled into the parking lot and I slowed down

to see where it stopped. It did so almost immediately inside the entrance, pulling up facing the sea. Instead of following it in immediately I drove on some four or five hundred yards to the entrance at the furthest end and parked up behind a number of vacationing cars. From here I had good visual.

A large couple in a slightly larger camper van were unloading everything that might be needed for a mid-afternoon tea break. Chairs, tables, parasols and a huge and extremely professional-looking hamper had all been pulled out and set up, not, as I might have imagined, on the beach but right there on the tarmac just in front of their transport.

Wishing them good day and enquiring how they were doing, I slipped round the back of their RV and, holding my binoculars in what I hoped to be a rather ornitho-logical fashion, I walked some way up towards the subject's vehicle.

The man had come round to the back of the van and opened the double doors. He was operating a button and an automated ramp was slowly unwinding onto the ground. Before long, with a certain sudden jolting, the wheelchair reversed itself slowly but precisely out. I had been observing this out of the corners of my eyes, my binoculars held up to the ocean view. But when the person in the wheelchair fully emerged I swung my binoculars through as if gazing down the coastline and fixed them firmly on the head that now lolled towards me.

In the wheelchair was a child. At this distance it was difficult to ascertain whether it was a boy or a girl but some-thing about the figure, crumpled as it was, indicated definitely that this was no grown person.

Now there was nothing further I could do except simply wait until they made their next move. Part of me, ridiculously, wanted to go up to them and engage them in conversation as if we were friends, as if I knew them. Rather than being a perfect stranger who was following them without their knowledge, let alone authority, I felt myself to have some distinct link with them.

After a few minutes of enjoying the waves and spray, the birds swooping and the shimmering sky, the child was reloaded into the van, which set off on up the ocean road. To the neutral observer there could have been nothing more normal about their behaviour but I was more and more mystified and I hurried to get back to the Dodge Stingray. Luckily, they were barely three hundred yards ahead of me by the time I pulled back out.

Soon we were driving through a near-endless stream of seaside resorts which ranged, sometimes in a matter of a few hundred yards, between the luxurious and perfectly painted to the somewhat shabby, kiss-me-quick type of establishments, burger stands and offers of larger and larger portions of French fries. Restaurants and bars that stank of cheap fixes lined the sea road.

Some time later the pair turned off down towards the beach and in through the gates of Atlantic View. This motel had little in common with the establishment in which I had spent the night before. This was a beautifully tended, spacious affair and although it was constructed on classical motel lines, that is to say a two-storey building with doors on the parking lot side and, I imagined, views out over the ocean on the other, each of the rooms was the size of a reasonable town apartment.

The subject had clearly made a prior booking. Hardly had the van pulled up underneath the arching porch of the reception area than a friendly man stepped out and came up to the car window. No, not only had the man made a booking but it was quite clear from the body language that the receptionist knew the subject. They had met before!

So was this a normal destination for a 'golfing holiday'? Adhering to the belief that the sport in question was simply a good walk ruined, I had no idea at all what was involved.

The man from the reception walked alongside the van as it drove up to the apartments and finally stopped at room number twelve. Of course, they would have booked a place on the ground, or rather first, floor, because this would obviously ease the access of the wheelchair. Very promptly the subject opened up the back of the van and repeated the performance with the hydraulic ramp.

Soon all three had disappeared inside the room with all their attendant baggage. Above and beyond the holdall that the man had carried out of his car before, he was now equipped with a large suitcase and several bags that at a distance looked as if they probably contained nappies. Of golf clubs, on the other hand, there was no sign. Whatever else had been transferred to the mobility van, the golf equipment had obviously been left in the sedan.

Soon the man and the receptionist returned to the door and bid each other farewell. I could see the subject trying to offer a tip but this was gently and cheerfully refused. As soon as the man returned behind his desk I swung the car into the reception area and made something of a meal about stretching and yawning when I got out.

When I went inside I, too, was greeted cheerfully and asked whether my journey had been a long but pleasant one. I agreed that it had. What was I doing? Passing through? Naturally I had little choice but to admit that I was 'on vacation from England'. This was, it was agreed, pretty neat.

Although I did realise, didn't I, that I should have made a reservation? They were very busy this time of year. Yes,

I agreed, the next time I knew that I was coming to Atlantic View I would certainly book in advance.

Before long I found myself in an enormous suite comprising a comfortable living room, decorated in light pastel shades, and a separate, equally roomy, bedroom and en suite bathroom. The vast picture windows gave out onto a spotless sand beach and more rolling waves.

Unfortunately, the only window through which to look back down onto the parking lot was a small frosted one in the bathroom at the rear. However I worked out that if I opened the small top vent and stood on the cistern of the lavatory, tilting my head to a fairly unnatural angle, I had an un-obstructed view of the subject's car. This was not at all, on the other hand, a satisfactory way to spend my time in this particularly attractive resort, I thought to myself as I removed a strange, lacy doily kind of loo roll cover from the toe of my shoe and put the toilet brush and holder back upright.

Oh well, I shrugged, that's the nature of the beast and, feeling annoyed by the lack of originality of this thought, I scanned the parking lot for any signs of movement. Opposite the accommodation building, set out around the beautifully clear, free-form swimming pool, were a selection of white tables and chairs and a four-sided bar surrounded by tall stools. Short of there being a sign to that effect, the bar could not have had perfect stake-out location written more clearly all over it.

Swiftly unpacking only the necessities of poolside life, I changed into my swimming shorts, which had last seen action in a pool in Africa some years previously and seemed in the passage of time to have shrunk alarmingly. Dressing in one of the pale-blue bathrobes that hung on the back of the bathroom door I flip-flopped my way across the tarmac in a pair of ill-fitting, little-worn sandals down to the pool. Making my way round to the far side of the bar and climbing up onto one of the high seats, I realised that this was an almost ideal lookout. There were a number of customers sitting on the other side of the rectangular serving area, who created reasonable cover, but if I peered over the top of them I had a clear view of the subject's door. Obviously, with the complications caused by the wheelchair, he was unlikely to be able to make a quick getaway. Anyway, they had only just arrived. I began to relax.

'What's it gonna be, sir?' asked an impossibly brown barman. 'Our special today is lobster roll – that's a one-and-a-half-pound fresh Maine lobster broiled, shelled and served on one of our freshly baked, foot-long subs. That comes with our very own home-made mayonnaise and our own special fries on the side. You can have that with a side salad and we have a choice of dressings, Italian, French, blue cheese, thousand island . . .'

'OK, that sounds great. Umm, French blue cheese, please,' I replied quickly lest I had lost my appetite by the time he had finished.

'You staying at the motel?'

'Yes, I am.'

'In that case, sir, you are eligible for a complimentary house margarita. Would you like that on the rocks or straight up?'

'Well, straight up but I don't know if . . .'

'OK, that's coming right up.'

Concerned that I should not be consuming alcohol in case I had to get back in my car again, I made to remonstrate with him again but he was already pouring a variety of different liquids from plastic bottles into a turbo food blender and sluicing out his badly worn cocktail shaker. Well, just the one wouldn't do any harm, I supposed.

There was no further sign of the subject and his fellow traveller as the afternoon wore on. Rather against my will

I got myself engaged in a lengthy conversation with a woman from Michigan whose husband, who was in nickel – which may have been code for something I didn't understand – had just left her. Apparently, she was looking for some action. Her words, not mine. The margaritas were unfortunately extremely good and at five o'clock in the afternoon worryingly potent.

With a supreme act of will I extricated myself from the clutches of the lady from Michigan and made my way to the motel reception. There was no sign of life but on the counter was a large brass bell with an instruction attached to ring for service. This I did rather over-enthusiastically and it rang out clear and loud until I cupped it with my hands to dim the sound. Leaning on one elbow I looked back out at the swimming pool and smiled. This was the life.

'Hey, how're you doing? Isn't it such a great day we got today?'

I swung round to greet the receptionist but to my surprise found nobody behind the desk. Turning further to my right I discovered myself standing in front of a large middle-aged man. I smiled and then, as the connection between my eyes and brain was finally made, gasped.

For standing in front of me dressed in a stripy summer shirt and shorts, smiling generously, was the subject.

'Hey, how you doing?' he repeated.

'Um . . . I'm doing good, er . . . how you doing?'

'I'm good. Yeah. Real good. So you must be from England, right? Just visiting?'

How did he know that? Oh, the accent, of course.

'Er . . . er . . . er . . . yes, that's right. Just visiting. On holiday, er . . . vacation. I mean I don't live here. I mean I'm just on vacation.'

'Well that's just great, isn't it? Well, my name's John.'

'Yes . . . I . . .'

Just at that moment we were interrupted by a whirring noise.

'Oh, I'm sorry, I didn't catch your name . . .'

'My name is Randy . . . well, no, it's not really. It's Will but some people . . .'

'Oh, Randy, that's great. Here, I want you to meet my son. Joey, I want you to say hi to Randy, he's over from England. Do you know where that is?'

Looking down, I looked down into the clear blue eyes of the little boy in the wheelchair.

12

Some Kinda Murder

'Well, I'll tell you, you could have pushed me over with your little finger when I turned round and discovered John, you know, the subject, standing right there and then his son comes in right behind him!' I explained to Makepeace when I visited him at the plush private hospital on the western fringes of Boston. He was recuperating well with the help of a physiotherapist who looked as if he had once had a promising career in the WWF.

Recuperation was what I most needed, I thought, as I nibbled on a couple of chocolates that I had brought my invalid friend. It had been with some relief that I had got back into town. I had felt completely exhausted for a couple of days. At least the outcome of the whole affair had become clear. There had been no girlfriend; there hadn't even been any golf. John, the subject, took three one-week holidays every year – almost a pilgrimage – to go and visit his son, who despite appearances was actually in his mid-twenties and the progeny of an earlier marriage to a childhood sweetheart. Joey suffered from extremely severe cerebral palsy which meant that although he had some capacity to understand what was taking place around him he had no capacity at all to communicate. Normal life in the outside world would have been a terrible struggle. A trust fund from his first wife's parents meant that John did not have to worry unduly about the boy's welfare, cared for as he was in great luxury and with great devotion at the sanatorium. Nevertheless he felt compelled to visit the boy at least three times a year and particularly over the week of his birthday, to take him out and make him as happy as possible. Perhaps if life had been otherwise he might have done things differently.

One thing, however, had become clear when he first started dating Susie. Such impediments as Joey would most decidedly get in the way of any future wedding plans. And so, because it had worked out like that, despite the fact that John and Susie had been married now for the best part of ten years, he had never in all this period of time found the moment, or even the necessity or desirability, to mention Joey's existence to his wife. It remained their little secret between the two of them. A complicity between father and son, if only half recognised by the boy, as they held the handrail of the little ship and watched the minke and the humpback whales exercise their perfect freedom.

As I explained to the interested staff at Chestnut Investigations Inc. when I went to report in, the afternoon after visiting Makepeace, the conversation had been extremely complicated. John and his son were heading out on a ship along the coast for a day's whale-watching the following morning. As I was here as a simple tourist I would surely like to join them? They could show me around the place, some of the sights. Perhaps I was busy?

Well, yes, no.

Busy? Yes, busy following them. But, no, sure.

Eventually, in some state of confusion I agreed.

Throughout the course of our day-long chat I had, of course, to pretend that I knew nothing about John. Not that he lived in Boston, not that he was married, not that he had a son, certainly, and of course not where he worked, what car he drove or any other detail about him. Above all I had to avoid suggesting that I knew he was in Maine on a golfing holiday. John could not have been pleasanter if he had tried and I was surprised and pleased to discover remained quite loyal to his wife, even if he admitted, as he put his arm around his son's shoulders and they gazed out together at the humpback and minke, that she could be a tricky one sometimes. On my return to our motel I had rung Nelson and explained the situation. He seemed pleased at the outcome.

'It's not always *cherchez la femme!*' He seemed particularly delighted with his French and also pleased that the case appeared to have resolved itself.

'OK, come away back to Boston,' he had suggested.

'But what are you going to tell Susie? I mean, what will go in your report? If she finds out about Joey who knows what she might do?'

I was still worried that my intervention might have some lasting effect on a familial situation that, if not perfect, at least made something out of a bad job, but as I suspected, Nelson had already given the various outcomes some thought.

'Well, contractually I am obliged to tell her whether her husband is being unfaithful to her. He is not and that should be enough for her. If she asks further questions then I will have no choice but to answer them. But I don't think she will. Whatever her reasons for wanting to know whether John was having an affair, the knowledge that he isn't should put the matter to rest. So now the mystery has resolved itself, thanks to you. Get yourself back to Boston. Think I'm going to need your help.'

Now, finally, back in the office, I was allowed little time to rest on my laurels.

'OK, OK, everybody clear out of my office right now. Everyone except Delray and Randy. I've got the Christiensens coming up right now for their first interview, OK?' Nelson made his way into the office with a huge pile of papers under one arm and a vast Styrofoam cup of coffee in one hand. He was puffing and panting after his trip all the way to the bathroom but he had a determined look in his eye.

'Randy,' he said after he waved Delray and me into two chairs alongside his own behind the desk and got Rita to arrange two in front. 'Randy, this is a case that we picked up from an attorney down in the South End? They call him Dutch. You don't know him but you'll meet him. Good guy. We just had to see if the clients could raise the finance on this. I think it could be a long one. We needed to check that they had the money. You know, like I told you, like I tell all the interns, they got to have the money. It's the American way.'

Actually, I discovered later that Nelson did protest too much in his exhortations that we should all follow the greenback. Much of his work, often after office hours, was conducted *pro bono* – for poorer members of the community. Even Buck Burnett was a member of a team that worked voluntarily one night a week, trying to pool information in an attempt to solve 'cold cases' – the ones that the police had failed ever to resolve.

'The easiest thing is for you to pick up from where we're at, at the moment. We don't have any case notes for you to follow yet so you're starting pretty much in at the beginning of this one. Is that OK by you?'

By now pretty much everything was OK by me and I had no expectations about how things would develop at all. I was just happy to slip into the groove of the case and see what transpired.

After Rita had arranged a tray of coffee cups and cakes on the desk, she skipped back to her own desk to answer the buzz of the downstairs intercom.

'It's the Christiensens, they're coming right up,' she called from her office and we sat expectantly.

A few minutes later, after some greetings from Rita, a couple were ushered in and asked to sit in the chairs opposite. They were possibly in early middle age, smartly dressed; the wife in particular had made an effort with her appearance.

They had a gentle air about them, they looked pleasant but they also looked frightened.

'OK, Mr and Mrs Christiensen. Here I've got two of my investigators, Delray and Randy. They're going to be doing most of the footwork on this one, but I, of course, will be in overall charge of the case. We need to get this one right. We need to be thorough. Now, I know how difficult it will be for you to give us the whole story but we have plenty of time so I think the best thing is for you to tell us your version of events and we will get on with the investigation.'

By the time they had finished the story it was only too clear why this couple should have looked so singularly ill at ease. Tony Christiensen drove deliveries; he was America's equivalent of a 'white van driver'. He didn't earn too much. His salary was supplemented by what Gracie, his wife, could earn from her part-time work cleaning houses downtown. Married young, the couple were the proud parents of three children. The eldest boy was now away in the army, way down south in Austin, Texas. Marine Corps. Only the year before, they had held the wedding of their daughter and a 'pretty good kind of guy'. She was twenty-five years of age, had finished high school and had worked her way through college. She wasn't one of them girls, like most of the ones on their side of town, just hanging with, hoping to rely on their 'baby daddies', the name, Delray explained later, used to describe the possible fathers of their numerous children.

The Christiensens lived on a housing project in East Stoneham. East Stoneham was a place that was to feature quite importantly in my life over the next few weeks. I could wish in many ways that it had not been so.

All that the parents needed now to concentrate upon was the upbringing of their youngest. Germaine had celebrated his sixteenth birthday three months earlier and they had been more than happy to take him out and treat him. Things were looking good for the boy. His high school grades were great and, amongst his teachers, there was even some discussion of a college future. There had been no signs, no signs at all, they stressed, that anything might be amiss with Germaine or his world.

'You know, he lived, breathed and slept baseball,' Tony told us half-proudly, half-plaintively. 'Before, he was just interested in the Little League stuff he was playing and, now he moved up, he just worried about how his team were doing this season. He wasn't into no gang crime; you wouldn't find Germaine involved in no kind of . . .' and here he paused '. . . some kind of homicide. Some kinda murder! No way!'

Previously utterly absorbed in listening with admiration to the story of this family, I now straightened in my seat, pinching myself by way of one of my regular reality checks.

Some kinda murder!

I stared amazed around the room but everybody else just seemed to take the concept in their stride.

It had been two weeks ago last Saturday and Marie – that was their daughter – had asked if Germaine would be available to go round and babysit for their two and a half year old son, while she and her husband went on a special church-organised trip up to Hampton on the coast.

Germaine, who had a soft heart, as many teenagers struggle so hard to hide, had accepted quite happily and had, according to his parents, set off on the twenty-minute walk to his sister's house. When he had arrived they had exchanged pleasantries, he and his brother-in-law, while Marie settled his nephew in a cot in the living room. Then she had departed with her husband, promising not to be back later than ten that evening. This was no problem for Germaine who relaxed on the settee and popped his DVD of the Baseball World Series 1975 to the Present Day into the player.

Unbeknownst to any member of the Christiensen family, on the other side of town, just at the moment Germaine was leaving for his sister's house, Antonio Rodriguez, janitor and caretaker in the orthodontic section of the Massachusetts General Hospital, was just knocking off work. Stripping off his scrubs and throwing them into the large laundry bin in the basement of the building, he grabbed his bicycle from the rack outside and push-push-pushed himself off and away. Before long he was pedalling in the general direction of home, one of the few to do so in a country convinced by the automobile. He lived perhaps fifteen or twenty minutes' walk from Germaine's sister and brother-in-law, also on a housing project just off Martin Luther King Junior Boulevard, the main artery that ran right through their part of town. It was an easy ride and Antonio enjoyed the trip; it allowed him to get the smell and the noise of the hospital out of his mind and hair. As was his habit, he picked up the evening edition of the *Boston Herald* at the corner store a couple of blocks from his house, sharing a joke or two with the store owner, a Guatemalan friend of his. He just loved that routine, going home.

Just as he was turning the corner, a group of youths stepped out into the road, taking no notice of the traffic, for, in that moment, it was their street. Antonio braked and wobbled but kept his balance and bicycled on, quietly remonstrating under his breath as he did so.

'Waddya say? Are you talking to me, Mexican man? Yo' sure better not be.'

As Antonio turned round he saw a foot come out and lodge itself in the back wheel of his bicycle. The machine came to an immediate and abrupt halt and Antonio, his arms buckling, was projected over the handlebars. He landed uncomfortably on one shoulder in the road. Quite suddenly, he was surrounded by a group of edgy young men.

'Waddya call us, Mexican man?'

It was all a mistake, Antonio knew that. He lifted one hand, peppered with gravel, holding his first two fingers up together in some long-remembered sign of peace and was about to mutter his apologies. The words never escaped his mouth because a large expensive trainer connected smartly with his cheek, smashing three teeth and causing blood to run immediately down his white shirt. This was, sadly, only the sign to unleash a hellfire of kicks and blows leaving Antonio covered in contusions, with several broken limbs. The hands that he held up and outward were pierced by long blades, a knife was thrust into his side, but it was the haemorrhage in his brain that meant that within minutes of the start of the attack his two young children, four and five years old, were fatherless.

There had been several witnesses to this horrific incident and the police had been called.

Although the individuals involved had disappeared in all directions, the witnesses to the attack were quite confident of their testimony. 'That little Mexican man, he didn't stand no chance.' 'They was five African-American youths involved.' 'All 'bout the same height, tall, real tall, over six foot, all round the same age.'

In fact, one of the five had been immediately recognised. Although he had not played any real part in the attack he was well known in the neighbourhood. Well known, ironically, because his father was a man of the cloth, the Reverend Bailey at the Pentecostal Church of Jesus just down there on the South Side. And so it was that Bailey Junior was quickly arrested. He maintained his innocence but agreed that he had indeed been present at this particularly nasty interlude. Fearful of some reprisal he refused, despite the remonstrations of his father, to name the other individuals involved. A house-to-house search, however, soon established three other suspects and they were quick to plead guilty to this insane and pointless act. They had little choice as in each of their cases forensic evidence had been found putting them at the scene of the crime and suggesting their personal involvement. In other words clothing and shoes were found balled up in the back of cupboards. They were covered in blood – the blood of Antonio Rodriguez.

The four of them were taken into custody at the local police station. From there they were very quickly sent on to the county jail where they were imprisoned on remand pending a pre-trial hearing.

What puzzled the police the most, however, was their inability to locate the fifth youth involved. The men, or boys rather, already incarcerated refused point-blank to name anybody else and seemed to be suffering from a collective amnesia on the subject.

· As usual, the police were keen to wrap up the case – clear their desks. It was all just statistics to them anyway.

Thorough, rigorous indeed, they questioned every young person of African-American origin in the area, photographed them up against the height chart and took their fingerprints. Just like usual. Despite further searches of these youngsters' homes they found no further evidence.

This was beginning to become frustrating. They were wasting too much time on these kids and on the dead . . . Anyway, the weather was still good for golf. So it was that they went back to the youngsters in prison. Now stripped of their fancy, oversized basketball outfits and weighty gold jewellery, the suspects wore the prison uniform orange jumpsuits sullenly.

So, again, who had been the fifth member of the gang?

The police officer in charge of the case, a man in an amphetamine hurry whom I shall call Officer S, chucked the photographs, mug shots of twenty different young people, down on the tin table of the interview room with a whack.

Which one was he?

Still the boys refused to answer.

Day in, day out, Officer S went back and eventually, early one morning when outside the wind suddenly turned round to the north announcing the arrival of winter and the Stars and Stripes smacked against the flagpole in the prison yard, they cracked. Perhaps it was simply because they were bored with the insistence of the policeman. Whatever the reason they collectively decided to remember which particular boy had been the fifth member of their gang.

'That's him, that's him right there. He the one wid us when we done the Mex.'

'You are quite sure this was the fifth person involved in the assault that caused the unlawful death of Antonio Rodriguez?'

Yes, they were quite sure. Never been surer. Now could they start discussing the possibilities of plea-bargaining with their attorneys?

Officer S scooped up the photographs, the one they had picked out on the top of the pile: the picture of a baffled, frightened-looking Germaine Christiensen.

When the police had come to their door, Germaine's parents had been paralysed by fear. They felt particularly guilty, quite impotent, as they watched their son being arrested and taken away.

Soon, though, they had mustered their strength again and realising, in their minds at least, that there was no way whatsoever that Germaine could be involved in this dreadful crime, they called for help. But where to call for it? Tony Christiensen took a detour out of his delivery rounds to go and talk to a police officer his daddy had once known when they had played baseball together back there in the seventies. The man was now retired but he knew the way it worked.

'Only thing you need is a good attorney,' he advised Tony. 'And the only thing you need to get a good attorney is plenty of good money.'

Not by any means wealthy, Tony turned despairingly to his family. Even though their hearts were with him all the way, they had no real financial assistance to give. They were sorry.

So that same afternoon Tony found himself signing a new mortgage agreement on their house – the house on which he had repaid the final instalment of the last one just a month earlier. Anything, of course, was worth it.

Through his father's ex-policeman friend he signed up

to a well-known, well-respected lawyer in town, who in turn, as nine out of ten American defence attorneys will do, employed a private investigator to work out precisely what had happened. The responsibility for this young man's future was suddenly heavy on our shoulders.

When finally their story was at an end the Christiensens looked expectantly, silently and sadly, at Nelson. They looked entirely beaten by the system.

If they were hoping to have some immediate answers to their plight they must have been disappointed for Nelson took the photographs that he had been given of Germaine and the hand-written timeframe that Tony Christiensen claimed proved that his son could not have been in any way involved, put them in a folder and closed it, placing one huge hand on top of it, his gold ring twinkling.

'Hmm,' he grunted and there was a long heavy silence.

'Have you had access to Germaine in jail?' he asked.

'Yes, yes, we have been most every day,' his mother insisted. 'You know, take him things. His magazines. His favourite candy. Pictures from his little nephew. But he's low, so low, Mr Mason.'

'OK, you make sure you keep going there as much as you can. Most important thing right now is to keep his spirits up.'

'Yes, but how we going to get him out of there? How are we, how we ever gonna get our boy free?'

Had I listened to this in a cinema, I would have dismissed it as schmaltz with healthy derision. Here, now, it was devastating.

'Hey, Mr Christiensen.' Nelson was wonderfully soothing. 'Tony, you just try and stay strong for Germaine. You gotta try and leave the rest of this to us. You understand?'

Tony nodded, proud and tear-stained. 'Yessir, I do.'

But I don't think he did understand quite what was happening.

How could he?

When the Christiensens finally left I was shattered.

But to my surprise, my annoyance even, the routine of the office immediately returned to normal, taking up its regular rhythms. When I left Nelson's office, Ernie was at his cubicle, engrossed in some matter of special scientific interest from which he was not going to be roused. Buck, with his feet up on his desk, was in the process of dismantling one of his medium-sized guns, cleaning each part with an old, furred toothbrush. He was concerned about the repairs to the Nissan Cherry, for which Nelson was threatening to make him pay, and even Delray was more interested in what he would be wearing that evening for what he described as a 'hot date'.

Rita was worrying about her mailing and billing system again. Sometimes, so infuriated did she become by technology, I thought that she was going to pick up her computer in her carefully manicured but powerful hands and lob it through the window into Chestnut Avenue below.

Nelson, himself, was moaning about having to go down to get himself a coffee at the deli. It was true that, at the speed he moved, considerable amounts of time would be wasted. Finally I offered to get it for him and was pleased to get out of the office where we had heard this terrible story and breathe the fresh, slightly misting air of Beacon Hill.

Only when I got back to the South End and the dark was drawing in did I remember that Mrs Walowski had invited me in for a drink to meet her sister, who was visiting from 'Milvorki'. This particular lady possessed a dress sense significantly less flamboyant than her sibling but, unfortunately,

also an accent considerably more impenetrable. Consequently, she must here remain nameless. When finally I had
recounted my experiences of the day, which I was quite
incapable of stopping myself doing, she joined Mrs
Walowski in a great deal of headshaking, a fair amount of
caraway cake-eating and no sympathy whatsoever. It
appeared she shared the general opinion that other people's
problems were precisely that – other people's problems.

'It is the same the whole world over. What can you do?
Just live your life. It's all you can do.'

They shook their heads some more as Mrs Walowski's
kitchen turned silent but for the gentle clinking of vodka
glasses and the sound of shoulders being shrugged.

Later, when I returned to my apartment, I collapsed on
the sofa and switched on the television to be distracted by
the endless chatter but all I could see before me was the
desperate face of Mrs Christiensen, a mother in real anguish
about her son. Somehow it seemed so strange that the others
in the office could have acted so calmly after their departure. No, not calmly, complacently.

After all, justice needed to be done.

When finally I climbed into bed, I could not help dwelling
on the thought that the boy, who I had never met, who I
might never meet, was at that very moment behind the
forbidding walls of the county jail, his bunk not lit as I was
now by the richly glittering, twinkling lights of the city, but
by the arc lights that blazed down all night from the barbed-
wired watchtowers.

13

Old Ma Mary

A nyway, there was no particular rush about the Christiensen case, announced Nelson, after I had made my way up the steep stairs of Chestnut Investigations Inc. the following day.

'Why's that?' I asked amazed, from the other side of his desk at which he sat looking even more colossal than usual.

'Cos, Randy, we know where the kid is. We know when his court date is coming up. Not . . .' And here he flicked through a file of notes, stroking his strange long locks down over his ears as he did so. 'Not for another two months. Put it like this, he ain't going anywhere no time soon. So, we don't rush it.'

Loath though I was to, I could see some kind of rather disheartening logic to his argument.

'We got one here that we really do need to get on with.' Nelson flicked another beige document wallet over the table to me and I read the file name on the cover as I unwound the strings that kept it shut.

CHRISTINE DONALDSON

Clumsily, I spilled the contents of the folder onto the floor as I opened it. What I picked up first was a picture of a girl, maybe twelve years old, with a radiant smile. Seemingly carefree in what looked like a formal school photograph. I could not help thinking of the picture of Germaine in his basketball kit. Both pictures possessed, beneath the gloss of the paper, a sense of overriding innocence, complete normality.

'So what's the background?' I asked, having heard Buck make much the same enquiry of Ernie only the other day. It sounded pretty good.

'Sixteen-year-old female goes missing.'

The photograph was clearly not a recent one then.

'Parents don't want to go to the cops right at this moment. Father's a university professor. Mother has her own little career doing TV spots, cookery, that kind of thing. Cable, but still in the public eye, you know. They don't want no fuss. Seems like the kid has a history of running away. Only this time it's different. Normally she's back in twenty-four hours. No harm done. Gone and stayed in a park with her friends. Fairly straightforward teenage kind of thing. But this time she's been gone for over seventy-two.'

'Straightforward? This kind of thing is pretty common?' I wondered aloud. 'I mean, do many kids just run away like that?'

Suddenly, as I asked the question my memory flashed back to an image of me packing a rucksack after a particularly bitter family dispute. It had been time to go, the world awaited, even though I was only twelve, and I was taking to the road. Although in my case it was only to the end of our road. Just past number 73, I had remembered there was a school trip the next day that I didn't want to miss. So, on that occasion, my globe-trotting ambitions were put on hold in favour of a visit to the Tower of London. Whether any of my classmates had felt the same desire to get away from it all, or even had attempted it, I was not certain. Somehow such personal things had been taboo, so we had contented ourselves with talking about music and sport and marks and, a little later, girls. That was, of course, when we were not engaged in that most English of pastimes: belittling one another.

'Hey, you know what, Randy? Over here it's like a family pastime. These kids're always running away. Problem is, sometimes they just don't come back again. Maybe the lucky ones, they get picked up for breaking the law, shop-breaking, theft, prostitution. Or maybe they're not so lucky, you know, they get found in a shallow grave. Sometimes they re-appear twenty years later. Carved a whole new life for themselves. But then sometimes they disappear and no one hears a thing. Ever again.'

One hundred thousand.

One hundred thousand was the figure that I eventually came across in later research.

One hundred thousand is the number of people who go missing in the United States every year.

This statistic was shocking but somehow not as shocking as the thought that this girl – I looked down again at her smile, her braces and her demonstrable happiness – this girl was out there somewhere and nobody who should know did know where she was.

'OK, let's get into the pre-investigation meeting. Let's see what Delray has managed to dig up.'

Delray was in his office next door to Rita's and here he had set up a white board covered with details, diagrams and photographs. When Nelson finally made his way there and sat down, not a procedure that was immediately easy to accomplish, Delray started. He described to us the precise location of the house, which was, it transpired, only a short fifteen- or twenty-minute walk from Chestnut Investigations Inc.'s offices – straight across Boston Common, down Commonwealth Avenue and a right into one of the large wide streets of brownstones that give central Boston such a dignified air. Christine went to an expensive private school a couple of hundred yards further on from her home. She had only one sibling – a younger brother, ten years old. Delray tapped him on his photographic nose – a grinning, freckled, toothless, smart-alecky boy.

'So,' Delray finished. 'Her known movements on the day she disappeared are as follows. Leaves for school. Eight ten. Normal time. Meets up with her friend Jilly Matthison, right on the corner here with Commonwealth. That's her right here.' He pointed out a picture of another smiling kid, and I wondered idly about the financial attractions of a career in orthodontics. Perhaps I was too old.

'They get to school. They have a normal day. There is no problem. Christine even gets merit points for a good piece of math work. School finishes. They head home. She says goodbye to her friend at the normal parting point and, whammo, she disappears. No one hears a thing since. The good news, if we can call it that, is that we don't have any ransom demand yet.'

Ransom?

Ransom equalled kidnapping.

Kidnapping equalled fiction.

Kidnapping equalled spies and secret agents, being tied up and chloroformed and thrown into the boot of a speeding car. It was James Bond and Pussy Galore. Well, anyway, it was really very much not for the real world. I almost laughed and then looked quite seriously at the two detectives who did not appear to find the situation nearly as odd as I did.

'You think it's a stranger abduction?' Nelson asked Delray.

'Stranger abduction? You mean abducted by a stranger?' I squeaked. 'A complete stranger?'

Aghast, I looked at Delray.

'Well, you got to take everything into consideration. Never gets talked about much in the press – it's all part of the contract between the kidnappers and the victim's family. Guarantee of a safe return. More abductions for cash than you'd think. Doesn't seem so very likely here, though, given the location. We are talking, like, right downtown Boston.'

'JFK got half of his head blown off and that was downtown Dallas. Can't rule nothing out,' Buck Burnett added helpfully as he walked past the open office door. His black eye was less swollen and was now a sort of orangey-blue. It didn't suit him.

'OK,' instructed Nelson after some due consideration. 'Here's what you guys are going to do. First, I want you to get in there and see the parents. Check out, umm, Christine's bedroom. Explain to the parents before that you have to go through everything, all her things. Then it's house-to-house, I'm afraid, guys. I want that whole street, every house between the family home and the school, interviewed. Talk to the teachers. See if they thought they saw anything strange in her behaviour. If she was going to skip, chances are she would have some kind of bag with her, although she may have prepared it in advance. This girl is nobody's fool, I gotta feeling.'

'When do we start?' I asked. For some reason I had skipped breakfast at Jimmy Wang's and would quite happily have slipped out for an hour or two to Canuca's Market on Charles for a coffee and a super sub.

'Hey, Randy, we can't waste no time on this one. Let's

go, let's go, let's go! I want both you guys round to the parents' place right now. I've spoken to them. They are coming back from their workplaces to meet with you,' he called as we made for the door, Delray picking up his brief-case of equipment from under the old-fashioned hat stand in reception. For the first time I noticed, under an old coat, a shoulder holster and something that looked distinctly like a bullet-proof vest.

'Hey, don't forget to talk to the kid brother,' Nelson added as we made our way down the narrow creaky stairs.

Although the walk was not a long one, Delray insisted that we used the car; in this case my Dodge Stingray that was parked up outside the offices. He maintained that it would be vital to have some wheels as they might be needed at short notice. I was under the impression he just liked to drive places or, more to the point, didn't like to walk to them. Anyway, I shrugged and we took the car.

A dozen or so granite steps led to the front door, which was massive and of highly polished wood. To my amazement a maid opened the door after a short conversation over the video intercom that Delray had pressed. I was rather pleased to hear him describe me as one of 'a couple of private investigators'.

The maid was not dressed in any sort of obvious uniform but the way that she kept referring to Madam-this and Sir-that in a very attractive Spanish accent made her role in the household quite clear.

We were asked to wait in the spacious, panelled hall. I wanted to hand the short, slight, cheerful woman my hat and cane. Unfortunately, I had neither so I just gave her a smile. Delray, normally resiliently cool, was sufficiently impressed by the surroundings to remove his baseball cap and even his sunglasses.

Shortly, almost noiselessly, I heard footsteps on the winding, wide, oak staircase. Shapely feet and ankles came finally around the last flight of steps, revealing their owner, a tall, blonde woman. Marlowe, it is well recorded, had a penchant for blondes. In a deeply politically incorrect fashion he makes a point of listing them, which I, of course, will avoid doing, except to mention my particular favourite the 'pale, pale blonde with anemia of some non-fatal but incurable type. She is very languid and very shadowy and she speaks softly out of nowhere . . . she is reading *The Waste Land* or Dante in the original, or Kafka or Kierkegaard or studying Provencal.'

Actually there is also 'the gorgeous show piece who will out-last three kingpin racketeers and then marry a couple of millionaires at a million a head and end up with a pale rose villa at Cap d'Antibes, an Alpha Romeo town car complete with pilot and co-pilot, and a stable of shopworn aristocrats, all of whom she will treat with the affectionate absent-mindedness of an elderly Duke saying goodnight to his butler.'

But Mrs Donaldson was in a category he didn't mention – the bottle blonde. From the way she swayed slightly it was difficult to tell what different kinds of bottle. Her make-up was almost imperceptibly wonky and the two-piece outfit, yellow and black, that she wore was from Hermès. This was quite obvious from the classic lines and the label that stuck out comically from the zipper at the back of her skirt.

'Oh, thank you, gentlemen. You must have come from Nelson Mason. Isn't he just such a dear? Please follow me. We'll hold this conversation in my husband's study, I think,' she explained in such a way that led me to understand that it was not really her role in the house to do much of the thinking.

We passed down a long corridor lined with prints of scenes from university life. Harvard, Cambridge, Oxford, Yale, they were all there. Stopping beside an engraving of the Sorbonne, the lady of the house, to my surprise, knocked on a door. Through the thick wood there was a muffled reply in the affirmative. Pushing hard, as if fighting against an air lock, she managed eventually to get the door to move.

At a desk, a desk that would certainly have impressed Nelson, sat a man. Initially I was surprised to remember that he was an academic. His immaculate suit and neatly parted hair gave him the appearance of somebody more involved in the world of business than education. This conundrum was soon resolved when he handed us each a card introducing himself as a Visiting Professor of Business Studies.

'OK, let's get on with this. I think we told most everything to Mason on the telephone when we had a conference call late last night. I know you guys are just doing your job. And Christ knows I want you to do it properly cos I'm the one paying! So if you got any further questions, shoot. But keep it brief, will you? I have a call coming through from Tokyo. As I say, there doesn't seem to be too much more I can add, but fire away.'

I glanced at his wife and she smiled at me weakly. Looking a little closer into her eyes I wondered if she was not under the influence of some form of medication. Her pupils were like pinpricks. Perhaps it was just the nerves, the worry about her missing daughter. This I could easily understand. There is only one thing worse than knowing the truth and that, of course, is not knowing it. I had often felt deeply sorry for people, interviewed in the press or on the television, whose children or other family members had disappeared off the face of the earth, sometimes decades before. Nothing, nothing was ever heard of them again. This woman, I guessed, must be feeling the same kind of concern.

Her husband, on the other hand, was coolly efficient in his answering of the half-dozen questions or so that Delray asked. If there was any sentiment that he attached to his responses it was probably best described as minor irritation.

'One question, something that's been worrying me,' asked Delray. 'This picture you've given us. How old is it?' He looked from the father to the mother and back again.

'Oh, she must have been coming up eleven in that picture. It was taken just before she went to camp at the end of elementary school.' Mrs Donaldson felt sufficiently animated at this memory to raise a vague smile.

'Well, maybe you have a more recent one because that was like five years ago, wasn't it?'

'Oh, well, yes, no, you see the thing is—' stuttered the mother.

'Gentlemen,' her husband interrupted, 'you have to understand that Christine has undergone something of a change over the last year or so. Not one we are too proud of, I can tell you.' He ripped one of the drawers of his desk violently open and with considerably more decisiveness than Nelson did his. 'It's all this shit they watch on TV. Total waste of time. Where is that goddamn file? OK, here you go. What would you think if your daughter ended up looking like that?'

A goth.

She had become a goth.

Now, what would Marlowe have made of goths? Would have been difficult to get dizzy with a dame looking like this. Who would want a moll with a mush covered in muck? Even covered up her getaway sticks in black cowhand's pants. Say, now you come to think of it, all her rags is black. Even got black all over her kisser and a great hunk of metal in her schnozzle.

In this photograph, presumably taken by a friend as the backdrop appeared to be a teenage bedroom, it was quite true that Christine was dressed entirely, but entirely, in black. Gone were the pigtails and the toothy grin, replaced by great black brows and eyeliner that had the disconcerting effect of making the eyes look larger but closer together. Her mouth, too, was painted black and the clothes that she wore complete with buckles, catches, zips and strange hooks were manufactured from a combination of denim, rubber and leather. They had, I imagined, been purchased in a shop that had the word 'Adult' somewhere in its name.

When I looked up the father was gazing out of the window seemingly lost for a moment in his thoughts.

'You know what? What I feel like most of the time? I just feel like I don't really give a damn. This whole society it's in free fall and there isn't squat I can do about it. Not me, not you, not anyone.' He sighed. 'You know . . . sometimes I think I don't really care if you find her or not. It's gonna cause me a lot less grief in the long run, that's for sure.'

His wife squeaked slightly at this last remark and the man sighed again.

'I only do it for her. She'll show you whatever else you need.'

After we had bid him farewell the three of us trooped in silence up the stairs and, faced with a choice of three corridors, took the first on the left. Down at the end along more of the thick, plush carpet stood a door with a brusque adolescent instruction not to enter. Below it was the picture of some fictionalised demonic face glaring out at us.

'OK, ma'am, I know this isn't easy for you but you have to check with us that as far as you are concerned everything is in place. Are you ready to do that? Please try and think as carefully as you can about what is there.'

'Oh, I don't know, really. Now Christine's started to buy her own clothes with her allowance it's more difficult. I don't spend so much time in there . . . now. Before, you know reading her stories . . .'

We went into the room. The atmosphere was something close to funereal. This was due partly, of course, to the mass of religious iconography that had been somehow perverted into some kind of cultish decorations. It was laughable but, still, a little sinister. Why was this girl drawn to the dark side of life? Even in the relatively short time since her disappearance a dust seemed to have settled over the bedroom and its belongings, as if this was now a place that had been deserted, closed down.

I stepped over a mass of shoes and boots covered with heavy straps and buckles, some of which would have come up to the wearer's thigh, and found myself in the middle of the room. Delray opened one of the cupboards and started to leaf through the clothes. 'Do you notice anything that might be missing here?'

Initially the wife shook her head but then I saw her pause and frown and lift up the pillows on the bed. There was nothing there.

'Anything missing?' asked Delray.

'Well, maybe,' stumbled the mother, trying to think straight. 'Maybe her nightclothes. No, probably in the laundry. I'll ask Dolores.'

'Be sure to let us know,' instructed Delray and I sensed a harder, irritated edge to his normally soft, laid-back voice.

Momentarily, I wondered what kind of nightclothes goths wore. Were they covered in skulls and crossbones like nearly all the other attire that this group of youngsters had adopted as their own?

Apart from the missing sleepwear and possibly a T-shirt, although this too was in some doubt, all Christine's belongings seemed to be in place. A search of her desk produced next to nothing and I was surprised not to find more paperwork. There seemed to be no letters, no poems, not even a diary.

'It's all in there,' said Delray, flicking his fingernail against a fancy, flat computer screen that stood on the dressing table.

'Did Christine have Internet access in her room?' he asked, leaning over the back of it to peer at the connections.

'Oh, er . . . you mean the Web, do you?' asked the mother a little doubtfully. 'Yes, of course, hey, you don't think we'd let our daughter get left behind, do you?'

'Does she have a cellphone? Or an electronic organiser?'

'Oh, yes, she has a cellphone. I have tried to ring it a thousand times but it just goes through to voicemail.'

'But you're certain she has it with her?'

'Oh, yes, I'm sure so. You know these youngsters, they never go anywhere without their phones, do they?' Mrs Donaldson attempted another weak smile and tucked a strand of yellow-blonde hair behind one ear.

'How many phones did she have?'

'Oh, only the one. I am pretty sure of that because when she got a new model part of the deal was to exchange her old one against it. Kind of an ecological, you know, a green thing, they said.'

'So, you mean, this one here has got to be hers?' With something of a flourish, Delray pulled out a slim black mobile telephone that had lain right at the back of a drawer of a bedside table and handed it to Christine's mother.

'Oh, yes. That's definitely it, I'm sure of it.' She looked it over curiously.

It was switched off or 'powered down' as Buck like to say. When Delray turned it on it began to bleep and vibrate as if it was about to take off like an angry and very large hornet.

'You mind if we keep this? We're going to need to read all those messages and listen to her voicemail. I think we better get our expert to take a look at this hard drive, too. That OK with you, Mrs Donaldson?'

'Oh, well, yes . . . I guess.'

Soon we were bidding farewell to the woman and stepping back down the wide open steps of the house. Once back in the Dodge Stingray, Delray deposited his files, the computer and the cellphone on the back seat and sighed with satisfaction.

'Sure looks like the little lady doesn't want to be found in a hurry!'

'You think she definitely has decided to run away? Not any question of her being abducted?'

'Oh, no. Whatever reason she's got she has upped and left. Kids do it all the time, and they love it if they think someone, you know, one of the 'rents is gonna get mad.' Delray, ringing Ernie to forewarn him that his Internet expertise would be required, instructed me to drive on, my man, in something that I think he believed to be an English accent.

Leaving the luxury of the brownstone in downtown Boston, we drove out along Commonwealth and then down towards Boston University, the mock-gothic Central College buildings and the Department of Theology on our right. We took a fork left, the road rising slightly as it ran up the side of Fenway Park, the home, of course, to the inter-planetarily renowned Boston Red Sox. On my last visit I hadn't noticed the huge Coca-Cola bottles on lamp-posts which lit up the surrounding sky on match days and neatly also advertised the team's main sponsors.

'You like baseball?'

'Oh, yes, I'm pretty keen,' I replied. 'Went to a game with Makepeace a while back, against the um . . . against . . .'

Such a keen fan was I, I couldn't remember.

'The Jets?'

'Yes, that's them, the Jets.' It may have been.

'Great game, wasn't it? Hey, it's the sport of champions. You and me gotta get ourselves to a game. Hey, by the way what is this cricket kind of thing anyway? I heard something about that before.' Delray was, pleasingly, forever curious but, sighing, I decided against any attempt to explain the niceties of the game. Instead I asked him where we were headed first and he pointed up ahead a couple of blocks where even at this distance I realised that we were about to enter a very different district. The culture shock could not have been greater, the contrast starker, between the tree-lined avenues where the Donaldsons lived and this, the housing project where until recently Germaine Christiensen had resided with his parents.

'This is East Stoneham. It's what we call the 'hood. Ninety-eight per cent African-American. Highest levels of unemployment in the state. Biggest concentration of drug users. More handguns here than in the rest of the Boston Metropolitan area. This is the real Wild West, my friend,' he explained cheerfully, almost proudly. 'We're just going to head on down to find Leroy. He's my brother. If anybody knows what's going down, Leroy knows what's going down. He's probably shooting some pool right now. That's what he normally does. Yeah, well that's all he does really.' Delray finished this explanation rather less upbeat. He was, however, quite correct in his supposition.

A few minutes later we parked up in an area strewn with rubbish that drifted in the cool air smelling of smoke and we pushed open the door of Poolside, a run-down snooker hall that seemed to have as many people hanging out on the doorstep as there were populating the two dingy rooms. Surprisingly, the tables were in remarkably good order and they were carefully, almost professionally, lit overhead by long gold-tasselled lighting units. Delray was clearly as well-known in the 'hood as Leroy. The two brothers greeted each other by clasping hands like arm wrestlers and bumping their chests together like two pouting, boxing bantams. Delray then proceeded to perform a number of extremely complex handshakes with the rest of Poolside's customers before introducing me quite affectionately as his 'good buddy from England'. I smiled and waved and was briefly confused as to whether Leroy really was Delray's brother or not because 'brother' or 'bro' seemed to be the most popular term of address amongst the population of East Stoneham.

'Hey, Leroy, why don't we take a break here and maybe go get ourselves a beer some place?'

'Sure, brother, why don't we do that?' Leroy grabbed me in a brief embrace around the shoulders and winked from under his bandanna and huge cap before saying goodbye to his 'homeys'.

'See you later, my brother. Later, bro.' The ritual lasted some good few minutes.

Soon we found ourselves sitting on a rough bench outside a roadside shack the like of which I had last seen in the backstreets of Lusaka. Delray had slotted a ten-dollar bill through an iron grille and received three bottles of Budweiser in return through a chink in the armour-plating that seemed to protect the sole inhabitant.

For a little while we sat and the two brothers chewed the cud about all things social and sporting, and, particularly, all things female. Then Delray paused a while.

'So, what do you hear about this Mexican guy who went down Thursday? Hear it was a hit from the guys over on the West Side? This guy involved in coke or crystal or something?'

This had never been mentioned in any of the conversations that we'd had about Antonio Rodriguez but Delray was just checking Leroy out, he told me later; checking to see whether his brother was going to play it straight with him.

'No way, bro. There wasn't any of that shit going down. This guy, he was just in the wrong place at the wrong time. I kinda feel sorry for the guy if you really want to know.'

'Who did it? Did you hear?' Delray asked the question directly.

'I don't know those dudes. I heard the cops got 'em anyway. Five guys they say. That's what the witnesses say.'

'Hey, did they all come forward, the witnesses, did they like co-operate with the cops?'

'You got to be shitting me! No way you're going to get Old Ma Mary talking to no cop. Well, not 'less she gotta, you know.'

'She was there? She saw that beating?'

'Sure she did, my bro. Was leaning right out of her window waiting for her dealerman to come by. She been in bed for days since then. She say she not gonna recover from that one.'

'Hey, Randy, what say we go and have a word with the old lady? You'll like her,' Delray laughed.

I smiled but I was not at all certain.

We left the Dodge Stingray outside the Poolside Snooker Club and made our way to Old Ma Mary's on foot. She only lived a couple of blocks away and Delray felt that leaving the car here under the watchful eye of Leroy, who had returned to his tables and his friends, was a safer option than taking it further into the 'hood. There was ample evidence of automobiles that had not benefited from their visit to East Stoneham.

As we made our way down the street past hairstylists,

music stores, cheap food joints and endless clothing emporiums and turned into a more residential area dotted with small wooden dwellings and low-level red tenement buildings, I was suddenly reminded of another place, another time. For a few minutes I could not find it but then a smell fixed the image immediately in my mind, transporting me back to the small town in which I had lived in Africa. But Africa had not been as bad as this. The closer I looked at the accommodation, the worse repair I saw it to be in. Here and there squares of hardboard and packing case covered broken windows, or what appeared to be simply holes in the wall. On a couple of occasions the owners had resorted to using cardboard boxes, their former contents advertised on their sides, and sheets of plastic that are more normally used by roofers or builders to hide unsightly construction work.

Before long, we found ourselves making our way up the dingy, stinking steps of one of the low-rise apartment blocks and walking along an outside corridor. Looking down I could see some children below, kicking a can around, and shrieking happily. They were watched lazily by a group of boys sitting around a music machine and playing a slow game of cards. Inside one of the hairdressing salons I could see excited girls pulling and tweaking their friends' hair and emptying dozens of cans of hair lacquer into the atmosphere to create just that perfect look.

'You're never gonna believe this place,' muttered Delray as he hammered on a battered and much graffitied front door.

He was absolutely right.

For a long time, a very long time, there was no sound or sign of life within the apartment but then, as I was about to suggest that we were wasting our time and should leave, something I would have been more than happy to do, the door was cranked open on ill-fitting hinges. A woman stood in front of us, her wide eyes staring at us enquiringly. All of a sudden I was overwhelmed by what seemed to be a combination of some extremely cheap form of scent and the smell of decomposition. Had I had a handkerchief I would have abruptly pressed it to my nose.

'Oh, hey, Delray, how're you doing? How's your mommy?' This short speech was enough for the lady as she bent over into a racking cough. She was clearly not well but when she looked up at us she smiled with a face of great gentleness. The laughter lines that might once have only appeared when she broadened her mouth into a smile were now deeply ingrained, the skin seemingly shrunk back over her cheekbones. Below a long aging T-shirt, which was all that she wore, I could see her collar bones sticking, jutting, out and where they were joined to the top of her ribcage the connection was clearly defined.

She seemed unwilling to let us into the apartment, which relieved me, but instead put her hand up as if to say 'Stop right there, hold on' and disappeared into her flat before reappearing with a packet of extra long Merit cigarettes and a throwaway plastic lighter. Clumsily she pulled one out and held it up to her mouth to light it. As she opened her mouth I felt my knees weaken when, as her lips curled back, I could see that all that remained of her teeth were some rotten, black and yellow stumps. She had pulled on some ill-fitting jogging pants to cover her much battered and bumpy legs. The waistband was loose and she held them hitched up with one hand, on the back of which she bore the scars of what could have been cigarette burns.

'So what's happening, Delray? I ain't seen you around here, in the 'hood, for a while.'

'No, Mary. Don't get so much time to visit no more.' Delray's accent had subliminally slipped closer to home.

'So you guys just come round to say hi, you and your nice friend here? Or how can I help?'

'Hear y'all had some trouble right outside – like a little while back?' Delray spoke to her gently as if anything too forceful would somehow damage the frail figure.

'We did?' Her eyes clouded and then she shut them tight in an effort to remember whether something had happened.

'You mean the Hispanic?' She snapped her eyes open again at the memory and looked at us both quite horrified. 'Yes . . . yes, I remember.'

As we drove back out of the 'hood later that afternoon I felt myself breathing more easily. Not because I had felt in any way threatened. Indeed, Delray's presence had made me feel almost like an unofficial guest, but the squalid housing and the pressures of population made for a brittle, difficult atmosphere.

Old Ma Mary had once been Delray's mother's best friend. She had looked after her children as a teenager and had known Delray all his life. Of course, he commented, she was only fifteen years his senior, which put her, if my mathematics was right, two or three years older than me. I could have easily believed that she was of my parents' generation.

'So, you know, like, what happened to her? She doesn't look very well.'

'No, you're right, she sure don't. She don't look good at all. Last time I saw her she didn't look so bad but she was all done up with her make-up and her wig. She was even gonna get herself some new teeth. Looks like it's gonna be too late for all that now. You see, that's what it does to you, that crystal meth. She's only been taking it six months. Sure, before she used to take a few pills now and again. But then you tell me any American citizen who doesn't do that,' he snorted. 'Still, she's not a bad person. It's just the way life worked out for her.'

Having been faced quite often with people coping with terrible dilemmas, just trying to play the hand that they had been dealt as best they could, I was often left speechless.

'Still, she gave us some pretty good information. Don't you think?'

I winced at the memory of what we had been told. Of how she had seen the boys hanging out in the street that afternoon but thought no more of it. There was always a lot of hanging out, particularly amongst the youngsters who had no useful employment. She hadn't really recognised them, partly because she hadn't been able to get too close, but mainly, commented Delray, because she was pretty strung out. She's not gonna make any kind of good witness, he commented.

'But what did you reckon was the most important piece of information?'

I thought about it.

Her breathless description of the repeated kicking that had eventually led to Antonio Rodriguez's death had been horrifying but she had had quite a good eye for detail. She had noticed that two of the boys were wearing Red Sox caps pulled firmly down over their eyes and that the other three had been wearing small black skullcaps of the type made out of rolled-up stocking material, of the sort much favoured by bank robbers.

'Well I guess we could work out whether Germaine owned any kind of hat like that.'

'No,' said Delray. 'He could have been lent one, bought it, thrown it away because he was scared of having been seen in it. But what part of her description couldn't he do anything about?'

'Well let me think . . .'

'Come on, what did she say about their appearance?'

I looked down at the flip-over notebook that I had purchased because I thought it fitted the part rather well. Then I discovered that it didn't fit my pocket and was lumbered with carrying the thing around all the time. I read back what I had written. 'About six thirty in the evening. Quite a lot of traffic. Seen her neighbour just come in. That's how she knew she had the time right. Asked neighbour. Watch pawned a long time ago. Five big guys on the corner . . .'

'Stop right there. What did you just read?'

'Watch pawned a long time ago. Five big guys . . .'

'You got it.'

'No, got what? We know there were five of them.'

'Yeah, but what does she tell us about their description? She says five big guys. What does your physical description of Germaine tell you? He is five seven, he only weighs in at ninety pounds. He's way underweight for his age. He's never gonna make a pitcher unless he puts some meat on his bones. No way Germaine's what you can call a big guy.'

Looking at the file and at the boy in baseball pose I saw that Delray was right. Never having met Germaine in the flesh, I had failed to picture his physical size. Now I even remembered that my partner had asked Old Ma Mary the question on two, if not three, occasions: 'You saying they is all big guys? All about the same height? Six foot or more, you say? You sure about that?'

'I think she's right. If they had all been differing heights it might be more difficult to be sure but if there's only one guy who's a lot shorter then that's going to be easy to remember, isn't it?'

14

Both Sides of the Tracks

A s soon as we got back to the Dodge Stingray and I
reversed us out of the parking spot in front of the
Poolside Snooker Club, Delray started to fiddle with Christine's cellphone.

'Hey, let's see what voicemail this little lady has picked
up.'

He loved referring to girls and women as little ladies.
Marlowe, too, had a wide variety of names to describe the
female sex. I shudder to think what would happen if I was
to use any of them. Heavens knew how, he had arranged
it so that the cellphone would play its messages through
the audio system of my car. Suddenly, shrilly, quite to my
surprise, I heard a female voice. It took little time to realise
from its anxious tone that it was Christine's mother.

'Hello, Christine, are you there? Can't remember what
time you said you were going to be back? Just to let you
know I am probably going to be out and your father is
busy. So you can just sort yourself out with a few things,
can't you? Dolores should have restocked the fridge. You
have any problems you can go next door. Don't wait up
for me. Not sure what time I'll be back. Your father will

ring you separately.' There was no sense of affection. No
suggestion of concern. Just a message left by someone who
was much too busy.

'Hey, it's me again,' said the same voice. 'I just want you
to take a message for me if that Dr Jefferson rings. Just take
any message he gives you. Don't ask too many questions.'

Then later: 'Honey? How come you aren't at home?
Where are you? I was expecting you to be here when I got
back. OK, ring me back when you get this.'

End of messages.

'So, what do you make of that?' asked Delray as he
compared the girl's flashy cellphone to his own.

'Sounds like a really happy family!' I replied and automatically felt sorry for this Christine.

'Yeah, doesn't seem to be a warm and loving one, does
it?'

Somehow, although it felt like a violation listening in to
these messages that were left for someone else, I could not
help being fascinated by the insight it gave me into the
gilded world in which these people lived.

'Hey, what strikes you as weird about that voicemail?'
asked Delray, replaying the messages.

'Nothing particularly that I can think of, except that her
mother doesn't seem to have too much time for her
daughter.'

'What about her friends?'

'How do we know? There weren't any messages from
her friends.'

'Exactly.' Delray paused as triumphantly as someone of
his understated nature could. 'And what does that tell you?'

'Er . . .'

'These kids, they live on their cellphones. You take one
away from them for more than, like, two hours, they're
gonna flip right out.'

'True . . . So that means that the phone has been switched off for nearly three days. In all that time, even when the kids must've known that she was missing from school, not one of them left a message with her.' I followed his line of deduction. 'Either that means she's mighty unpopular or . . .'

'Correct,' said Delray closing his eyes and leaning back in my passenger seat. 'Either she is some real little Miss Poison or, and I like this one more, she has fixed up some kind of conspiracy. That's assuming her mother is right and she doesn't have another cellphone.'

'So, you mean the only people who don't know what's going on right now are the parents.'

'Affirmative, except it won't just be the parents. It's going to be the adults. Bet your bottom dollar that none of those teachers of hers knows what's going down.' Delray was scrolling through the list of names and muttered something to himself. 'Hey, Will, let's get over there and talk to some of them.' He checked his watch and added that it was about now that school would be 'out'.

We drove down a side street just up off Charles and Boylston and pulled over opposite the gates of a neo-Edwardian building.

Schools in America have always confused me, and I have always found the American education system impossibly difficult to understand. However often I hear children described as being in one grade or the other it never seems to make any sense. As I understand it now, children go first to elementary school then on to junior high school then to senior high school, but then, of course, a junior high school is also known as middle school. If this is the case then the senior high school is simply known as high school. This is quite straightforward.

Of course, as in all schools, depending on which year you are in you will have a certain title. So, obviously, if you are in seventh grade you are a seventh grader, in eighth grade you are an eighth grader. In ninth grade, the first year of senior high school, or high school if you went to a middle school, you are a ninth grader but you are also a freshman. The year after that, in tenth grade, you become a sophomore and the year after that a junior. In your last year, perhaps understandably, you become a senior but then when you leave high school, which could actually have been senior high school if you had been to a junior high school, and go to college or a university (the difference between the two is too confusing to be discussed here), you become a freshman once more. When you have been a freshman at university, which is not the same as being a freshman at high school if you have been to a middle school or a senior high school if you have been to junior high school, you then become a sophomore. Once you have been a sophomore, you then become a junior for the second time and then, finally, in your last year, a senior again. Anyway, it has taken some time but I am very pleased to have now clarified the system.

Christine's school was obviously a senior high school (or a high school), but quite a small-scale establishment and when we heard an electronic bell ring inside, the youngsters leaving the gates were in tens rather than hundreds. Out on the sidewalk stood an extremely hassled-looking teacher, a clipboard held rather uselessly at her side, who bid the students farewell as they left the gates. We climbed out of the car and crossed the street. I was beginning to really feel quite the part, particularly when Delray presented his card to the teacher and indicating me said, 'and this is my partner.' I tried to nod my affirmation of this as coolly as I could. I don't think that I was grinning too widely.

'We're here about the girl who's gone missing? Maybe you can help us some?'

'Girl that is missing? Which one?' She laughed rather hollowly and checked her watch. She was not having a good day. 'These girls' – and I noticed now that indeed it was only girls leaving the gates – 'are always "going missing". You know what that means most of the time? Just another spot of rehab. Anyway, you mean Christine? Well, I'm quite sure she hasn't been kidnapped. She's much too smart for that.'

'Could you tell us a bit more about her?' Delray asked gently, leaning against one of the iron posts of the school railings.

The woman glanced at him and me and seemed to have a change of heart. 'I'm sorry. The principal says we shouldn't be talking with anybody from outside the school community. I'm sorry, gentlemen, if you wish to put any more questions you'll have to put them to the principal herself. And what a pleasure that will be for you!'

Delray made it clear that he understood the restrictions placed upon the member of staff and thanked her as we made our way in the direction of the school office. Almost as we were getting out of earshot in the hubbub of young voices I overheard the member of staff call after us, 'You need to speak to Susie Graham, you got me? Susie Graham!'

'You hear that?' I asked as we ran up the steps one by one and pushed open the heavy wood and glass doors.

'Sure did,' he replied. 'Don't you forget that name. Write it down.'

'Susie Graham. OK.' I had my notebook in my hand, of course, but could I find my pen?

The school secretary was very severe, which was no great surprise. We were, after all, men. I imagined that a girl with a cut knee or a broken heart would be admirably cared for by Miss Sullivan.

Miss Pleasance is not available today, we were told. 'We have had some parent–teacher meetings today and Miss

Pleasance still has some parents of the new girls she needs to talk to. You will have to make an appointment.'

And that was that. At least, that was that until Delray sat on her table. She rolled back some feet in her executive chair and stared at him horrified.

'You better tell that Miss Pleasant that there is a girl out there who is missing. She could be dead or alive but she's more likely to be the former unless I get some co-operation from you people.' Delray suddenly sounded three times his age. To my delight, Miss Sullivan was reaching for the telephone console before he had even finished and slid back off the desk.

'She will . . . she will see you right now. This way, gentlemen, this way.'

Miss Pleasance, for the main part, lived up to her name but as far as any insights into what might have happened she was seemingly helpless.

'Perhaps you could give us a list of her best friends? We would like to have a word with them. See if they know anything. See if maybe Christine was hanging around with a boy or some boys or something?'

'Oh, no, I don't think so, no, I don't think so at all.' Miss Pleasance shuddered at the thought of such an outrageous happening. 'I think I should get her form teacher in here. Miss Eames will be able to fill you in on some of the details.'

Fairly shortly a young woman, out of much the same mould but with distinctly finer detail than the rather dumpy Miss Pleasance, appeared and sat very decorously on the only other spare chair in the headmistress's office.

'Yes, well there are, of course, quite a few. Christine was a popular girl. There was, let me see, I think the easiest thing is I write them down for you. Miss Pleasance, if you could just pass me a copy of the school list then maybe we can let these gentlemen have their home telephone numbers.'

'Oh, I don't know if that is quite in order, Miss Eames?'
The headmistress looked distinctly nervous and drummed
her fingers on the desk. 'You know how it is these days,
people don't like their information given out.'

'Oh, Miss Pleasance, come on. This is an emergency,'
exclaimed Miss Eames, who was getting quite into the swing
of our investigation.

Once it was agreed that we could have the telephone
numbers as well as the home addresses, Miss Eames noted
them down in a careful hand and passed over the list of
names to me simply because I sat closer to her than Delray.
I took it and inspected it rather professionally, then, perhaps
a little too quickly, handed it on to Delray.

'Just one thing here, we heard a name. What was it, Will?'

'Sue something. Sue Brabham, was it or was it Daniels,
Sue Daniels?' I blundered.

Delray flipped his notebook open and read 'Susie
Graham.' And winked and smiled without looking at me.

Making a mental note to write everything down from
now on I hastily agreed that yes, indeed, it was Susie
Graham. I then found my pen.

'Yes, Susie Graham. We have a student of that name.'

'Would she have been a friend of Christine's?'

Miss Eames and Miss Pleasance looked at each other
bemused.

'No, you see, they didn't get along at all well. In fact we
even had to put them in separate classes just recently. Unfortunately, they were engaged in a terrible fight just after the
ballet and contemporary class. Yes, just before the summer
break. Like nearly three months ago, maybe more, and they
vowed they would never sit in the same room as each other
again.'

'Do you know what this argument was about?' Delray
asked.

'Well, you know these young people, it could be about any number of things. You never quite get to the bottom of it.'

'I daresay,' pondered Delray. 'Had they had a history of antagonism then?'

'Oh, no,' said Miss Pleasance, quite surprised. 'In fact they had been pretty good friends down in the junior department but you know how kids are, they grow up in different directions, so somehow they just fell out with each other.'

As a matter of fact I did know how easily young people fell out of favour with one another. For ten years I had taught in secondary schools in the United Kingdom and although the memory of those years was almost faultlessly a happy one, I could remember when lives were believed to be about to fall apart. Arguments over the most minor of things could fester if not cleared up quickly. More often than not I had found myself unkindly telling some unfortunate boy or girl whose world had come crashing down after some unkind act or remark, that nothing was really that bad. Of course I had the benefit of hindsight.

Most boys would soon find themselves back on cheerful terms with their classmates or a chastising teacher but I knew it to be true that many girls who had fallen foul of each other, or who had been admonished by me for whatever reason, had held these injurious remarks close to their chests. Sometimes it would take weeks to be forgiven, sometimes months, sometimes even terms. I wonder now, if I met one particular girl who must be, I gulp at the thought, in her early thirties, whether she would let bygones be bygones or whether she would just walk on by.

We thanked the two teachers and left the building.

'You know where we're going to look next, buddy?'

'Are we going to do the door-to-door interviews, now?' I was rather keen on that idea.

'No, we're going surfing,' said Delray as he wandered over, seemingly aimlessly, to a girl who was still waiting to be picked up. I followed on hurriedly.

'Hey, how're you doing?' asked Delray.

The girl, far from looking shy, turned to him chewing gum and smiled broadly. She was doing pretty good, she guessed.

Delray, with a skill required of all good investigators, had a happy knack of being able to drop into the mannerisms and speech patterns of his interlocutor. I am sure that within a few minutes this girl must have felt herself to be talking with a friend she had known for some time, even someone of her own age.

Oh yeah, she had heard about that Christine girl. She didn't know her too well because she was in another stream but she knew the girls that she hung with – a couple of them were her good friends.

'Hey, you mind if we ask you a few more questions, maybe in a couple of days?' asked Delray.

The girl seemed delighted to be in the thick of the action. 'Sure, that will be no problem. You want my cell number?' It was alarming how readily she proffered it.

Delray took it. He jotted it down in his notebook and then, looking up at her, he asked, 'You got an email address I can use? Kinda might be a little bit more . . . discreet.' He obviously had chosen his words carefully and they did just the trick. Her eyes widened with the excitement of being involved in a true mystery and she happily handed it over.

'We'll be in touch.' Delray smiled broadly and dashingly. The girl, twisting her hair, lifted her hand in a half wave and smiled.

'Back to the office, my man.' Delray used his pseudo-English accent again and laughed. I didn't mind – I had been practising my American one a great deal in the bathroom mirror back in the apartment. Heaven knew what Mrs Walowski downstairs made of it all.

We drove back to Beacon Hill in silence. Both of us, I knew, were wondering what the fate of these two young people from different sides of the tracks would turn out to be.

Once we were back in the office we held an impromptu meeting with Ernie Vinh. Ernie and I had still hardly exchanged more than a handful of words in the time that I had been working at Chestnut Investigations Inc. but now he was quite cheerful when he greeted me.

'OK, here's what I want you to do,' said Delray.

Some of the computer terminology confused me but I understood the gist of Delray's plan. Ernie was to search the Net for any traces of Christine. It was very likely that she would have a Web presence on one of the numerous social networking sites. Once we had located that we might get a little closer to identifying her movements.

'What a lot of kids are real unguarded about is not so much what they post on their sites but more what they let other people post on their space,' explained Ernie as he manipulated his keyboard with the same fervour and panache as the organist at Boston Cathedral. 'Most employers go straight to them. If your friend has left a message thanking you for the great marijuana on the weekend, it's not going to improve your job opportunities, is it?'

Once we had tracked Christine down on the computer we could pursue our line of investigation through her 'contact list'. Once there, he could get a little closer to finding out what she did in this alternative world. A world that we discovered later her parents had next to no idea about. Ernie Vinh drifted into his habitual silence as he worked. With cool concentration he zoomed around various websites and chat rooms and something called message boards. For the next hour or so Delray and I read and reread the witness statements and police reports concerning the Antonio Rodriguez homicide. But all the time out of the corner of my eye I could see that Ernie was still clicking and clacking on his keyboard.

Heaven knew what Marlowe would have made of all this technological wizardry. Probably he would have been bored and appalled. Something else we had in common. Fortunately, Ernie was acting as our online gumshoe.

'Here you go, guys,' he said, with not any real emotion in his voice, just a faint smile of satisfaction at a job well done. 'Welcome to Miss Christine's kingdom.'

We closed our files and came over as Ernest turned the screen towards us. Displayed on it was the computer equivalent of a scrap book. Somehow he had succeeded in working his way onto one of the popular spaces that teenagers used to describe their lives and to pour out their anxieties about their homes, their loves, and their schools. And pour it out Christine most certainly had done. There was any amount of information about her likes and dislikes, about her interests, about her friends and also, here we looked more closely, her boyfriends.

'They have got to be on the dark side. I like a black side to a guy. I don't want all these roses and shit. I want a guy who's gonna take me on a night ride. That's why, Sean, you're my devil in disguise!'

'We got any idea who this Sean guy is?' asked Ern.

We didn't.

'I guess, yeah, I guess he's the guy we need to track down. Can we get back into one of those chat rooms like where all those girls, her school friends, are hanging out right now? Maybe we can find some stuff about who he might be.'

Delray, fifteen years my junior, was considerably more au fait with computer technology but I sensed that he found it as tedious as I did.

All the flashing and strobing taking place on the screen, all the nicknames and passwords and screen names and slang, short cuts and teen terminology soon started to become deadly dull. Before long I found myself being nudged awake by Delray. He suggested that we should head for the Harvard Gardens Bar for some refreshment. I agreed hurriedly. Marlowe would have approved.

Ernie Vinh refused our invitation monosyllabically. He was not a drinker and, in fact, he was just heading off to teach a t'ai chi class, before returning to the office for another zoom around cyberspace.

It was quiet at the Harvard Gardens and we easily found two seats at the bar. Delray ordered a Dr Pepper, undoubtedly the most disgusting soft drink ever concocted, and I chose a beer randomly from the fifteen or so available, in the certain knowledge that they all tasted pretty much the same. We moved to a booth and chatted about the day's events but failed to make any great deductions. A few minutes later Delray's cellphone started to beep. As private investigators have the habit of changing the ring tone of their cellphones on a regular basis, so as not to be recognised by one particular sound, Delray failed to identify that it was his telephone until the second after it had stopped ringing. Flicking open the lid he checked to find out where the call had come from. When he saw he looked aghast, checked his watch and asked me what the date was. I had no idea. Excusing himself he hurriedly dialled a number.

'Hey, Mom.' Delray was at his most apologetic. 'Yeah, yeah, sure I remember. Yeah, I'm coming right over. I'm just having a chat with my new English friend, you know, I told you about him? What's that? OK, OK, I'll ask him.'

Turning back to me, snapping his phone closed, he smiled.

'Just had to ring my mom. Going over there tonight for some food. I told her all about you. She says, you want to come over?'

By now I was not at all surprised at another display of American hospitality and readily agreed.

'Should I grab something to take with us? Maybe a bottle of wine or something?'

'Oh, no, whatever you get don't get a bottle of wine!' Delray looked quite nervous. 'My mom is very religious. We don't do any drinking or anything like that at home. She can smell alcohol fumes like four blocks away.' I laughed and then looked down at my beer which I suddenly realised I had finished. Suddenly, I could feel the booze seeping out of my pores. This was ridiculous.

What would Marlowe have said? Hardly hard-boiled.

Instinctively, I reached into my pockets for some chewing gum and found none. In the men's 'comfort station' I found a vending machine selling great round balls of toothpaste-flavoured chewing gum. I bought three, popped them all into my mouth and started to chew. A few minutes later my jaws ached so much I could hardly speak.

Some twenty minutes later, we pulled up outside a low-rise tenement block on the north side of East Stoneham. Here the gardens and streets were litter free and well-tended. In side streets children, sporting big leather gloves on their left hands, hurled fat softballs to each other while others skipped or practised dance moves quite happily as the dusk settled.

'Here, have a squirt of this,' said Delray and produced a small canister of breath freshener from the glove box of his car. Thanking him, I took it and opened my mouth. Now, this is by no means a small target but somehow I misjudged the direction of the spray and was immediately blinded by something that was mentholated and extremely strong. Wiping my eyes I eventually managed to fire a puff of Icy Blast where it was intended and scrambled, disorientated, from the car. By the time I had followed Delray to the top of the stairs, I could just about see again but still looked as if I had been chopping onions all afternoon.

Doreen, Delray's mother, was a slight woman with a welcoming smile and a gentle manner, who was much too polite and sensible to ask what had happened to me as I blinked a greeting. She had only just returned from her work as a secretary at the public hospital and was in the process of hanging up the jacket of her smart two-piece suit when we arrived. She had a very endearing way of describing us as 'boys' which is an experience I undergo only too rarely nowadays. Delray produced two bottles of Coke and showed me around the compact but spotlessly tidy apartment. There was any number of pictures of Delray dressed in suits at various graduation ceremonies or holding awards won at sporting events. There were also photographs of his twin brother Leroy, who did not appear to be engaged in any of the same activities. Doreen smiled from several snaps. Most were of church outings, of groups standing outside ecclesiastical edifices. One of these I recognised immediately.

'So you have been to London? I recognise that place. It's the evangelical church on Marsham Street. I stay just by there sometimes.'

'Is that right?' asked Doreen, delighted. 'Yes, we were there only last year. Let me tell you all about it.'

And tell me all about it she certainly did. By the time that Delray offered to drive me back to the South End he looked almost catatonic.

Amazingly, it was midnight before I made it back to the

apartment. Boy, could Doreen talk. I toyed with the idea of having a late-night large Scotch straight up with a splash of soda, no ice, sipped over a few pages of *The Big Sleep*, but I decided it was way too late.

Delray was calling round at eight the next morning. He was going to take me to court.

15

No Place I Wanna Be

When we, Delray and I, drove to the office the next morning some time before nine o'clock I was amazed to discover Nelson and Ernie hunched over the computer in the corner of Buck's office. I wasn't sure I had seen Nelson *in situ* at such an early hour before. One of the attractions of being a private eye, he had told me soon after we had first met, is that you don't have to be in the office any particular time. It remained a mystery to me where Nelson lived and although there was definitely a Mrs Nelson Mason – Buck had told me this with grimaces – I was never to meet her. There were no children, it appeared. I suppose I could have followed him home. Surveillance, of course, was my new game but I didn't want to so I didn't.

In fact, it transpired that the two of them had been up the entire night and had somehow managed to work their way into the 'community' of youngsters on the Internet. As I listened to them talk I realised that Ernie, in this virtual world, had assumed the identity of a fifteen-year-old girl. He had even created a page for himself, or rather herself, in which Ernie listed her interests and what types of music she enjoyed. He had also drawn up a computer portrait of herself. The cartoon-style picture was of a rather dour-looking girl whose hair hung lank over her eyes. I was surprised he had not added a few spots of acne for good measure. If I had been designing my own person on the Internet I suspected I might have created somebody rather more glamorous. Ernie and Nelson decided finally to log off as most of the youngsters who had been up all night tapping on their keyboards were now packing their bags for school.

'What a goddamn life. I thought sitting in front of a computer screen was something you had to do, not something you wanted to do,' grumbled Nelson as he lumbered back into his office and collapsed behind his desk for a snooze. Ernie, probably some twenty-five years his junior, looked quite bemused at this thought but turned back to his screen and carried on typing.

'Look,' he said to me, somewhat to my surprise as I knew how normally taciturn he was. 'Would you get yourself one of those?'

Looking over his shoulder I saw a picture of a boy who advertised his age as slightly over fifteen, demonstrating with a tug of his underpants a silver ring that had been pierced into a part of his anatomy that had me wincing and looking away.

'Wonder if he has shown that to his grandma?' muttered Ernie and chuckled in, what was for him, a rare moment of humour.

'Oh, Delray, make sure that you introduce Randy to Dane. Dane is Germaine's defence attorney. Attorneys are jerks but Dane is a good guy,' observed Rita as she unpacked her zero-calorie lunch box onto her desk and shrugged her coat off before hanging it carefully on the hat stand in the reception, thoughtfully dusting the green-shaded, brass desk lamp with her fingers as she did so.

'Randy may have to work one-on-one with Dane if we get pushed for manpower, so you guys need to know each other, OK?'

Both nodding, Delray and I left and climbed into his low-slung sports car, the tinted windows of which meant that it was difficult to see out on a sunny day and certainly impossible to look in.

'Great little surveillance number,' Delray assured me. Little was the operative word as I folded myself in three in order to get into the passenger seat.

The County Court House was not at all as I had imagined it. Instead of a grandiose, Georgian-style, red-brick, white-edged building with a fluttering Stars and Stripes on a flag pole on its roof, this place was an ugly, squat, concrete building two storeys high. Of course there was actually a Stars and Stripes fluttering from a flag pole on the roof top. This though was no real surprise because, as I had mused only a few days before, when in downtown Boston, it was almost impossible to find oneself in any metropolitan area of the United States, turn through 360 degrees and not see a flag of some dimension, small, large or absolutely enormous. Why were these flags so numerous? Australia was equally enthusiastic to 'fly the flag'. Was it a question of patriotism? Was it simply a love of the nation of many people's adoption? Perhaps it was a rallying call in a country that seemed to have otherwise little social cohesion? Or was it just something in which to wrap yourself, something behind which to hide? Having already discovered that it was a dangerous pastime to question Americans' attitude to their country, I decided not to bring up the conversation with Delray, as we climbed up the few steps to the Court House. To date I had found little sign of any citizen of the United States ready to ask themselves questions on this subject.

Despite my disappointment at the lack of grandeur of the buildings where such important proceedings were to take place, I was, of course, pleased to discover, when we eventually walked into the sterile concourse with its shiny floor, that there were a number of people, dressed in fluttering black gowns, walking around clutching files under their arms.

One of these figures came over to see us as soon as we entered.

'Hey, Dane, this is Randy. He is working alongside us on this one. He's from the UK but you don't have as much problem understanding what he says as you might think.' Delray didn't appear to be joking.

'Hey, Randy,' Dane said and looked at me curiously with blue eyes that twinkled out of a face that was clearly well cared for and surrounded by hair and beard that must have been expensive to maintain. I wondered whether his first name was some reference to his original roots. A Viking perhaps? 'How're you doing? You know, I spent a bit of time in the United Kingdom. I went to your Bristol University. You know it?'

I nodded. That was where Kelly wanted to go, of course, but I didn't mention this to Dane.

'You ever meet a guy over there called John Dickenson? He was a professor. Lectured in divorce law. Great guy.'

I had a serious think and then shook my head. This was always happening.

Suddenly Dane switched into professional mode and turned his attention to Delray. 'Look, here's the deal. You know this is just a pre-trial hearing, fact-checking really. Germaine is just gonna show up here with the other four guys. All they're going to do is ask his date of birth, you know, the normal procedure? Address. You know, the normal deal.'

'Yeah, yeah.'

'What I want you to do is take a good look at the other four guys. We need to note their addresses, then I want you guys to go back and do some background checks on them. Some of the people who end up in this place, it's like they were born to. Sort of like a fate thing. But not this Germaine kid, not him, he's a different kind of person.'

'Is he OK?' I asked suddenly, surprising myself.

'Oh, yeah, well, he's OK, bearing up. Hard, though.'

'Let's get going. They're about to start,' Delray said, glancing over Dane's shoulder.

The courtroom was small and if I had been hoping for oak panelling and pictures of George Washington then I was disappointed. There was, of course, a flag and behind the seat where the judge was already sitting was a huge crest of the United States. The judge himself was busying himself with some papers whilst talking into a mobile telephone. We sidled down a row of benches and found ourselves sitting next to the Christiensen parents. Sadly, they looked no happier or more comfortable than the last time I had seen them at Nelson's offices. I smiled at them and they smiled back but before long the court session commenced. There was something curiously relaxed about the whole proceedings and when the very overweight police officer, his belt of handcuffs, gun and pepper spray only just visible below his heaving stomach, called the court to order and told them that they might be seated, everyone in the public gallery settled into their seats as if awaiting some theatrical experience.

In this they were to be disappointed as the proceedings were extremely brief. Over to my left, to the judge's right, was a raised stand in which there were half a dozen or so chairs left lying around loosely as if they had been vacated recently and carelessly. These were soon to be filled by the accused.

Five figures walked, or rather shuffled in as they were all manacled at the ankles and at the wrists, a chain connecting the two and then a chain connecting each man to the next by the waist. If it had not been for the orange jumpsuits and flip-flops I could not have more sharply, however much I would have willed it some other way, been reminded of a chain gang of slaves on the plantations. The first four men to come in were enormous. Each of them showed signs of long days spent in weights rooms. They also displayed an interest in do-it-yourself tattooing. Forced as they were to keep their hands on their laps by the strange formation of the chains, I could see that the forearms of the four were covered with strange markings, rather like the doodlings of a bored author. And I should know.

The fifth pair of arms in the row of detainees was much smaller, slighter. There were no tattoos. When I glanced up to its owner, the boy I immediately knew to be Germaine Christiensen, I was taken aback, shocked, as if physically struck by two things. First, was an ugly, brutal black eye that puffed and swelled up onto his forehead and down below his cheekbone. The white of the eye was bloodshot completely. Was he blinded? Second, I could not believe how youthful this boy looked. His face was smooth. He showed no signs of a beard. He was childlike. When he glanced round, startled by his surroundings, he had no interest in anything other than seeking out his mother's face. He found her and he looked her deep in the eye and then he could not help but begin to cry. She leant forward to him as if to go to him, touch him, kiss him, hold him, but she could not.

When he lifted his hand to his face to wipe away the tears that came tumbling down his smooth cheek, his hand was yanked violently back by its handcuffs. The man next door to him did not like to be disturbed as he sat and stretched and yawned whilst the clerk went through the terminally boring but vitally important procedural matters of the court, checking the names, the dates of birth, the addresses and the rest of the strange, merciless information that was required.

When finally the proceedings came to an end, although they had barely lasted perhaps ten minutes, I felt a huge relief to be able to stand up and leave the room. The detainees, with the exception of Germaine, did not appear to share my concerns. They laughed and joked with their jailors and with each other. They did not even bother, as far as I could see, to look out their state-appointed defence attorney in the crowd. He was a harried-looking man with smudged glasses and greasy grey hair swept over the top of his head into a little ponytail tied up with an elastic band at the back of his head. He was in possession of a serious hygiene problem and smelt rank as he pushed past me onto his next case.

Not for the first time did I have a sense of the surreal. How was it possible for these young men, barely men, one of them only just twenty years old, to make so light of what, to all intents and purposes, would be or could be the rest of their lives? On the way out of the Court House I had asked Delray what he thought these young men might receive by way of a prison sentence if found guilty.

Delray was studying criminal law and had just been looking at sentencing guidelines for the varying states. Massachusetts had done away with the death penalty, and there is little point in wasting time in any observation here about how sensible that was or how horrific it is that so many states in America carry out such abominable acts in the name of us all. Here, at least, only a custodial sentence was possible. Delray frowned a little while he considered the circumstances.

'Well, let's say these guys go down for first-degree, maybe even second-degree homicide.' He paused again. 'Well, I gotta say they're looking at somewhere like fifty to fifty-five years to life. Might be wrong.'

'Fifty years! Or life? What does that mean?'

'Or life? Well, that just kinda means that they'll do fifty years or die in prison before that.'

'Oh, yes, I see. Of old age, you mean?'

'No way, well maybe, but more likely not of old age. There's guys being killed every day in American jails. You know those two defendants, the ones sitting in seats two and three. No way they are ever gonna get out of jail once they get inside. They got the whole wrong attitude. They'll end up dead in there.'

And this all, shocking as it was, was not nearly as horrifying as the possible fate of Germaine. He was risking fifty years in prison.

Fifty years in prison!

Fifty years for something he had not done.

Of that I was sure. Certain now that I had seen him for the first time. He was certainly innocent. I would have been happy to put money on it.

Perhaps I spend too much time thinking about it. It wasn't my problem. But of course it was.

Anyway not to be silly, nor ridiculously idealistic any more, I should get back to the bald facts of the case.

Through teaching, just because it interests me, I believe strongly in being able to judge a great deal about someone simply from their face. Some people are good at dissimulating. Pretending that they are someone else. Playing a role. But somewhere along the line in off-guard or stressful moments, everyone lets the mask slip. Then is revealed the true personality. However much someone may hide it again, from that single glimpse you will always know with whom you are dealing. Germaine had, if anything, been unguarded and I had seen someone who I did not believe could have any involvement in this horrific incident.

'You see how small he is? Even if that kid is wearing some disco dancer stack heels, no way he's ever gonna look like the other guys. You agree with me, Randy?'

'No, yes, you're completely right. There is no way anybody could fail to notice the difference. I wonder how he got that black eye?'

'How do you think? You don't need to ask yourself that question, my friend.' Delray shook his head and for a moment looked slightly shocked himself. 'Those four guys, they will be abusing that kid, beating up on him so bad. No way they're gonna let him stand up in court and tell the truth.'

'Why not? What do they care if he goes down or not?'

'Because if he doesn't go down then there's still someone out there the police got to find. The police don't want the problem but those other guys, you can bet my ass, they are covering up for someone. Germaine goes down, everyone's happy.'

'But why would the police arrest him just on the say-so of the other defendants? They can't be reliable witnesses, can they?'

'You gotta understand one thing, buddy. Quicker the case is closed, the happier the cops are. They got five arrests. They're feeling pretty good about this. Happens all the time, guy. Better get used to it. Hey, if the police did their job a bit better we wouldn't have so many cases, would we?' He laughed but with no mirth.

Delray had insisted that we follow the police van straight to the County Jail where Germaine and the other defendants were being reincarcerated. My experiences at the Court

House had almost been enough for me for one day but I now sensed some urgency. Now that I had seen Germaine and seen the wheels of the judicial system start, like a meat-grinder, to crank slowly into operation, I realised that there was a job to be done.

Perhaps I had not given due thought to what a visit to an American prison might entail. Jail is somewhere I am happy to say I have not, to date, spent any time at all, apart from an unfortunate interlude in Zambia but that was absolutely *not* my fault. My image of incarceration was a combination of something dank and Dickensian and some vision summoned up by a newspaper colum-nist's rant about the easy life in British jails. I had some vague idea about snooker tables and TVs and foam-filled sofas, even coffee machines, but maybe with some chains and the odd rat gnawing. It wasn't a very clear picture at all.

The reality of the County Jail, and it was just that, a county jail, not Sing Sing, not a high-security number, shocked me profoundly. For a start, the main building material was not concrete or brick or wood or glass, it was steel. The floors were steel, the walls were steel, the doors and gates and bars were all steel. The whole place resonated with a clanging metallic din that assaults the senses and is designed to induce madness. It stank of inhumanity.

Almost fulfilling my Victorian vision, the warden who accompanied us on our way to the interview room where we were to talk to Germaine had a huge circular bunch of keys at his waist and he unhitched it perhaps six times before we reached the tiny but sound-proofed interview room. Three glass walls built against one of the steel ones of the prison. It was simply furnished with a table, perhaps four feet by four feet, and three chairs.

Just sitting there next to Delray opposite the empty chair I had the sensation of suffocating. The total lack of anything personal was completely soul-destroying. It was really as if you were sitting in suspension, as if time no longer had any sense or meaning. Perhaps it didn't. I noticed Delray glance through the glass partition and down the corridor, and as I followed his glaze I could see a group of men walking towards me. Fancifully I thought of a wedding party, the groom arriving with two best men accompanying him on either side. The flash of orange was his bright wedding attire. The dark uniforms, the sign of the importance of the occasion. But it was Germaine, barely sixteen years old and shackled.

If he was innocent, even if he was guilty, and was sentenced to jail, there would be no wedding party for Germaine Christiensen. There would be no 'moments' in his life. No girlfriends, no eighteenth birthday, no engagement, no wedding, no fortieth birthday, no fiftieth birthday, no career, no retirement. No nothing.

'Germaine, I want you to meet Randy. He is helping me out on this case. You OK with that?'

Germaine, who did not meet our gaze, just shrugged and hunched over his hands that rested in his lap.

'Hello, Germaine,' I said without anything else to say.

Germaine lifted his head quickly and looked at me quizzically, his black eye shocking. Perhaps my accent somehow resonated with him. Perhaps it reminded him of some TV programme. Perhaps his favourite comedian. Perhaps a children's fairy tale and some funny English character.

'OK, Germaine, there's a few things we've got to go over. You understand that, don't you? But listen, first, how're you getting on in here? How're you finding everything?'

Germaine looked up at us both, sharply now, searching

out our gaze with a look that was both open and honest.
Then he sighed, then he shrugged, then he answered the
question.

'This ain't no place I wanna be.'

And then he started to cry.

16

We Shall Overcome

So difficult had the experience of visiting the prison been, that, feeling admittedly guilty, I was relieved to be distracted from the memory of it and of Germaine's obvious pain, by a summons to Chestnut Investigations Inc. to see Ernie.

Although Christine had been tracked down in cyberspace, we were still no closer to finding out where she was to be found in the real world. Ernie Vinh had continued to make his researches on the Internet. He found himself being drawn into a weird semi-world in which I think he had begun to half believe himself. He really had started to believe he was a fifteen-year-old girl.

'No point in messing around too much more with this,' declared Nelson. 'We need you to get back to see the parents. Randy, you will have to go it alone. I need Delray to get back up to East Stoneham.'

'Oh, I see . . . Are you sure . . . ?'

I thought about it, worried about it and realised, finally, that I rather liked the idea.

'Well, OK. But do you think they'll know anything further? They seemed pretty spaced out, I mean distant, from the whole thing when we spoke to them last time,' I said, and Delray agreed.

'Listen, I've known cases where teenagers go missing and the parents've been involved. That's to say they've coalesced with the child's decision to leave home. They're delighted to get rid of the little monster but they can't admit it to either the rest of the family or other people in the neighbourhood. That's why they come to us. Show the community they're doing everything they can. More often than not they regret it because we find the kid again. Sometimes it comes out that the parents know, sometimes it doesn't, but I often have a pretty good idea of what's happened.'

'You mean that there are parents out there who would willingly see their thirteen-, fourteen-, fifteen-year-old child leave home never to be seen again?' I asked incredulously.

'More than you would think. A lot of these guys, they come from traditional, maybe slightly old-fashioned, Christian families, no great education, boring jobs, they get married young because that's what their parents did. They have a few babies and then they start seeing the other guys, you know, people on the TV, movie stars, having a good time and they say to themselves why should I let myself be tied down by a couple of brats who don't even seem to appreciate what I do for them?'

'That's awful!' I exclaimed.

'Yes, but it's true. People in this country are extremely easily gulled by what they see as commercial success. They want stuff and they want it now. The more, the better. If anyone gets in their way, hell, what's it got to do with them?'

What Nelson had to say appalled me. It was now almost as if the Donaldson parents were becoming suspects.

'Anything you want me to ask them directly? I mean anything that you really want us to know specifically about?' I asked.

'Ask them if they know anything about what she got up to on the Internet. I'm willing to bet you a hundred bucks each that neither of them will have a clue. Ask them how old she was when she got the computer in her room. Twelve or thirteen, I would guess. Also, and this is probably more important, ask them what they know about this friend, what did you call her? Susan, Susie?' He consulted the file. 'Yes, Susie Graham. I would like you to try to get hold of her if you can. Might be tricky because you'll probably have to get the parents' consent to talk to her. I wonder if that's the Graham who's a hotshot attorney up in Cambridge?'

That afternoon I headed back out towards Christine's parents' mansion. On the way I pondered what we had learnt in our long and often very difficult interview with Germaine. He was at his wits' end. He was unable to fit in with any of the other prisoners because he was too terrified of being attacked. So when the rest of the inmates went out into the recreation yard he stayed in his cell. This meant that he was incarcerated pretty much day and night. This only compounded his worry about what would happen to him and, touchingly, how his parents were coping with his predicament.

'I didn't ever see my daddy cry. You know, he just wanna be strong for me. He ain't meant to cry. He meant to be strong. But every time they come over here or I like talk to them on the phone he's crying, man.'

He worried too about the financial implications. His father was only a delivery guy and he couldn't be earning much more than the minimum wage. (Later I asked Delray about this and discovered that indeed there was a minimum wage in the United States. I was impressed to hear it existed but disappointed to hear how much it paid.)

'Listen, Germaine, you and me and Randy here, we got to go over what happened that afternoon. You getting me?

We need to go over like every little itty-bitty piece of information because there ain't nothing we can overlook. You
understand me?'

'Yes, sir,' replied Germaine.

'OK, let's hear it right over from A to Zee.'

Germaine told us the details of that day as he must have
done several times before to his attorney, his parents and
the police. How many times those same old details must
have gone around and around his head, again and again,
night after night, here in the stark, stark steel-clad prison.
Just as we had read in the statements he had given, he told
us that he had left his house at four fifteen and made his
way to his sister's place, getting there shortly after four
thirty. How had he known that he had arrived after
four thirty? Because his sister had chided him for being a
few minutes late to look after the little boy. She and her
husband had to get going at four thirty sharp and he had
looked at the clock in her kitchen to realise that he was a
few minutes behind schedule. He had sat and watched his
baseball DVD on the television and his nephew had fallen
asleep beside him on the settee. When asked what else he
had watched he could name a number of the programmes
and which channels he had seen them on. We could easily
check the veracity of this by looking at the listings but then
he may well have known what was on at that moment
anyway – or even checked afterwards? Had he eaten or
drunk anything while he had been there? Had he needed
to go to the grocery store while his nephew slept? No, no,
he had just watched the TV until his sister and brother-in-
law had returned around seven fifteen.

'You mean you just sat on the settee and watched TV for
three hours?' I asked.

'Yeah, sure, why not?' he replied, but there was no real
question there. That was just what he had done.

'Those guys you were in court with? Did you know them? Did you hang with them? Did any of your buddies hang with them?' Delray had asked.

No, those boys had left his high school a couple of years previously, failing to complete their school certificate, and he hadn't seen anything of them since. In high school people had tended to mix strictly with their own year group. These older boys, apart from being known to be loudmouths and occasional bullies, had had nothing to do with him or his friends directly.

Did he think that they knew who he was?

He shrugged. He doubted it.

Knew his name?

He shook his head.

All this rang true from my teaching experience and I said as much to Delray in the car.

'Yeah, but you don't know what happens after school hours, you know, in the 'hood. They all hang out together in the street and the big kids bring on the little ones, start using them as messengers and then get them into more serious shit. You know what I mean?'

So did Germaine know what their names were?

No, sir.

Not previously, he insisted. Now, of course, he did. He had learnt them in prison and had heard them read out with middle names and all in the Court House. Had he ever joined a gang? No, never, his mom was real scared at that idea. That's why he had joined up with the baseball team and that's what he practised like five nights every week because they had a great ground with floodlights. That's where his friends were. That's what he enjoyed doing. That's where he should be now – in the ball park. He glanced up above his head, as if looking for the sky, trying to find some natural light. There was none.

'You got any girlfriends, Germaine? You know, any girl anybody might be jealous of?' Delray asked but not crudely.

'No, sir,' he replied without any hint of embarrassment, as if the idea had not yet occurred to him. 'No, sir, I just, you know, hang with my buddies down at the baseball. Sometimes I go to my grandma and sometimes I hang out with my sis and my brother-in-law. He's pretty cool, you know? He was pitcher for his state university baseball side. He has loads of really cool memorabilia. Stuff you could never find, like, even in the big stores.'

Briefly, Germaine had seemed to come alive again, his eyes flashed and his crumpled body took back its healthy form. So it was doubly crushing for him to realise, as he focused back on his surroundings, what dire straits he was in.

When we had come away from our meeting, I didn't feel we'd really progressed any further. Nothing proved that he was involved in the case – nor did there appear, apart from some suppositions about timings and distances that we had made, to be anything to prove beyond doubt that he had not been there. We had discussed how long it would take him to get to the scene of the crime and back again and agreed that as a young fit guy he could have made it all the way there. But that meant leaving the nephew all on his own. That meant being seen in the street by a witness. That meant being almost certainly covered in some blood spatters, and no forensic evidence had been found on him or in his house at all. But above and beyond this there seemed to be absolutely no motive. Why would a boy who had, it seemed, gone babysitting for his nephew at short notice, suddenly become involved in a killing that seemed to be an entirely random, if not isolated, case?

There was a clear look of regret on Germaine's face as we left but he raised a small smile and said he hoped he would catch us later. If nothing else, I thought, we had helped him pass some time, taken him out of those grim surroundings at least in his mind for a little while.

Suddenly, I felt extremely sentimental, almost handicapped by my emotions.

Marlowe would have had more sangfroid, would just get the job done. Prove the boy innocent. Walk off into a Californian sunset.

Pathetically, I just felt consumed by the whole situation, brought down by the circumstances, disabled by the system, appalled, pointlessly, by the injustice.

The contrast between Germaine's and Christine's upbringings struck me again forcefully as I headed downtown. With some help from Ernie I had done a little research on the background of the parents before setting out. I had discovered that the father had come late to education. He still sat on the board of directors for a number of companies whilst lecturing two days a week at a business school. From what we could gather, his business interests meant that he certainly no longer had any need to go out and earn his crust.

Ernie had logged me onto an information website called something like Safesearch, a database that PIs could sign up to, and here I was able to find out any number of pieces of information about the life of Christine's parents. It was astonishing how easy it was to uncover enormous amounts of information about regular US citizens on the Internet. The key to everything appeared to be social security numbers, and as the parents had already provided us with theirs, in total innocence, no doubt, about what information we could tap into, our task was made very easy. By simply punching in the number we automatically had access to, and reliable information on, the whole of the father's adult life. Every time he had moved house, every time he had paid rent, every time he had raised a mortgage or loan it was recorded right down to the last minute. Every time he had changed his car the tag number, the colour, the model and the age of manufacture were all carefully noted. Deaths and births were all clearly recorded and interconnected and it was easy to see that his mother had died when he was very young and that his father, it appeared, was still alive and living in Vermont.

Although I was bowled over by the amount of information about private individuals that was available with a few scrolls and the entering of a few passwords, I was not sure if I had uncovered anything of any great use. Moving on down I clicked directly on the wife's name, which turned blue and then threw up her particular life story in dates, facts and figures. Here I discovered that many years previously she had given birth to a daughter who would be some ten years Christine's senior. Checking dates I saw that the daughter had been born eighteen months before the couple married. Given the reasonable length of time between the two events it might well have been, I concluded, that the child had been born of a different relationship. Whatever the truth, the baby girl had been christened Julia and had received her mother's maiden name. Just by clicking on her name I was then able to pursue the paperless trail through all the passages of her life.

I was an intruder but I could not help myself. It was all in a day's work for a PI, wasn't it?

Julia had left home some years before and her last reported address was somewhere just north of Cambridge. Delray mulled over this information when I passed it to him and we decided that it was a lead worth pursuing.

'Ask the mother about this Julia when you see her. No point in giving ourselves work trying to find out whether she's still at that address or not. Better we go straight to her when we find out for sure where she is.'

The traffic was flowing freely on the Massachusetts Turn-pike as I headed out to the considerable luxury of Back Bay. Parking up outside the house, I made my way up the steps and, swallowing hard to drown some butterflies that had recently hatched in my stomach, knocked on the door. Again I was picked up by the video surveillance camera and Dolores, the surprisingly buoyant maid, who recognised me straightaway, came to the door and ushered me in. As she did so she explained that Mr (I almost thought that she had said 'Master' but I think it was her accent) Donaldson was away – on a business trip – and only the mother was there to meet me. Mrs Donaldson looked much as she had done the last time: pale, unhealthy, twitchy and, on close inspection, rather untidily dressed. Rather more distracted than concerned. Vague rather than worried.

'So your husband had to go off on a business trip, is that correct?' I asked, not entirely able to keep a note of incredulity out of my voice.

'Yeah, yeah, now where did he say he was going? Some-thing he couldn't get out of, it was something like an annual conference in some place, where was it now? Oh yeah, he's gone to South Beach, California for the annual conference of America Hotels. He couldn't miss that one, of course; he is the chairman of the board.'

(Later, back at Chestnut Investigations, Delray rang the cellphone number with a spurious excuse prepared, and although it was not answered we were able, through the help of one of Ernie's friends at the telephone company, to confirm, through the tracking device built into the handset, that we were indeed calling a phone at that moment in time located at or near South Beach, California.)

'Righto. I see. Now I wonder, do you think, maybe, perhaps you could tell me a bit about Julia?'

She looked surprised but not, I thought, aghast.

'Julia? How do you know about her?'

This was a good question as I had become a little confused about how secret the methods we had used were meant to be. Ernie, typically, had not been very forthcoming on the finer legal points.

'State records . . .' I muttered vaguely and fiddled with my file. 'Now, where am I? Oh yes, would you mind, you know, very much, if I asked you how close Julia and Christine were?'

Softly, the mother let out a low sigh but I think something about my Sergeant Wilson style of interrogation and my unmistakable English accent relaxed her. She was tired, she said, and although she seemed to barely have the energy to do so she told me the story of her first daughter. She was the outcome of a brief, and I could not help feeling, probably deeply unsatisfactory, affair with a married man when she was barely out of her teens. She hadn't known much about much and when Julia was born it was a shock to the whole family. Nevertheless, her own mother had rallied around and whilst she was finishing her studies spent most of the time looking after the little girl. When she'd met Christine's father she had been away at school and her first daughter had not really featured in their relationship, their engagement or finally their wedding. But as time went on Julia began to spend more and more time with her natural mother and her husband accepted it, busy as he was with his numerous engagements, as long as it kept his new wife happy. Christine was born and they formed, for a while anyway, a fairly traditional family unit. Julia had finished her school studies with no small degree of success and moved away to university to major in Humanities.

Imperceptibly, days slipping by as they do, it seemed to her mother that her eldest daughter had fallen out of contact.

There was no obvious reason. It was just that Julia was busy with her life and they were busy with theirs. As time had gone on they had actually lost track of her whereabouts. She had been in Europe for a while and then travelled in Africa, which surprised them because they had themselves only ever holidayed in the United States.

'Why she wanted to go abroad, we never could understand. So dangerous, you know, with all those diseases . . . all those bla . . .'

'Did you know she was living in Cambridge up until the end of last year?' I handed her the address, annoyed. No, more than annoyed.

'No, we didn't hear of that address. I *am* pleased she is not too far away,' she added absent-mindedly.

'So obviously you wouldn't know if she was still there?'

'No, no . . .'

'Well, can you tell me how the relationship between the two sisters was? I mean were they close? Were they in regular contact, do you know?'

'I, well, that is, I guess I don't really seem to know.'

I could imagine Marlowe sighing with frustration at this point, so I did it for him. The only thing we were managing to glean from Christine's mother was how ridiculously, embarrassingly little she seemed to know about her daughters and their lives.

'By the way, ma'am . . .' I particularly liked this form of address although perhaps it sounded a little odd with my accent – rather as if I was addressing royalty. 'Do you know a friend of Christine's called Susie Graham?'

'Yes, Susie, yes.' She suddenly brightened at being able to remember something – anything – anything at all. 'Of course, she was a friend of Christine's for a long time.'

'*Was* a friend? You mean you don't think she's a friend of Christine's any more?'

'No, well I'm not really sure. Well, I didn't hear too much about her recently. You know what young girls are like . . .' She drifted off, her sentences dangling, in the now only too familiar fashion.

Only as I was leaving did she appear to come back into focus. Had I ever been to Norfolk? 'You know, Norfolk, England.'

Making an executive decision that this was not going to pertain to the case I told her that I hadn't, although actually I had, and hurried my way down the steps and back towards the Dodge Stingray.

When I got back to the offices of Chestnut Investigations Inc., Delray had still not returned from East Stoneham so I killed time by rather guiltily entertaining myself looking people up on Safesearch. My efforts at snooping were not very successful as I only knew many of my American friends by their first name. The only person I managed to track down was Jolene, the cheerful barmaid of Crazy Joan's, who had given me her card. In America even hospitality staff have their own personal business cards, and her full name and address allowed me to work out her movements over the last ten years. Disappointingly, she had not got very far. On the other hand, she had been on particularly fine form organising a karaoke evening when I had stopped by for some late-night fortification after my visit to Delray's mother.

Kelly, who initially I had hardly recognised as she was wearing so many clothes, had performed a particularly impressive turn as Marilyn Monroe singing 'Happy Birthday, Mr President'. Later she had sung a couple of war protest duets with Vietnam Vic and then led the remaining and, I'm afraid, rather drunken customers in several rounds of 'We Shall Overcome'. I had been hoping to ask her out on some sort of a date, although I was not really sure how this was done in America and was painfully aware of the fact that she was fifteen years my junior. Fortunately, or unfortunately, she cut in first and asked me what I thought of Henry Kissinger. This conversation was much complicated by the fact that I believed this particular gentleman to have lent his name to a type of cigar. In order to extricate myself from the ensuing terrible confusion, I invited myself to join them on the march they had planned for the following Sunday. Of course, I had forgotten this by the time I had got my coat on.

As Delray and I headed out to Cambridge to see if we could track down Julia, we discussed what the next best course of action would be in the Germaine Christiensen case. Delray suggested, and I didn't feel particularly comforted by the idea, that we should return to jail. He had hoped to track down some more witnesses in East Stoneham but had had no luck. If we went back this time we would interview the other suspects hoping to extract from them some admission that they had framed Germaine.

'I want to talk to some of the cops involved in this case too,' said Delray thoughtfully as we pulled up outside a low, red-brick tenement block which was suitably atmospheric for private investigators. We pressed the intercom button that, although nameless, corresponded to the number we had seen in the records. After a few seconds and a little crackling, a strange, de-humanised voice responded. We asked if Julia was there.

'Who is this?'

We explained.

'Private dicks, huh? Well, she don't live here any more. But you know what? It's your lucky day. You know why?' Our interlocutor was strong on rhetoric. 'You wanna know why? Well I'm gonna tell you. You know where she is now? You know where she moved to from here? Well I'm gonna tell you. She moved to the apartment right across the hall. If I look through my peephole I can see her goddamn front door right there in front of me. She's in number nine, that's all you've got to do. Ring number nine, OK? Must be your lucky day.' And then with a degree more static the person hung up, leaving his or her gender inconclusive.

Julia was a young pretty woman, with immensely long, mousy hair. She was wearing a plain kaftan and a be-jewelled stud shone brightly in one nostril. Despite her hippy lifestyle – the apartment was filled with Indian religious iconography, in rather stark contrast to that found in her half-sister's bedroom, and the rooms smelled sweetly of joss sticks – there was something deeply normal about her in a way that simply could not be applied to her mother. She explained that yes, she had, to all intents and purposes, cut contact with her parents. Not really out of any bitterness or anger, just simply because she didn't feel she had anything in common with these people who, as far as she was concerned, she explained, were much too middle-class in their attitudes. She found more enjoyment in the arts and crafts shop where she was now the deputy manager, and amongst her student, 'boho' friends.

Yes, she was fond of Christine but Christine was going her own way too, growing up. They had been in occasional communication and yes, Julia was sure Christine did know that she was living at this address. Why? Because she'd been there. No, not that recently. In fact, must have been easy six weeks ago. Christine had just phoned out of the blue. Asked if she could come over. With a friend. Why, was there a problem?

She was clearly concerned but had seen nothing strange

in Christine's behaviour. They had just drunk tea and the girls had gone back into Boston on the T.

We thanked her and were about to make our way back down to street level. Just as we were walking out of the door Delray paused and turned to Julia again.

'Just one last thing . . .'

'Sure.'

'You said it was a girl that came over with Christine?'

'That's right. A girlfriend of hers. Seen her before someplace but it was the first time I'd met her, you know.'

'Sure. You don't happen to remember her name?'

'I'm not sure but . . .' Julia tossed her hair forward over one shoulder and began to comb it through with long fingers. 'If you told me I would remember, I'm sure.'

If we had it would rather defeat the object of the exercise but I said nothing.

'Susie, was it?'

'Susie Graham?' Delray and I asked simultaneously.

'Yes, that's right. Why, is that relevant?'

'It most certainly is!' replied Delray, triumphantly.

'Is it?' I asked.

17

Gothic, Like Dracula

Susie Graham lived out at Charlestown, a perfectly ordinary suburb, with her parents, who turned out to be
perfectly ordinary people. That Sunday afternoon in
October, a week before Thanksgiving, was a perfectly ordinary Sunday afternoon in October. Ordinary for two
gumshoes going about their business.

Whilst Mrs Graham called up the stairs of a large airy
wooden-framed house in comfortable gardens, the father
shook his head. When questioned, it appeared he knew
next to nothing about Susie's school life. Something of a
trait, it seemed, even, or perhaps particularly, at this elite
school. Of course, he knew what grades she was receiving,
that she was a bright girl. He had been to listen to his
daughter sing in the choir and even though he wasn't
particularly sports-minded had attended the end-of-year
sporting competition in which she had taken part. He was
often at home; his job with a well-known computer
company out the other side of Cambridge did not take
him away very often. But when Susie returned to the house
it was more about family matters that they talked. About
their trips up to New Hampshire to their house just north

of Portsmouth. Of the sailing boat that he and Susie's brother, who had now left home, were building in the little boat yard that they had there. Susie had enjoyed horses very much at one stage, which is when she had met Christine. Yeah, the girl had been to their house occasionally, Mr Graham remembered. He hitched up some spotless chinos as he sat on the arm of a primly bound, straight-backed sofa. The trousers, combined with a plain polo top and loafers and no socks, gave the impression that he was in uniform.

'Did you know about the dispute that your daughter had with Christine back awhile?' asked Delray as we sat in a spacious family room, the curtains pulled down halfway against the bright sunshine outside.

'Dispute? Oh, no. Nothing like that. I guess, now you come to mention it, we don't hear so much about Christine any more.'

'Did your daughter not tell you about that at all? I understand it was noticed by all her teachers.' I asked. I knew that a lot of youngsters kept things from their parents but equally that often, if the dynamics of the family were right, they were keen to have someone to talk to close to home.

Through the opening of the door I could see a diminutive, bespectacled girl coming up the stairs from the basement.

'Oh, there you are, honey. I've been looking all over for you. There's some investigators here. They have come about your friend Christine.'

'Why would I have anything to tell them about Christine? She's not my friend,' I heard the girl say as she turned away back into the kitchen and could just hear her mother's muted reply.

'I said, I am not her friend. How many times do I have to tell you?' Susie was most persistent.

'Well, please go in there and say hello politely?' I could hear the note of tired exasperation as Mrs Graham raised her voice slightly. A few moments later Susie released a suitably adolescent harrumph and came round the corner into the living room holding a glass of milk. Around her mouth was a white line that had been left by her drink. It looked almost as if it had been applied for comic effect.

'Hi, hi,' she squeaked, in a voice very different from the one I had just heard her using to her mother. The girl smiled widely, almost grotesquely, I thought suddenly, revealing dental braces, and popped up onto her toes in order to stick her hand out to shake ours. 'How may I help you?' came the next formulaic question.

After she had sat down next to her father and wrapped her arms around her knees, Delray went through the questionnaire that Nelson had insisted would be the official approach to taking witness statements. It was intellectually quite acute and covered a range of aspects from how the witness first met and knew the victim to the history of their relationship right through to their last meeting, but as Susie started from the premise that she was no longer a friend of Christine she maintained she had little information to divulge. Even when Delray tried to take the information back again to where they had first met and why they had first become friends, Susie did not seem to wish to follow his lead and simply repeated the fact that she had had no contact with Christine socially for some time. They weren't friends any more. Remember?

Finally we called the interview to an end and thanked Mr and Mrs Graham on their doorstep.

'Oh, I hope you didn't think she was too rude. You know how these youngsters can be sometimes nowadays?'

Surprised, I shook my head. 'No, she seemed very charming and helpful, even if she couldn't give us any information we particularly needed. You must be pleased that she is so bright and open.'

'Oh, she's not like that normally, I can tell you,' The mother blurted out and then hid her face in her hands as the father raised his eyes heavenward.

'My wife doesn't mean that. She just means that sometimes, you know, these girls can get pretty difficult at this age. Anyway at least you didn't see her with all that muck all over her face.'

'What do you mean by that?' Delray asked sharply.

'Oh, you know, all that stuff. The make-up and the black clothes. What do they call it now? Gothic. Isn't that it? Gothic, like Dracula.'

'So how long would you have said she has been interested in gothic stuff?'

'Oh, a few months now. In fact it was that Christine girl who got her into it. We were quite pleased when she stopped coming over because we thought that perhaps now the phase would be over. Unfortunately that doesn't seem to have been the case so far.'

'I wonder, I just wonder, if we might just ask Susie if we can take a look at her room.'

'Oh, you don't have to worry about asking her. She just had to go for her piano lesson next door anyway.'

'Well, I don't know.'

'I'm sure she won't mind,' murmured Delray soothingly.

I was quite sure she would but nevertheless we trooped up the stairs to the first floor and then on up to the second. When the door of Susie's room was pushed open and once we had accustomed ourselves to the difference in size and the changed location of the windows, we could see that it was a carbon copy of Christine's.

'So what did you make of young Susie, then?' I asked Delray as we drove back through the rush-hour traffic from

Charlestown towards the North End. I think I was rather hoping that he might describe her as 'a piece of work' as Philip Marlowe might have done in the rich prose of Raymond Chandler or, perhaps, 'some kind of broad' *à la* Spenser. Delray, however, was not this kind of private investigator. For him it was an obsession with facts and concrete evidence. For this I admired him very much even though I would perhaps have preferred a little more cloak and dagger.

'Well, she's a bright cookie.' Cookie was a start. 'Yeah, there aren't any flies on her. You think she's hiding something?'

'Yes, I think quite probably she is. But what? She couldn't have known that we were coming, could she?' I thought of the bright-eyed, overly helpful cheerful-looking girl that we had interviewed, and then compared that image with the bedroom that we had found with its posters of bands named The Devil's Lot or Satan's Children. 'We only decided to visit them this afternoon.'

'You more than most, Will, you should know what a school grapevine is like. There's going to be any sort of gossip and information floating around and if she wanted to find out what was going on there isn't any doubt she would have done.'

'No, that's true, I guess, but she did seem quite certain that she had no time for Christine, that they certainly had not had anything left to do with one another.'

'The lady doth protest too much, methinks.' Delray smiled.

Shakespeare! Or was it Shakespeare?

I decided to keep quiet. Another thought struck me.

'You don't think there is any question of foul play? Like she might have done something to Christine, do you?' Then I laughed. All this private investigation stuff was going to my head. I was becoming quite fanciful.

'Can't rule anything out, can we?' Delray nodded thoughtfully as I swung the Dodge Stingray into a parking slot outside Maria's Restaurant on the North Side.

'This is where you can get the best linguine in town. Linguine and clams, my friend, you're going to love it.'

And love it I did. Never mind the fact that several thousand miles of ocean separated this restaurant from Naples from where it derived its origins. The pasta and its sauce were as authentic as it was possible to imagine – right down to the fragrant, almost raw slices of garlic. I hoped we weren't going to spend the afternoon interviewing any key witnesses.

'You know what doesn't add up, Will?' Delray asked as we sipped on about the only two good coffees in America.

'What's that then?' I am never very sprightly after a big lunch and this had been American big.

'Susie goes round to Julia's with Christine six weeks ago but according to everyone, Susie, the school, backed up by both sets of parents, they fell out over three months ago.'

'Could have muddled the dates?'

'Not all of them surely?'

We paused and split the bill. I chewed on a toothpick. It felt right.

'Thing I can't get over,' said Delray as he stirred his coffee thoughtfully. 'Thing I can't get over is this goth business. We know both these girls, they are still goths. You know, of all the different groups there are – punks, new waves, rockers, heavy metallers, you know, all those different types – the one that sticks together the most is the goths. It's not any coincidence one of their favourite bands is called The Cult. These guys go on having affiliations with other goths for years. They are like a breed apart.

'Also, I don't quite get why when we turn up she's all

dressed up like one of the Brady Bunch. How come if her parents know she dresses as a goth and she is used to that look, why then just when we turn up does she look all like a goody-goody?'

'Well maybe she was just having some down time? Maybe she was just relaxing?'

'No,' said Delray as we finished our espressos and got ready to pay the bill. 'No, it doesn't work like that. These guys do everything 100 per cent. They eat, sleep and dream that stuff.' If the circumstances of her disappearance had not been more mysterious then I would have given a short laugh at the memory. Despite my own forays into 'trendiness' in my youth, I had never particularly adhered to any of the particular groups based around musical interests that were prevalent in the 1980s. It was simply because punk was all but dead, the new romantics looked, whichever way you chose to admire yourself in the mirror, totally ridiculous, and my parents would have killed me if I had shaved off all my hair to become a skinhead. In hindsight this was a good thing as having a full head of my own natural hair was only to last until I was about thirty anyway. I could understand why my friends so slavishly followed these fashions in the same way that they followed football clubs or admired particular heroes. It was very comforting. It meant, in a world that they found, as they discovered it, often a little baffling, there was something that they could have some confidence in. There was something that they could share with friends every morning at school. I, personally, was reticent in letting myself be attached to any particular 'cause', not wanting to nail my colours to a particular mast. Perhaps that 'unclubbable' trait has remained with me ever since.

At least then, twenty, twenty-five years ago there was a fairly carefully delineated choice of options. Now, these young people were presented with such an amazing range of activities and interests that choice must simply have been the hardest thing. When I was at school you could be sure that if you had discussed with your friend what it was that they had watched on the television the night before you would find some common ground. Then there had only been three channels, perhaps a little while later four. Now there were literally hundreds and the socially cohesive nature of television had evaporated for ever.

With a jolt I was shaken out of this reverie when Delray reminded me that we were now heading back out to the County Jail to interview those guys that had been arrested along with Germaine. Rita had received permission from the prison governor and had rung Delray and left a message to give us the green light. A part of me, a fairly well practised part of me, started to grope round for excuses as to why I should not go. Fairly often over the last ten years I had found myself faced with an offer I would do anything to turn down. So, I had become something of an expert in, if not exactly fibbing, then at least alluding to colourfully imaginative reasons that might take me away from the matter in hand. The thought of the greyness, the darkness and the brutality of the prison filled me with dread.

Just as I was about to come out with something I simply had to do, the frightened tearful face of Germaine flashed in front of my eyes and in me swelled up, if not a sense of crusading fervour, at least a great deal of sympathy and of responsibility for him, and for his family.

'Let's go,' I said, sliding off the bench seat and out of our alcove.

'What I'm going to try and do is get these people on my side, OK? We know that there isn't any doubt in our minds that they were responsible for this crime. You have to

overlook that, act like nothing has happened,' said Delray
calmly. 'They're going to be interested that you're British
but no more than that. Don't expect that they will even talk
to you if you ask them a question. These guys are born
with suspicion in their blood. Even if I can talk their way,
they going to be mighty suspicious of me. But I seen Nelson
do it. You have to work on them. I don't think we're going
to find much out from them on this occasion. Not like
they're going to be just about to admit they got it wrong
and fingered the wrong guy.'

'Why did they pick on Germaine, then? We are pretty
certain that he wasn't involved in any way, aren't we? So
why have they got it in for him? Do you think there is some
story, something that was going down in the 'hood?' Had
it not been for the serious nature of the case I would have
grinned widely at my use of this last phrase. Actually I did
grin widely but I soon stopped.

'No, no, I don't think he's there for any reason except
that he was in the wrong place at the wrong time. You
remember what happened? The police get a description that
there are five people, they get four of them but they need
the fifth to get this whole thing cleared up. So they pull in
every kid in the neighbourhood and they take their photo.
Then because they don't have any obvious suspect they
throw down these pictures in front of the guys and ask
them to pick him out.'

'So why do they pick him out? Because he's the only one
they know? We know that they do know him, right?'

'Yeah, but maybe you got it the wrong way round. Maybe
they pick him out because he's the only one they don't
know. You know what I mean? They know him but they
don't know him?'

'No, I'm not sure I do know what you mean.'

'Goes back to that gang thing. You know, with the girl

and all? I bet if we go back and have a look at those pictures we will find out all those guys they are in the same gang. Except Germaine.'

'You mean they are protecting them?'

'Well, one of them, yeah. Because we know there were only five guys there. But I bet that they are protecting one of their own. A guy in one of those pictures or a guy who managed to slip the cops. It's gotta be one of their homeys, that's for sure. Oh, and another thing, I think it's time we went to see some of those officers of the law. What do you think of that idea?'

I wasn't at all sure I was any more enthusiastic about that idea than I was about meeting the inmates here at the prison. Yet again I wondered what I had got myself into as the first guy was brought in and loomed over us menacingly in the small glass-sided interview room. As Dane, the attorney, had said, it was as if these guys had been born to end up this way. Their destiny was to get sent to prison at an early age and either spend the whole of the rest of their lives there or significant periods thereof. It was all over for them and they seemed to recognise that. It didn't seem to mean, however, that they wanted to co-operate with us in any way.

As we walked across the parking lot away from the doors of the medieval-looking prison which strangely reminded me from the outside of the Tower of London, I felt drained by this crime and punishment.

I shall never make a statistician, that is for certain, but I made some efforts to consider and calculate the levels of crime in America. After all, its lawlessness is almost, perversely, one of the country's selling points. The Wild West, as we would like to perceive it. Unfortunately, closer inspection of the data makes for rather disappointing reading. Take burglary, by example: there are significantly more burglaries recorded per thousand of the population in Scotland than there are in the US, and in Australia there are nearly twice as many.

Homicide, a category that you might think that America should by rights have 'got licked', is slightly more promising. There are nearly five times as many people murdered in America per capita as there are in the United Kingdom, but there are four times as many more people killed in Russia as there are in the States. Of course, if you want to significantly improve your chances of being bumped off, a trip to South Africa, which has eight times the homicide rate of America, or Colombia, with an impressive twelve times as many, should be your destinations of choice.

Naturally it does depend very much on where you go in the US. A trip to Delaware or Iowa, Maine or New Hampshire means, rather unexcitingly, that you run practically no risk at all of anybody trying to do you in. If, in the other hand, you are looking for a riskier holiday destination, then the capital Washington and the District of Columbia lead by example and are by far the most dangerous destinations. That said, Arizona, South Carolina and New Mexico are all keeping their murderous end up.

'Well, better get back to the office and have a debrief with Nelson.' Delray interrupted my deliberations. 'Also I want to find out whether there's anything new going down in the Christine case.'

'Sounds like a good one.'

As it turned out there was something going down in the Christine case.

It was called a ransom note.

18

Making Deductions

'Of course the parents have had to contact the police. They were nervous about it. Didn't want to but they didn't have much choice. Otherwise they could have been arrested for non-assistance to a person in danger, and in this case still a minor too,' explained Nelson reaching inside the ever-thickening folder on Christine and pulling out a clear plastic evidence bag.

'Oh I see, of course, that is absolutely normal, I suppose,' I replied but despite this felt a totally perverse feeling of irritation, perhaps quite human but also quite idiotic, that someone else was getting involved with my case. I brought myself up sharply with the realisation that if every missing person had access to more resources, more people out there rooting for them, there would certainly be fewer tragic consequences.

'Here is the note,' said Nelson, flicking the plastic bag across the table. 'They have a perfect colour reproduction, of course. The police let us have the original but only after the parents insisted. So, what can you tell me about that, then, Randy?'

Actually, I wasn't sure that I liked having my deductive

skills put to the test like this. It was like being offered a glass of wine by a grinning host and asked to say where it came from. I invariably got it wrong and usually was hardly capable of working out more than whether it was red, white or rosé. I decided to change tack a little.

'So, how did the parents get hold of this note? How was it delivered?'

'The maid found it on the inside doormat, shoved through the letterbox. She took it straight to Christine's mother who rang the police immediately and us straight afterwards. We received the call at four thirty p.m., isn't that correct, Rita?'

'Affirmative.' Rita checked her file.

'How long do you think it had been lying on the mat for?'

'Probably just a second before the maid found it,' suggested Nelson. 'The maid went to answer the doorbell. After she had picked up the note and opened the door she found that there was no one there.'

'Not necessarily connected.' Buck Burnett was leaning in the doorway, as involved as the rest of us. He really did have the hide of a rhino. If I had been stopped by a store detective fondling items of lingerie in Macy's Intimate Apparel Department, as he had been two days earlier when he was supposed to be on surveillance, I would have been hiding in the bottom drawer of my desk. Guilelessly, he had told us he was just playing a part. 'What part was that then? Local perv?' Rita had asked rather acidly. Buck had at least had the decency to blush.

Picked up by security while on surveillance in a store. Honestly.

'I don't reckon kids are coincidentally just going to start on a spate of rat-tat-tat on people's doors the same day as someone starts sending ransom notes, do you?' Nelson could not help replying ever-so-gently sarcastically. 'That said, I'm not suggesting it's the kidnapper who delivered the note. It was found in a blank envelope and could have been handed to a kid to deliver.'

'Yeah, right, that's what I was thinking,' said Buck defensively, and Nelson, who couldn't bring himself to be too unkind to Buck, smiled briefly at him.

Sometimes, I, too, found it in my heart to feel sorry for him. Things so regularly went wrong that, in all honesty, it didn't seem very fair. Only just after the Nissan Cherry had returned from the body shop, he had had it impounded whilst out on a moving surveillance.

In fact, the case was straightforward, a regular worker's compensation. The subject called into work, incapacitated he said, supplied a doctor's note, bad backs being hard to prove, taken several weeks off, claimed the sick pay and, here the employer's suspicions proved correct, played squash most days. Of course without his car, which had been illegally parked, Buck was unable to pursue the subject. Finally, he was forced to explain that he had just 'run' to a bakery to pick up a couple of doughnuts and a coffee. Admittedly these last were practically official equipment for private investigators, but it had, after all, been he that had lectured me on the importance of paying attention, watching closely at all times. Nelson had made him pay the cost of the impounding of his vehicle out of his wages. Buck had looked most regretful.

'OK, so, the cops are gonna start making enquiries round the area pretty soon.' Nelson continued with the 'sitrep' – the situation report. 'Morrison's on this one so we should get good co-operation, get an information exchange going.'

Morrison was good, everyone agreed.

'OK, Randy, let's get back to it. Tell me what you can about this paper and what's written on it.'

The paper was a simple sheet of A5, that is to say half

a piece of the metrically sized A4. (A4 paper in the US has taken over from the foolscap shape that until recently was so popularly used. The global nature of computers, and more specifically their printers, has meant that Americans have been forced to accept this foreign intervention. Nobody talked about it very much.) The piece of paper had, I could see from the lower edge, been torn, but neatly, from a full sheet of A4. It looked without microscopic inspection to be like any other sheet of white computer printing paper. Perhaps it had particular qualities that would make it more easily identifiable but I did not have the skills to spot them and I said as much.

'OK, not bad,' Nelson grunted. 'Now tell me more about the message. Not what it says because that's pretty clear but what about the way it's written?'

I agreed. Its message was very obvious.

'Christine will be returned to you safely if you follow our instruction's. Wait for further information.'

The note made clear that she was safe, or at least it suggested so, and alluded surely to a forthcoming ransom demand. As yet, no particular reference to a sum had been made but according to Nelson this was quite usual. Make contact first and advise the victim's relations of an impending demand for money.

The lettering was blue. Not an official navy or dark blue that appears on highlighted text on a computer, but more of an artistic, pastel shade which was pale against the white paper. In the semi-gloom of Nelson's office I had had to tip the paper once or twice into the light of his desk lamp to make the message clear. Rather than the dull Times New Roman 12-point script that I use to bash out my manuscripts this was an all together more fanciful style. It was more modern and eccentric even than Arial, the font much favoured by slim bespectacled designers and the like. This was typed from swirly characters, almost comic book in effect, in fact, almost childish.

I said as much to the assembled room and also pointed out that despite the fact that the spelling was literate an apostrophe had been misplaced in the message.

'Childish,' mused Nelson. 'Yes, that fits, doesn't it?'

'Does it?' I answered, rather pleased by his approbation.

'Yes, I think you're right, boss. This is a hoax. This is a set-up. Childish, yes, I like the childish. It gets delivered to the door at about the right time that kids are coming out of school. Someone rings the door bell and runs away. How childish does that sound?' Delray said.

'OK, yeah, fits in with your theory right at the beginning about the voicemail messages. Isn't that right, Delray?' reminded Rita Martinez. 'You know, for twenty-four hours there's not one single message from any of her friends.'

'But why would anybody want to pretend that they had kidnapped someone?'

'Throw us off the scent.'

Annoyingly even Buck had reached this conclusion before me.

'It's not so much that someone has kidnapped her, more likely someone's hiding her.'

Delray and I looked at each other and for the second time in two days spoke the same name simultaneously.

'Susie Graham.'

When Delray and I returned to the Donaldson home, the atmosphere was a very great deal more fraught than before. When we walked into his office, Christine's father was on the telephone to the police department but within a fairly short space of time he replaced the receiver and looked at us. A glint in his eye suggested that he very much preferred things this way. Now there was an adversary, now there was a game to be played. He was back in control. Perhaps, too, the situation was not all of Christine's making. Perhaps he could find room for some forgiveness, some rapprochement.

'Do you know how many kids disappear in this country every year? That guy told me. It's incredible. What's more incredible,' he added quite calmly and here he glanced at his wife, 'what's more incredible is the number of them who are never seen again.'

Christine's mother started to cry, the most genuine response that we had seen from her in all our meetings.

'The police said they'll try and put out some information on the local news channel. They're going to keep an eye out for her on the streets. Why the hell would she be on the streets? If some guy has abducted her he's not going to be taking her shopping, is he?'

'Sir, we have to cover all the possibilities. One of the possibilities is that this message is some kind of hoax. Possibly a joke, a prank played by one of her schoolmates.'

Mr Donaldson looked thunderstruck. As I watched, he computed the possibilities of this being true and when he realised its likelihood, the fight sucked out of him again. This time it was replaced by rage.

'Who could possibly come up with a prank like this? It's so horrible. Don't they realise what pain they are causing us?' The mother was beginning to wail now. It was if she was coming round from a deep anaesthetic sleep. It was most disconcerting.

'If I ever found out the person who had sent this as some kind of joke like you say, I'd sure as hell strangle them right here and now.' Her husband was clearly building himself into a fury. He was raging against a feeling of complete impotence.

Delray was remarkably reassuring.

'Whichever way it pans out, if someone still wants to

ask for a ransom, or if she is being hidden, then that has to be a good sign for the welfare of Christine,' he said. 'But like I say, I think we have to explore all the different avenues. Let's just go over these friends again. Can you give me your list of people that you know she is in regular communication with? We have looked closely at her phone but she has deleted all the text messages that she sent to them and if we want to get records of numbers it will take us quite a while, the police as well, to get the records from the phone company.'

The parents paused for some considerable time whilst they thought and came up with much the same list of names as the school had provided us with. There was only one exception – they had included a certain Lisa Edwards. Thank you, we said as we left, and hurried back to the car. We telephoned Miss Pleasance, the headmistress of the school, who, when she heard of the ransom message, understood the urgency of the situation and agreed to contact Lisa's parents to ask their permission for us to interview their daughter. The moment she received it she asked her secretary to go and find Lisa.

Lisa was an all-American girl. 'Well, sir,' she replied when we asked her how she had come to know Christine. She thought carefully. 'We only became friends, you know, like at the beginning of this year. I came from San Diego and I didn't know anybody here too much. Christine was really nice to me even though I'm not like her . . . You know.'

'You mean you're not a goth?' I asked.

'Yes, sir, that's correct. She is going to let me try some of her clothes and stuff like that.'

Lisa was blonde with smiley blue eyes and a few freckles left over from the summer. It would be a shame to cover all that up under spade-loads of make-up and lipstick, bottles of black hair dye.

'You know that her parents just received a ransom note?' asked Delray gently. 'This means that your friend could be in some serious trouble.'

'Ransom note? You mean like kidnapping? You mean she might have been abducted?' Lisa squeaked, her eyes wide with amazement. 'No, no, you must be talking about a different case. Christine hasn't been kidnapped, I'm sure she hasn't.'

Lisa looked completely confused but tried to remain guarded, like a boxer who has just received a hard punch and is wondering where the last blow came from, all the while trying to protect themself from another.

'Why are you so sure?' Delray jumped upon her answer.

'No, no, no . . .' Lisa seemed to shrink back into herself. 'No, I mean, what I mean is, she couldn't be, could she? There isn't anyway I'm sure. It must be a mistake, that's what I meant.'

'Can you think of anybody she's mentioned to you that might have wished her harm? Did she have any concerns of any nature that she may have shared with you?' But now Lisa had retreated into herself and refused to say anything at all of any importance but just repeated how much she liked her friend.

'Isn't that nice? For the first time we know that somebody's lying. That is really good news. I think it's time to go and see our friend Susie again.'

We found her in the art department standing in front of a canvas on which she was painting a picture that was in the style of William Blake in the underworld. In appearance, she was transformed from our first meeting and now wore as much of her cultish make-up and clobber as the school allowed.

She grimaced when she saw us but adopted a sunnier disposition when we approached to ask our questions. OK, she agreed quite quickly, she had not really fallen out with Christine. Yes, she had accompanied her to Julia's. Why had she pretended to have argued with her? Oh, it was just a silly joke; just messing with some of the other girls' heads. Nothing important. Now, her eyes widened, she was very concerned about her friend, she really was.

'Do you think it's likely that Christine has run away or do you think there's a real possibility she has been abducted?' asked Delray. 'You will have heard we have received a note?'

Susie frowned and nodded and turned her face slightly away. I could see the row of empty holes pierced up the edge of her ear; eight I counted.

'Oh, I don't think so, no.' It was almost as if she didn't think it was a very good idea. 'She was talking about a guy who she said she knew. I never met him. She said she didn't know him that well but she really liked him.'

'What was the name of this man? Sean?'

She looked surprised and glanced at both of us.

'Oh, no. Sean was history like last summer!'

Poor old Sean.

'No, she never said nothing to me about his name or anything,' Susie replied quickly, and I was under the distinct impression that she was becoming increasingly uncomfortable, backing away from us. 'Really, I don't know any more about him. Maybe she made him up.'

Finally we had to let her go because she, like Lisa, brought the shutters down and refused to give us any further information.

We were sitting in the Dodge Stingray at the end of school when Susie appeared from the school gates.

'We're going to take a risk on this one. We will chance it that she is taking the T back home to the Charlestown stop. It's a hunch but I'm guessing she is not going any place different,' said Delray as he pointed for me to follow the girl, who was now a couple of hundred yards away. Surveillance of somebody on foot whilst in a car is remarkably difficult but I followed Delray's instructions to the letter and we watched her enter the train station.

'OK, step on it,' Delray said. 'We are going to have to get there pretty fast if we want to arrive before her. T's slow but more direct.'

Fortunately the afternoon traffic had not yet got going and the bridge out of the West End, the Zakim Bunker Hill Bridge, was pretty much clear. We turned right onto New Rutherford Avenue and then left again out onto Harvard Street. Before long we were in a residential area and, turning round Winthrop Square, we headed out onto Walnut Street. I was in a state of high excitement by the time we stopped outside the tube station where a few minutes later Susie appeared. Delray punched me playfully on the arm.

'Good driving, partner.'

I smiled and pulled the sun visor down over the driver's seat as the girl, her school bag hung over her shoulder, glanced back.

'OK, just pull up over there by the gas station. From there we should have a view of her going into the house.'

I did as instructed and we pulled up on the forecourt the other side of the petrol pumps. From there some distance off the other side of the freeway we saw the girl head up the side street towards her house. The front of the house had a porch with wooden steps running up to it, but instead of this Susie took a stone-laid path that ran up the left-hand side of the house.

Delray looked at me briefly and I glanced back questioningly.

'OK, come on. Let's just see what this is all about.'

Leaving the car on the forecourt, we hurried across the

traffic, darting around the moving vehicles and hooting horns. I stopped a while on the central reservation but when I saw Delray skipping across to the other side I followed him with my heart in my mouth.

Delray had now decided that he was on the right scent and without any further ado he headed up the path that Susie had taken. There were no cars outside the house and I presumed that the parents had not yet returned. As quietly as we could we crept along the path that was bordered on both sides by large bushes. At the end of it, right at the back of the house but still at the side, there was a wooden panelled door such as might be found on a potting shed. It was slightly ajar. We stopped and listened and distantly we could hear some droning rock music. I could smell something. At first I thought it was a scent coming from the garden but I soon realised that it was the odour of something sweetly burning. Incense! It was some kind of burning perfume.

Delray pushed the door slightly open and we both looked down a badly lit flight of stairs into the basement. As I glanced back along the side of the house and saw the way that the incline of the garden ran away I realised that this must lead to a second basement, a basement below the one that was accessible from the house. Whether there was any communication between the two elsewhere we didn't know.

Slowly, cinematically, we made our way down the steps and pushed at the door that we found at the bottom. As it swung slowly open I almost wished that Buck Burnett was with us. He could at least have led the way, his enormous revolver in his hand. When we pushed open the door we found, their faces lit by flickering candles, two young girls.

One was Susie Graham.

The other, her pantomime make-up unable to disguise her expression of surprise, was Christine.

19

The Big Sleep . . . Almost

The war protest was to take place on Carlton Square. Unfortunately it had been timetabled to coincide with a farmers' market. The stallholders looked confused by the arrival of several thousand protestors but at least if there should be any confrontation with the forces of law and order then we would have ample quantities of tomatoes and eggs at our disposal. I had met Vietnam Vic at Crazy Joan's where he was having a couple of Wild Turkeys to put 'fire in my belly'. I decided, catching the reek of the whiskey, that my stomach was quite warm enough as it was. Shortly after we set out to join the protestors, to my delight, Kelly appeared on a street corner near the Christian Science building. Fortunately, as it was quite a nippy morning, she was not dressed in her normal Silhouettes outfit but had changed into an elegant brown overcoat and leather boots. She wore a long scarf wrapped around her neck and a woolly hat, pulled down most fetchingly over her blonde hair.

She could have been in *Love Story*.

When we arrived on Carlton Square, the three of us arm in arm, a substantial crowd had already gathered. Not sure of my role, I decided to play the part of the observer. I had my notebook in my hand and decided that should anybody need to know I would simply say that I came from England and that I was a writer. All quite true. Suddenly, with something of a sinking feeling, I remembered how little I had achieved on my book since I had been in Boston. Anyway, who cared about that now, this was much more fun. A tide was turning in America against the war in Iraq and if perhaps I had expected a certain degree of opposition to the protestors from patriotic passers-by, nothing was said. When a speech given by a prominent Vietnam veteran and presidential candidate came to an end, Vic applauded enthusiastically, perhaps assisted in this endeavour by the Wild Turkeys, and Kelly, quite overcome by the emotion of the moment, turned to me and whispered, 'Isn't this just great?' I agreed that it was and thought it even greater when she leant up onto her tiptoes and kissed me on the cheek.

Somehow the Susie Graham and Christine case managed to irritate me in a way that was quite unusual. Once we had discovered the girls, Delray attempted to find out what the reasons for Christine's disappearance were. Without saying it in so many words, Christine gave us the definite impression that she did not think it was any of our business. When Delray asked her questions about her welfare and her feelings towards her parents, she shrugged, and when at one stage she plugged music into her ears and turned it up, I was sorely tempted to pick up the machine and its owner and kick them up to the first floor. Instead, we rang Susie Graham's parents, who appeared, mildly grateful, and took control of the situation. Christine's parents, although clearly relieved that she had been found again, expressed annoyance that they would need to come over to Charlestown to pick her up. No, Delray suggested, he did not really think it was a good idea that she go back on the T. Our report would be in the post to them the following day. After that they could decide what further course of action they would take.

'They're the customer. They pay and you give them what they want – nothing more, nothing less. That's the way to do business in America. If they don't ask for it, don't give them it.'

None of the participants seemed to realise the trouble that had been caused, the damage that was being done, but that was not our problem, it seemed.

Sitting side by side on two high stools at the window bar in Luciano's delicatessen on Charles Street, we looked out at the wet, streaky street, wrapped our hands round large cups of skinny latte Americano something – which, it must be admitted, was delicious – and gazed down again at the police report. The edges of the photocopied paper were grimy with our fingerprints. We had leafed through the statements taken by the cops so many times.

'What say we have a look at Old Ma Mary's statement again?'

'Why do we always go back to her statement?' I asked. She surely, with her drug addictions or afflictions, was no reliable witness. I added this thought to Delray. He smiled.

'She's a good lady. We can't just judge everybody by their problems. Anyway, we're not going to use her as a witness. Let's just go back to see what she said.'

We found the relevant page, which was already covered in fluorescent marker pen and underlinings in black ink.

'OK, read me that paragraph right there.' Delray stabbed at it with a piece of doughnut.

'You mean the bit after it says about the four males, sorry, five males hanging on the street corner?'

'Yeah, where the cop asks her for a physical description of the individuals involved.'

'OK, here we go: "Five boys attacked the Mexican. I guess they were between eighteen and twenty-five years of age and all of them were approximately between five ten and six two tall. They were all big guys."'

'You remember? She always said they were big guys. All five of them. Go look at the statement given by that officer who first interviewed Germaine. See what he says. What you call him? Officer S?'

'Yes, Officer S. He was the guy who first interviewed Germaine when they took him into custody. Here is the bit. "So, Germaine, you know what we heard? We heard five guys, four big guys and a little shrimp of a guy, they are responsible for killing the Mexican. You are that little guy, aren't you?" He just made that up! How come he did that?'

'Because he's got Germaine in front of him and Germaine is a little guy, remember. All our friend Officer S wants to do is get himself one conviction. If that means bending the truth a little bit then he's going to do that.'

'So you mean that he's just going to make stuff up to get Germaine convicted. Why?' Again an atmosphere of fiction and fantasy seemed to surround the whole case and I almost physically had to pinch myself to return to the real world and realise that this was very much non-fiction.

'That officer, he's allowed to say anything he likes to the witness that he is interviewing. If it's going to get some form of confession then the police see that is all good. What he's not allowed to do is produce his lies as evidence in a court of law. And, you can be pretty certain that's what he's doing. It'll come to court and no one will question the testimony. If the public defence investigator is on it, he's not probably going to have time to get down in the 'hood and interview them witnesses. Probably too scared to as well.

Come the court case it'll be four big guys and a little guy. Not even Germaine would notice the set-up. Why would he?' Delray finished off his enormous cup of coffee in a single swallow and scooped up the Germaine file.

'What say you and me, we go and pay Officer S a visit? He must be about to come off his shift right now.'

We took the Dodge Stingray downtown and pulled up in the parking lot opposite the main police headquarters. Outside the building there were literally dozens of squad cars parked up alongside any number of prison vans and dog-handling cars.

'He'll probably be taking one of those police cars home with him tonight. If he lives in a gated community, or even just in a regular street, his neighbours like him for taking it home. Makes them feel nice and safe and secure when they see it parked up outside his place. Also, good for him. He can go and have himself a few beers and just jump right back behind that steering wheel. Who's ever going to pull over a cop car? What does our Latin tell us? Now let me get this right. "*Sed quis custodiet ipsos custodes.*" Lot of people forget the "*sed*" but I think you will find that that is the full quotation. True today as it was then, don't you agree?'

'Indeed, indeed,' I muttered, and desperately scratched around for my remaining Latin. All I could remember was something about Caesar being sick in a bus that everyone thought was tremendously funny but which wasn't, even at the age of nine.

'That's the man. Look, right over there.'

The glass doors of the headquarters had been pushed roughly open and a group of seven or eight police officers had appeared. They looked in off-duty mode with their hats in their hands. A number of them had loosened their ties and they were all chatting cheerfully one to another. It appeared that they normally took their handguns and cans of Mace home to the dinner table. Out of the crowd appeared one individual who headed for a particular car with the certainty born of possession. Even at a distance I could see that this man was powerfully built. Big, but not because of excess subcutaneous fat or the kind of pneumatic muscle developed from many hours spent in a gym. Just the brawn of a bruiser.

Although now I felt strangely practised in all matters of surveillance it was with a certain frisson that I headed after the cop car out into the traffic and up the hill towards Cambridge Avenue. Turning right and dipping down past the Holiday Inn and the numerous Italian restaurants and late-night bars, we reached the traffic lights at Mass Gen and weaved our way through the cones of the seemingly permanent roadworks underneath the train tracks flyover. To my surprise he turned left into Charles Street and after only twenty or thirty yards pulled over and parked. There was some sort of display of powerful arrogance in the way that the car was parked at an angle to the kerb and some distance from it, its offside rear light almost asking someone to knock into it and fall into a whole heap of trouble.

'Keep going. He'll be going to the Tens,' confirmed Delray.

'Going where?'

'Tens. It's a bar. You never been there?'

'No, never been there yet.'

'Kind of a dive. Suits this guy, I'd say.'

Parking a little more neatly than the policeman had done, we quickly crossed the road and took a few steps up to the front door of the bar, which pushed open easily and allowed us into the air-conditioned cool. Thanks to the rigorous anti-smoking laws passed in the state of Massachusetts the bar was no longer redolent of the sweet fug of tobacco smoke but instead smelt, disgustingly, of beer and disinfectant and customer.

We approached the bar and I peered into the recesses of the room. My eyes soon became accustomed to the darkness of the surroundings and the banks of television screens that flickered incessantly. After we are all dead, after the Apocalypse, those TV screens will still be flickering and chattering, flickering and chattering, I am sure of it. By now I was almost completely inured to the almost ubiquitous neon-lit advertising slogans. There must have been a sign promoting every single product that was to be found behind the long Formica-topped bar where a suspicious, ratty little man was polishing a glass with ill-concealed dissatisfaction. We went up to talk to him and as we did so I had a chance to check out the contents of all the cubicles in the joint. Although we had clearly watched Officer S enter the building he was nowhere to be seen. Delray Drummond, I could tell, had realised this already, almost by a process of osmosis.

'Hey, buddy, how're you doing?' asked Delray in what I felt to be the most neutral of tones.

'Good, good. What can I do for you gentlemen?' he asked in a way that was about as unhelpful in its intention as it was possible to imagine. Wiping his hands on a sopping dishcloth, the man only gave me the most cursory of glances but he stared resolutely at Delray. As I leant my elbows and back on the bar I could not help but realise that Delray was the only African-American in the room.

'Thank you, sir. Thank you. We were, my partner and I, we were just wondering if you could help us some, sir,' Delray asked with seemingly excessive deference and a slight twang about his accent. This, quietly, was his own way of getting back. 'We were looking for an Officer S. We just saw him come in right now. We just wondering whether you don't have some kind of back bar. Maybe for private members or something?'

'No, we don't,' snapped the barman. 'And anyway, who wants to know? You friends of his then?'

'Wouldn't say friends. Let's say we work in the same line of business,' replied Delray succinctly.

'You got some kind of ID?' the barman snapped now in a tone that could only be described as abrupt. Delray produced one of the embossed cards from Chestnut Investigations Inc. and managed to place it carefully on the bar, all the while giving the impression that he had just flicked it there. Perhaps it was all really just a game?

I could almost see the words Private Investigator mirrored in the pupils of the ratty man's eyes and his eyebrows lift accordingly. He picked up the card by one corner and spun it back across the bar at Delray, who deftly slipped it up and put it into his top pocket. Over the noise of the jukebox and the chattering of the other customers, silence suddenly reigned.

The barman's mouth moved and seemingly some seconds later his words reached us. 'You guys better get out of here. You guys better get out of here real fast. Outta here, right now,' the man said.

After two or three seconds had elapsed, the time it took for his instruction to sink in, I was already preparing my exit, moving in slow motion backwards across the barroom floor in what I believed was known as a moon walk. No problem for me at all to get out of there if that was what the ratty little man with the mean mouth required. Halfway to the door, I realised that Delray had asked him another question. I did not catch it but only too quickly did I witness the man's reaction. Reaching below the counter he pulled out with one hand a pump-action shotgun. Ridiculously, sensationally, he held it by the forward grip and jerked the gun up and down. Again, above the sound of the bar I could hear the unmistakeable sound of a cartridge being automatically inserted into the breech. I had heard this sound countless times before. Until now every one of those times had been whilst I had been watching a film. I suddenly felt very, very sick but, to my astonishment, found myself walking back towards Delray. What I had in mind, I have no idea but I wondered then whether it was all going to be over.

Life.

Here, in this shabby bar stinking of detergent. In a foreign country. This was not at all how I had imagined it.

'What did it matter where you lay once you were dead? In a dirty sump or in a marble tower on top of a high hill? . . . you were not bothered by things like that. You just slept the big sleep, not caring about the nastiness of how you died or where you fell.' Marlowe was right, of course, he always was. He was correct too to have gone off for a couple of double whiskies after a narrow squeak. If I ever escaped this episode I determined to spend the next few years financially shoring up the distilleries of Scotland.

At that moment a door swung open and Officer S appeared, apparently from the men's room, buckling his belt, on which his own gun was holstered.

Bloody guns.

'Hey, hey, hey. Charlie, don't lose your cool.'

For the first and last time I felt that I had to agree with the police officer's suggestion.

'Officer S, I want to introduce myself. I am Delray Drummond from Chestnut Investigations Incorporated. I only want to ask you some questions concerning the Germaine Christiensen case. You got a few moments?' Delray impressively ignored Charlie the barman and directed his focus on the barrel-like police officer. I felt this might be a moment to enter the fray and, gingerly, rejoined Delray in front of the policeman. For this act of courage I was introduced as Delray's partner.

Officer S seemed uncertain about the way to act but finally ushered us over to an empty booth. He did not offer to buy us a drink, which was a pity because by now I felt sorely in need of one.

Delray asked some fairly informal questions to begin with. How long had the officer been with this particular police department? Had he ever worked on gang crime before? What was his experience of homicide cases? What was his witness interview technique? What was his suspect interview technique? I could see Delray drawing closer to the important material. So, clearly, could Officer S, who batted back the questions with text-book answers. Always by the letter of the law, etc., etc.

'Would you ever give a suspect misleading information to get him to admit his guilt?'

Officer S looked nervously between the two of us and licked his lips. Then he thought some more and appeared to relax.

'Sure I would. Nothing wrong with that. Got to get to the truth. That's the important thing, isn't it?'

'Sure, absolutely. We want to get to the truth too.'

'So, would it be true or untrue to say that there were four tall African-Americans and one much shorter guy present at this particular homicide?'

'Oh, look, that's just to get the guy to spill the beans.'

'So under no circumstances would you claim in a court of law there were four tall males and one short male?'

'Er . . .'

'In fact, all you could truthfully say is that all the

witnesses said that there were five tall African-Americans present. Is that correct?'

Officer S, to my delight, was looking increasingly uncomfortable.

'Well, I guess I would just say what the witnesses saw,' stammered the officer.

'So if you could only say that five tall African-Americans were responsible for this killing then that must mean, must it not, that Germaine Christiensen could not have been involved?' Delray was growing positively Rumpolean and I was deeply proud of him.

'Yeah, whatever. Look, guys, I gotta go. Come on, lighten up. What are you trying to say? It's not like it's real important or anything.'

20

Release!

It might not have been a real big deal to Officer S but it certainly was to Delray and me as we sped back in the direction of the offices of Chestnut Investigations Inc., on Chestnut Avenue, Beacon Hill. Thumping up the stairs, we interrupted Nelson's rereading of a Lord Peter Wimsey novel. We waited until he had unscrewed the monocle from his eye and we had his full attention. After Delray had given him the final details the great man looked down at his huge hands spread out pensively on the desk top and grunted.

'You gonna get that officer to sign a statement? It's his whole career on the line. You gonna have to be seriously persuasive.'

'We can put in our evidence that the officer agreed with us that it was just an oversight on his part.' Delray folded his arms and let out his breath softly.

'Except that it clearly was no oversight on his part. He was lying through his teeth in order to . . . in order to. Why was he lying? Why did he have it in for Germaine?' I asked, at a loss. Suddenly I couldn't see the point of the policeman's actions.

'Oh, don't think that this is anything personal about Germaine. Not like he doesn't like the guy or he's holding any personal grudge. Not even probably a racist thing.'

Nelson swung from side to side in his office chair and stared down at his desk.

'No,' he continued. 'Somehow that might be better. Even if he had some perverted reason for it. But you can bet your last dollar this guy was nailing Germaine simply because he could not be bothered. He wants to get the case closed. He wants to go home to his wife and kids.'

The silence was heavy for a few minutes.

'OK, what you got out of the police officer is going to be useful for us. Should sound pretty good in court.' Nelson paused. 'But it isn't good enough, we need to get to the bottom of who it really was. The fifth man. That'll wrap it up. That way, it won't even get to court.'

'What are you proposing, boss?' asked Delray. 'Go back over those witnesses again? See if we can find out more?'

'You, you know any other way?' asked Rita Martinez as she delivered a pile of files to Nelson's desk. 'You gonna need to go back and see those boys in prison. Tell them you proved Germaine's a set-up, a patsy, and he's gonna walk. Only way they gonna plea-bargain now is to spill the beans on the fifth member of the gang.'

Buck Burnett loomed in the doorway and appeared about to say something. Nelson raised his eyes to the leather-clad detective and shook his head.

Poor Buck.

'You know, you'll get some private eye agencies,' explained Nelson, turning to me again, 'they'll go and put the frighteners on the prisoners, tell them something bad's gonna happen to their family. Hope that way they're gonna spill the beans. It doesn't work. Not on three counts. One, it's illegal. Two, these guys have no respect for what little friends and relations they have. Three, where can you go from there? They say they won't co-operate, what you gonna do? Take them some candy?'

'Hey, boss, maybe we go back and we work on the pastor's son? You know the one, the one who was present but witnesses say was not actually involved in the homicide? Strikes me he might be the easiest guy there.' Delray had the boy in his mind's eye.

'Yeah, I see where you're coming from. But I think maybe you go and see the bad guys first. Just gauge their reaction. See how nervous they are. Could give you a good line of questioning when you see the other guy. I'll get Dane to book you into the jail first thing Monday morning.' Picking up our files, we stood and Nelson flicked the blinds and turned out the desk lamp. Silently we trooped down the stairs and into the early evening light of Beacon Hill. It was Friday evening and Buck invited me for a beer at the Harvard Gardens Bar up on Cambridge Avenue but I wasn't much in the mood for a beer and, unkind though it is to say, for Buck's company either. Instead, I skipped across the traffic and made my way back to the South End.

Mrs Walowski was having a furious row with her Korean friends on the doorstep. Drink had been taken, as the Irish like to say, and tempers had flared. No doubt the kernel of the argument was something culinary but I was not in the mood for any involvement. Instead I made my way through the small angry crowd and the dizzying exhaled alcohol fumes and up to the apartment. On the radio some cool jazz was playing and I sat by the window, the lights out, sipping on a large Scotch straight up with a splash of soda, no ice, and watched the traffic glide up and down the highway out towards the Mystic River.

If really we could get the information that was required,

was this truly going to make a difference to Germaine's liberty? Although the whole process that had found him in his tragic circumstances was astonishing, the concept that this gumshoe work could achieve the positive effect of his release from prison and the arrest of the genuine guilty party seemed even more fantastical. I had been deeply disturbed by my encounter with the police force and was none too thrilled about the prospect of having to return to the jail and interview the inmates. As I glanced again at the ever-increasing traffic on the turnpike I remembered some of the statistics that Delray had given me as we had sat in surveillance on Christine's house.

Germaine's future was just one tiny move in this ongoing tournament, this year-round game of cops and robbers. Somehow there seemed to be no stopping it, no respite, in a world where inequality was obvious, drugs rife, and, as I had seen, firearms almost ubiquitous; there would be no end to this all-absorbing pastime. It was to this idea that I returned again and again: that this was all, somehow, because of its unending nature, just a permanent and abominable game. The endless channels of crime reporting and court cases were fodder for the spectators. For them it was all a distraction. If you got bored with one case of murder you could try another and, as long as you remained uninvolved, it was no doubt great entertainment.

Despite my revulsion at the cheapening of human tragedy that I had seen too much of recently, it only made the plight of the likes of Germaine that much sharper, their helplessness that much more acute and, to my mind, the honour in their defence that much greater.

On the other hand, I thought, as I made my way later to bed, why did I care? What was it to me? In a different land, amongst strangers, why did I care about the outcome of this case as much as I did? I didn't know but I was quite sure that I did care what happened to Germaine Christiensen. So it was the next day that I felt a certain resolve as I folded into Delray's blacked-out sports car and we made our way to the County Jail. As we passed through the various checks and Delray said howdy to the guard on duty that morning, I was not sure whether I wanted to see Germaine again in prison circumstances. It was not the purpose of our visit and there was no particular reason why we should run into him but somehow I would have felt a profound embarrassment at having to look him in the eye. As we clanged down the corridor to the interview room I recognised, perhaps rather unimaginatively, how I valued my freedom. For the past decade or so I had been allowed, pretty much, to go where I wished and to do what I wanted. This did not mean that along the way I had not tried to make some payment for my liberty, but nonetheless I had been free.

We had to see the four inmates separately and, as agreed, we arranged to leave the pastor's son till last. There was something deeply dismaying, depressing, about the unambivalent refusal of the first three inmates to co-operate. They did not make me feel angry. More, I was left with a feeling of profound emptiness by their total inability to react to me and Delray with anything that was less than hostile. It was a complete clash of cultures. I had no expectation that they should recognise anything in me beyond the obviously humanoid that should attract their curiosity or their empathy but Delray was certainly one of their own, and I expected that at least there would be some common ground. But no, these men seemed to be isolated from the rest of the 'normal' world. It was as if they had accepted their fate. That fate was prison. Their destiny, more likely than not, a death behind bars, or a release and a return to prison, and then a death behind bars. It seemed that by their early twenties their mould had hardened completely and that there would never be any changing them. I wondered about their families. Particularly their children. All three of them had started families young although none lived in a 'stable relationship'. Nor, of course, now were they ever likely to do so.

Dispirited, we stepped out of the jail for a break and to breathe some real air. Delray and I sat on the hood of his car and drank ice-cold sodas and sighed. There seemed little point in attempting any other communication. Shrugging and tossing his can into the trash, Delray made for the gate and I followed him in.

The routine was much the same. We went in, we were searched. We made our way down a soulless corridor and then down another until we reached the strange glass room. In a rerun of the first three visits I could hear the whirr of electrically activated locks and the clunking of a door that opened an airlock between one world and another. Another figure shuffled in, manacled and head bowed, and sat in the plastic bucket chair. This time, however, we both noticed, Delray and I, a perceptible difference in body language. Here there were no legs splayed back and shoulders thrown wide. No head cocked back at an angle and a regard that looked both slyly and disapprovingly down at us. Here instead was the figure of a young man that even my unprofessional eye could see was on the verge of some terrible mental collapse. He could not help but jiggle his knees up and down and they bumped against his hands that were clasped together in front of him almost in some form of supplication. There was no arrogance in his eye, only deep and lasting worry.

'Hey, brother,' said Delray softly.

'Hey . . .' said the man softly and licked his lips. There

was a long pause before Delray started on the delicate task
of trying to draw the truth from this young man. An age
later on I glanced up from the bowed figure and saw
through the glass a clock on the wall far away, enmeshed
in wire. It seemed, though, as if its hands had hardly moved
on at all. Here again there was some strange cinematic time
warp where things ran as fast as a car chase or seemed to
slow down like a fading pulse. One thing was very clear.
Marcus, for that was the first name of the pastor's son,
was frightened. Terribly frightened. Perhaps more terrified
even than Germaine. At least Germaine knew his innocence. Marcus was only too aware of his guilt. This was a
guilt that he carried as heavily as his friends had lightly
shrugged theirs off. This was not a result that he and his
parents had ever foreseen for him. Perhaps Marcus had
just been in the wrong place at the wrong time. Germaine,
of course, had not been in the wrong place at the wrong
time but still found himself in equal trouble, I thought
darkly as Marcus glanced up at us imploringly. His expression was difficult to read in the dark corner of the
interrogation room but his eyes expressed the horror only
too clearly. Now, for the umpteenth time, he told the story
of his day. How he had gone to high school, how he had
taken a walk at lunch in the direction of home where he
had forgotten one of his economics papers and had met
the other boys in the road. Partly because he was scared
of them, and partly also because he was concerned about
a lesson that afternoon with his least favourite teacher, he
allowed himself to be convinced to play hookey for the
afternoon. Nothing much had happened, of course, it never
did. They had taken the bus into Cambridge, had walked
round the mall and taken the bus home. This, it appeared,
was a fairly well worn route for the youngsters of the area.
It seemed to be a deeply frustrating one, too, as they were

not able to shop to their heart's content as so many others they saw browsing in the windows were. The other guys were full of tall tales about girls and guns and cars and all the other veneers that made up their personalities. We were again nudging closer to the moment of the attack and, as if he could see it coming closer like a car crash about to happen, Marcus seemed almost to put up his hands in front of his face at the horror of what was to take place.

'It was real bad, weren't it?' said Delray dipping deep into the dialect of the 'hood.

'Yeah, man. Oh, my sweet God, it was so bad.' Now Marcus was gazing at the ceiling. Looking for the light, his eyes were wet with tears.

'Who's there, man? C'mon, I need names. You four guys? But Germaine, he ain't there, man, he ain't never been there, did he?'

No, Marcus shook his head miserably. No, he wasn't there. Delray let out a long slow breath or perhaps I did.

'So . . . ?' I asked unable to stop myself.

'So . . .' said Delray simultaneously. 'So who was the other guy?'

'No way, man,' cried Marcus, and his voice was horrible in its desperation. 'No way, man. I ain't ever gonna be able to tell you that on this earth, man.'

Silence. A long heavy silence. A silence during which all three of us reassessed our position.

'OK,' said Delray brusquely, his complicit accent and tone changing. He stood up abruptly and snatched at the zip of his leather jacket, pulling it up and turning away from Marcus. 'We gotta get out of here.' He paused. I tapped on the glass door and the guard who had been sitting immobile, asleep with his eyes open, jolted into action and hurried to the door as much as it is possible to hurry if you are clinically obese.

'When you guys coming back?' asked Marcus plaintively. 'You gotta come back and check I'm OK, yeah, right?'

'We gonna come back,' said Delray, and I was surprised, almost shocked at the harshness of his voice. 'We gonna come back when you got something to say.' We made for the door. Delray seemed calm and in control of the situation. I did not. Marcus seemed to sense this.

'Hey, man, c'mon, you guys gotta help me.'

'No, Marcus, you gotta help yourself,' said Delray magisterially and I wished I had said it myself.

As we left the prison building Delray muttered something to the staff sergeant, who nodded in agreement and made a note in his ledger. We walked across the parking lot in silence and got into Delray's car. It was cold out now but somehow the adrenaline and emotion that had been pumped up in the little interview room were keeping me more than warm.

'So . . .' I started, but something in the way that Delray snapped the ignition key and roared the engine into life told me that he was not feeling conversational. We left at some speed. To my surprise we did not head back to Beacon Hill to report our findings as I had felt we should, but instead headed out north and soon found ourselves at the shopping mall that the young men had visited so fatefully some weeks before. Wordlessly, and to my considerable surprise, Delray made a quick and efficient tour of numerous young people's stores clutching up video games and any number of novelty items as well as heaps of confectionery. To sweeten our interviewees up. Literally.

'OK, it's go-back-to-jail time,' he said, and back to jail we went. Twenty minutes later Marcus gave us the name of the fifth man who had killed Antonio Rodriguez.

* * *

Snowflakes spiralled like sparks under the arc lights that illuminated the parking lot and strangely small front door of the County Jail the night that Germaine Christiensen was released without charge.

It suddenly struck me that this was the first time since we had met that I had seen Nelson Mason outside his office. He and I leant expectantly against the Dodge Stingray out of which he had eventually managed to clamber. To my right Delray Drummond was pacing nervously back and forward as if he feared that at the eleventh hour something would go wrong. That the reprieve would suddenly be rescinded. Rita Martinez had arrived with Buck Burnett and the two of them spoke solicitously to Delray, who leant his forehead gently on the roof of his sports car, unable to cope with the tension.

All of us held back from the two silhouettes touching shoulder to shoulder between us and the door to the prison. Germaine's parents looked visibly thinner than they had when we had first met. The strain had been terrible on them, perhaps just as terrible as it had been for their son. The snow that fell began to settle on the tarmac and a light but bitterly cold breeze blew it up against the sides of the empty cars, pushing it like shifting sand.

I glanced surreptitiously down at my watch as I had done seemingly every thirty seconds since we had arrived. Seven p.m. had been the time fixed for Germaine's release and if the act was to be punctual then we had only three further minutes to wait. I glanced up at Germaine's sister, who leapt out of a car that had only now slid to a halt. She rushed over to her parents, complaining bitterly about the weather and the traffic conditions that it had caused. Nobody wanted to miss this moment in time. Almost as if we could hear the clocks chiming through the city simultaneously on the stroke of seven the door opened and, from the darkness within, appeared a figure, gaunt but youthful.

And pale, so very pale, beneath the arc lights.

Walking at a determinedly regulated speed, Germaine attempted to keep his composure but when he was still some twenty yards away from his parents he dropped the plastic bag that contained his only prison belongings, and ran for his parents. It was he who needed to feel their embrace so badly but all of us at that moment felt an extraordinary sense of belonging to these events.

In some ways, as an outsider, a foreigner, I felt relieved to be able to stand at a short distance from the intense emotions that erupted like small geysers throughout the course of the party that evening at Christienson's small house. Painfully tired, Germaine could only keep repeating his thanks and his love for the people who had helped him. I looked round the room at my new friends: Nelson, Delray, for whom my admiration was boundless, Rita, who kept the whole show on the road, and even Buck, who in his funny sort of way was trying to do the right thing, these people were rarities.

A few days later Delray and I stepped back up the steps of the mansion in downtown Boston. We were there at the request of Christine's parents, who had told us that she had something to say to us. Her apology and thanks was painful to listen to in its sugariness and I suspected its lack of sincerity. Nevertheless it was said and drew a close to the whole affair. Or at least for Chestnut Investigations Inc., it did. Christine and her parents had employed the services of any number of psychiatrists and family counsellors who had been called upon to try and carry out the major repairs that were needed to reconstruct this family unit. As we wrapped our coats around us and headed back out onto

Newbury Street, Delray and I agreed that there seemed to be little happy future for them and that the quicker Christine could fly the nest and her parents could resolve their differences together or separately, the better it would be. Somehow, their tawdry history was more depressing than the far more dangerous case of Germaine Christiensen. Although the rupture to his adolescence had been terrible, I knew, we knew, that everything good that the human heart has to offer would be given to him to help him heal.

Marcus, the pastor's son, received a sentence of ten years in prison. A harsh sentence that stood as nought alongside the thirty-four years that each of the other defendants received for the murder of Antonio Rodriguez. Had it not been for the services of Chestnut Investigations Inc., Germaine Christiensen would have been nearly fifty years old by the time he was released from prison.

When, finally, matters urged me back to England I took my leave from my private-eye friends and, as we sipped champagne from the plastic cups of the water cooler machine, Nelson Mason asked me how I had enjoyed working for him. The answer, of course, was very much.

'Maybe you should come back again, help us out some more.'

'Thanks. I sure will but you owe me big time, buddy,' I told him rather authentically.

'Oh, yeah, and how is that then, Randy?' His great face juddered with amusement.

'Yeah, you owe me, Nelson. Now I got two books to write.'

Epilogue

C hristmas is approaching again and the birds that have spent the day hop-hopping on my front lawn in perfect freedom have now disappeared up into the trees. It is only teatime but dark already and the sudden cold edge to the wind has brought memories of Boston rushing back.

Only half an hour ago I put the telephone down after a long conversation with Nelson Mason. As soon as I heard his voice at the other end of the line I could picture him, massive, impassive, immobile and imperturbable behind his huge desk at Chestnut Investigations Inc. In the next-door room I could hear the clickety-clack of Rita's keyboard. Amused, I imagined her staring fixedly at Buck before casting her eyes heavenward as he explained his latest disaster. I thought I could hear Delroy's cheerful tones, perhaps talking on another line to one of his 'lovely ladies'. Perhaps he was just updating Ernie on the progress of his latest case.

They were busy, Nelson said. They had managed to clear up the big construction insurance fraud that Jack Make-peace had been investigating undercover and that meant that they had extra reason for celebrations this festive season.

'Who knows what the New Year will bring, Randy, who knows? But sure gonna be a busy one. Always is in private investigation.'

Had he heard anything subsequently of the fate of the individuals involved in the cases that we had covered together? How often I had wondered what became of them all.

Well, Christine had moved out of the family home and in with her sister, which seemed like a surprisingly sane solution to what had surely become an unbearably tense domestic situation.

'Course, the parents still have to support her right up until she finishes her college education. She took them to court. Got an order compelling them to do so. Interesting little triangle of self-interest, that one, wouldn't you say, Randy?'

A court order! Against her parents. I had not known whether to swear or to laugh. In the end I had just spluttered.

'Oh, by the way, you're going to be interested to know about that John you did the surveillance on up in Maine. You remember?' I was unlikely to forget. 'Yeah, well he split up with that Susie. Last I heard he's moving out of state. Heading out to Vermont or Connecticut. Yeah, that's what I heard. Sounds like he came clean about the boy. Gonna have him live with him. Got a full-time carer. Guess you have got to be pleased about that one, haven't you?'

Although Nelson was not asking for my personal reaction, I was pleased. I always am when innocent parties have something go their way.

What about Germaine, I asked instinctively.

'Well, you need to know he got hit pretty hard by the whole experience. Became very timid. Stopped going out. Even gave up on his baseball. The parents, they were pretty shaken up too. Oh, you better believe it, they were pretty much at their wits' end.'

My heart bulged in my chest and my eyes stung as I thought of the broken family, somehow so adrift and lonely in the big city. There and then, standing in my kitchen, looking out into the dusk, I felt as helpless as they did. I didn't know what further to say.

'But they had a stroke of luck,' Nelson continued. 'And boy, did they need it. You remember the son-in-law? A pretty neat kind of guy. Well, turns out he's got relations out in Idaho and when they heard the story they invited all of them, the whole family, to go live with them out on their farm. Apparently they have got some kind of homestead vacant they can all use. Dad's going to drive the farm machinery and Mom can find work in the local town. Germaine, I heard, can carry on his studies in the high school there. Got himself some part-time work on the farm too. So that's pretty cool.'

Pretty cool it certainly was. My spirits lifted and I smiled down the phone as I told Nelson how pleased I was. In the reflection of the window I could picture Germaine astride a tractor, the smokestack puffing merrily as he drove off to a happier place, a brighter future, with the sun on his back.

Finally we bid each other farewell, Nelson and I, wishing each other a happy Christmas with a pleasing and genuine fondness.

'Oh, by the way, Randy, you better keep me up to date with your movements. I know how much you like to move about!'

'You better believe it, buddy,' I replied cheerfully.

'Yeah,' he laughed. 'Who knows when Chestnut Investigations mightn't have another case for you . . .'